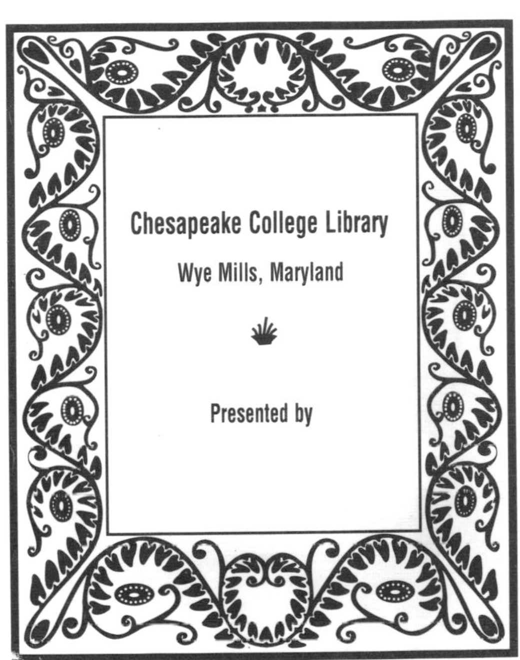
Chesapeake College Library
Wye Mills, Maryland
Presented by

A GUIDE TO THE
OXFORD ENGLISH
DICTIONARY

A GUIDE TO THE OXFORD ENGLISH DICTIONARY

DONNA LEE BERG

Oxford New York
OXFORD UNIVERSITY PRESS
1993

Oxford University Press, Walton Street, Oxford OX2 6DP
Oxford New York Toronto
Delhi Bombay Calcutta Madras Karachi
Kuala Lumpur Singapore Hong Kong Tokyo
Nairobi Dar es Salaam Cape Town
Melbourne Auckland Madrid
and associated companies in
Berlin Ibadan

Oxford is a trade mark of Oxford University Press

Library of Congress Cataloging-in-Publication Data
Berg, Donna Lee.
A guide to the Oxford English dictionary / Donna Lee Berg,
p. 206 cm.
Includes bibliographical references (p. 205).
ISBN 0-19-869179-3
1. Oxford English dictionary. 2. English language—Lexicography.
3. English language—Etymology. I. Oxford English dictionary.
II. Title.
PE1617.049B47 1993 423—dc20 91-41383

Typeset by Latimer Trend & Company Ltd, Plymouth
and printed in Great Britain
on acid-free paper
by The Bath Press, Avon

CONTENTS

FOREWORD

The *Oxford English Dictionary* is recognized throughout the world as the most complete historical record of the English language ever assembled. It has served several generations of scholars, students, librarians, and writers, as well as people from all walks of life with a curiosity and an interest in exploring the origin and history of words. To some the Dictionary represents the ultimate linguistic authority—even though the *OED* itself has never claimed to be prescriptive. Others have referred to it as a 'national monument', but, far from being 'carved in stone', today's *OED* exists not only in print, but as a dynamic computerized inventory of language which is being constantly updated and revised. Given its somewhat intimidating reputation, it is understandable that the first-time user of the Dictionary may approach the twenty densely printed volumes with a certain amount of trepidation.

This book is written with the hope that it will relieve the anxieties of the novice reader and perhaps enlarge the experienced user's understanding of the Dictionary. Its organization takes into account the fact that readers frequently avoid the lengthy explanatory introductions with which authors and editors optimistically preface dictionaries and other reference books. Most of us prefer to plunge into the contents, reluctantly exploring the introductory material only when we are puzzled by some convention used in the text. Alternatively, we may simply ignore what we cannot readily understand, and, consequently, deprive ourselves of valuable information. With this in mind, *A Guide to the OED* is designed, like a map, to provide users with directions and information, when needed, with a minimal amount of effort. It is deliberately organized as a reference book so that each of its major sections may be approached independently, if so desired. In this way, it attempts to address the needs of both the scholar and the casual Dictionary user by providing the option of reading the text in full or randomly exploring its contents.

Part I is a guide to the major components in a typical dictionary entry. Each element is discussed in turn and illustrated by examples from the text, so that one may read the section in its entirety or simply refer to a single element, such as the pronunciation, etymology, or quotations. Part II is intended as a 'companion' to the Dictionary and consists of alphabetically arranged articles on a variety of topics. It includes grammatical, lexicographical, and linguistic terms found in the *OED* and defines their use within that context. In addition, there are numerous biographical articles on the editors and other individuals who contributed to, or in some way influenced, the Dictionary. It also contains historical articles on subjects such as lexicography, philology, and etymology, as well as subjects of more recent interest such as the New OED Project, the Dictionary database, and the current Reading Programme. A *Chronology of Events Relevant to the History of the OED* supplements the two major sections and provides a quick overview of the more than one-hundred-year history of the *OED*. Full bibliographical details of books and articles cited in the text will be found in the *Bibliography*, which also includes some additional sources that may be of interest to readers wishing to pursue a particular topic further. In addition, readers who are statistically minded may wish to consult *OED Facts and Figures*.

Finally, while the text normally follows standard British spelling and usage, alternative terms, such as 'period' for 'full stop', are given in a few instances where British usage might cause confusion for North American readers.

ACKNOWLEDGEMENTS

A Guide to the OED is the result of a fortuitous convergence of interests—a fascination on my part with the *Oxford English Dictionary* and the desire of the Oxford University Press to provide modern readers with a reference book which would combine technical and historical information about the Dictionary in a convenient format. My own interest developed as a result of my association with the Centre for the New OED and Text Research at the University of Waterloo in Waterloo, Ontario, Canada, and from my professional career as a librarian. As one of the partners in the Press's New OED Project, the Centre had the responsibility for developing a database model for the Dictionary which happily provided the Centre's staff with on-line access to one of the world's major dictionaries, and the opportunity to work directly with the editorial staff of the *OED*. It is probably fair to say that our admiration for the compilers of the Dictionary and our appreciation of the immensity of their accomplishment grew in direct proportion to our involvement.

I am therefore indebted to individuals on both sides of the Atlantic who provided the support and guidance which helped bring this volume to print. My special thanks are due to Professor Frank Tompa, the Director of the Waterloo Centre for the OED, who granted me unrestricted access to the Dictionary database, and to the other facilities of the Centre, without which much of the information contained in this book could not have been included. I would also like to express my sincere thanks to the present and former staff of the Centre and the technical team—Elizabeth Blake, Tim Bray, Heather Fawcett, Linda Jones, Darrell Raymond, and Tim Snider—who were always willing patiently to answer questions, to provide me with guidance in my computer searches, and to read and comment on copy. My thanks also to Professor Jack C. Gray of the University of Waterloo who provided some of the statistics on author citations. And, of course, this work could not have been completed without the full co-operation and support of the senior editorial staff of the *OED*, in particular John Simpson and Edmund Weiner, Yvonne Warburton, and Sara Tulloch. I am also grateful to Elizabeth Knowles of Oxford University Press for clarifying some of the facts surrounding the story of Dr William C. Minor.

In addition, my research involved a number of printed sources, and a list of the major titles consulted is included in the *Bibliography* at the end of this volume. I would, however, like to mention two authors whose works were especially helpful. K. M. Elisabeth Murray's charming and informative biography of her grandfather, entitled *Caught in the Web of Words: James Murray and the Oxford English Dictionary*, was an invaluable source of biographical and historical information. The two works by Hans Aarsleff which are cited in the *Bibliography* provided many insights into the historical development of lexicography and philology, and the role of the *OED* within that intellectual framework.

DONNA LEE BERG
University of Waterloo
1991

PART I

A USER'S GUIDE TO THE *OED*

DICTIONARY BASICS

WHAT IS THE *OED*?

The *Oxford English Dictionary* (*OED*) is a unique reference work. It is visibly unique because of its size, and linguistically unique because of its comprehensiveness and its inclusion of chronologically arranged quotations illustrating changes in the meaning of words. In lexicographical terms, it is a *diachronic* dictionary; that is, it not only defines the language of the present day, it also records its use at any period within the Dictionary's coverage. The diachronic, or historical, approach benefits users in several ways. First, in addition to explaining what a word form means, it also, by documenting its history, explains *why* it has come to have a particular meaning. Secondly, it enables the reader, through both its definitions and numerous quotations, to view how individual words (and the language as a whole) were used at any point within the time period covered by the Dictionary. In addition, the illustrative quotations, which form well over half the Dictionary's text, are in themselves a rich resource for both literary and social history. Quite aside from its usefulness to scholars, the *OED* can also inform—and entertain—the general reader, for it is difficult to open a volume without discovering a new word, an interesting quotation, or a reference encouraging further exploration of the Dictionary's contents.

PUBLISHING HISTORY

The second edition of the *Oxford English Dictionary* is a consolidation of more than a century's work by four generations of lexicographers. The *OED* was initially published in a series of 125 slim fascicles between the years 1884 and 1928. The first complete edition in ten volumes was published in 1928. In 1933, this edition was reissued in twelve volumes together with a single supplementary volume containing additional entries and a select bibliography of the works cited in quotations. The Dictionary was further updated by the 4-volume *Supplement* (which also included the material in the 1933 supplement) published between 1972 and 1986. The present 20-volume second edition, published in 1989, integrates the first edition with the 4-volume *Supplement*, and adds approximately 5,000 new words and new meanings of old words.

THE SCOPE OF THE *OED*

The *Oxford English Dictionary* is the only English language dictionary that presents a comprehensive history of the English language and illustrates its development by quotations from both scholarly and popular works. Virtually any source of the printed word is used, including journals, magazines, and newspapers; Biblical text and government documents; manuscripts, collections of letters, and diaries. In total the second edition of the *OED* contains nearly two and a half million quotations.

The scope of the Dictionary's coverage is as inclusive as it is broad. Its 290,500 entries attempt to cover the documented use of words currently employed in the English language, or known to have been in use at any time since the middle of the twelfth century (note, however, that many words included in the Dictionary have histories preceding 1150, since it is only words that were obsolete by that year which are excluded). Including variant spellings, obsolete forms, combinations, and derivatives, some of which have entries in their own right, the *OED* contains 616,500 word forms. However, given that the reach of English vocabulary extends to rapidly expanding technical and scientific fields, as well as to slang, jargon, and dialect, not even the *OED* can hope to achieve total inclusiveness. In addition, the passage of time with the accompanying increased rate of growth of the language, as well as historical and social changes, have necessitated adjustments to the original policy. For example, words which were considered too vulgar to appear in print in the first edition were added to the *Supplement*, and it is recognized that much still remains to be done in revising and updating scientific and technical vocabulary. Coverage of regional forms of English, particularly of English-speaking regions and nations outside the British Isles, such as the United States, Canada, Australia, South Africa, and the West Indies, was considerably expanded by the *Supplement* and continues to be actively pursued.

It should be noted that geographical place-names, names of persons, proprietary names, etc. are included only if they are used attributively, allusively, or possessively, since the *OED* is not an encyclopaedic dictionary. It does not attempt to include names of persons or places based on criteria such as importance or size. Nevertheless, the *OED* contains in the neighbourhood of 10,000 headwords in this class.

Contrary to the popular view of the *OED* as an authority on the 'correct' usage of the language, the Dictionary is intended to be *descriptive*, not *prescriptive*; it records, non-judgementally, the history of the language as mirrored in the written words of a democratic mix of novelists, playwrights, journalists, scholars, scientists, legislators, politicians, diarists, saints, and philosophers.

ARRANGEMENT OF ENTRIES

Like most modern English language dictionaries, the *OED* is made up of a series of individual *entries* arranged alphabetically by *headword*. A headword, in the case of the *OED*, is the word, combination, phrase, variant or obsolete form, or, in some cases, acronym or abbreviation, which is the subject of a Dictionary entry and appears at its 'head'. All headwords in the second edition of the Dictionary are printed in **bold type**. For users of the printed text (as compared to users of the electronic or computerized version of the *OED*) headwords are the usual entry point to the Dictionary.

It is important when one is searching for a word or phrase to understand what the term 'arranged alphabetically' means. Headwords in the *OED* follow a strict letter-by-letter order, ignoring capitalization, punctuation, and spaces between compound words or phrases, thus:

A (letter of the alphabet)
absolute (word)
ABTA (acronym)
ante- (prefix)
Athoan (proper name)
at-hold (combination)
Athole brose (proper name/combination)
at home, at-home (combination)
-athon (suffix)

a-three (combination)
à tort et à travers (phrase)
atour (word)

ON FIRST OPENING THE *OED*

Opening the pages of the *OED* for the first time, one is probably struck by the quantity and density of the text, although users of the first edition will be pleased to note that the second edition follows the *Supplement*'s policy of more generous spacing. Three columns of typical entries are shown in Fig. 1.

The user may then observe that there is a variety of typefaces. For example, the eye is initially drawn, as the editors intend it to be, to the large bold type of the headwords, such as **Mayfair, mayflower, may-fly**, etc. This typographical convention, as in most dictionaries, is a finding device to enable the reader to scan a page quickly for the desired word.

The next thing that may be apparent is that some paragraphs within entries are printed in larger typeface than others. As might be expected, these different typefaces represent two kinds of information. The larger print is used for the 'primary' information in an entry—typically, the description of the headword and the definition of its senses. The paragraphs in smaller type contain supportive or supplementary information. Included in this category are the quotations that illustrate usage of the headword senses, and explanatory notes supplementing etymologies and definitions. The designations 'supportive' and 'supplementary' in no way imply that the information they contain is less important than the 'primary' information. On the contrary, the quotations play an essential role in defining the senses and illustrating their development in the context of the language.

Finally, the first-time user of the Dictionary may notice that in addition to entries comprising several paragraphs or several pages, there are entries as brief as a single line, for example, **mayed, mayghe(e, maygne, -gnelle**. The *OED* contains two distinct types of entry, which for purposes of differentiation are referred to in this guide as **main entries** and **cross-reference entries**. Main entries provide the most comprehensive information about a headword's history and meaning, while the function of the cross-reference entry is to direct the user from irregular, obsolete, variant, were Maydukes. **1841** *Knickerbocker* XVII. 154 The air is impregnated with the fragrances..of the blossoming may-dukes. **1874** *Rep. Vermont Board Agric.* II. 359 This variety, and the..May Duke, Late Duke, and other Dukes,..are hardly less hardy than plums.

mayed, obs. form of MAID *sb.*[1]

mayer (ˈmeɪə(r)). [f. MAY *v.*[2] + -ER[1].] One who 'goes a-maying'.

1756 TOLDERVY *Hist. 2 Orphans* II. 152 They set out on foot to join the merry mayers. **1825** HONE *Every-day Bk.* I. 566 Parties of these Mayers are seen dancing. **1893** 'Q.' *Delect. Duchy* 23 All but a few of the mayers had risen from the table.

mayar, -ary: see MAYOR, MAYORY.

†ˈ**Mayey**, *a. Obs. rare.* Also **-ie**. [f. MAY *sb.*[3] + *-ey*, -Y.] Flowering in the month of May.

1604 T. WRIGHT *Passions* I. iii. 14 To..enioy the roses till they flourish, not to let wither the Mayie flowres of their flesh. *a* **1618** SYLVESTER *Maiden's Blush* 470 And up hee comes as fresh as Mayey-Rose.

Mayfair (ˈmeɪfɛə(r)). [MAY *sb.*[3] + FAIR *sb.*[1]]

a. A fair held in May, esp. that held annually from the 17th century until the end of the 18th century in Brook fields near Hyde Park Corner. **b.** The district of London, very fashionable since the 19th century, between Oxford Street and Piccadilly, occupying the site of the old fairground. Also as quasi-*adj.*

1701 B. FAIRFAX in *Tatler* (1786) I. Notes 418, I wish you had been at May-fair, where the rope-dancing would have recompensed your labour. **1709** *Tatler* 24–26 May, The Crowd of the Audience are fitter for Representations at May-fair, than a Theatre-Royal. **1748** H. WALPOLE *Let.* 3 Sept. (1903) II. 336 A chosen committee waited on the faithful pair to the minister of May-fair. **1754** *Connoisseur* 17 Oct. 227 Catalogue of Males and Females to be disposed of in Marriage to the Best Bidder, at Mr. Keith's Repository in May Fair. **1848** THACKERAY *Van. Fair* li. 453 Yesterday, Colonel and Mrs. Crawley entertained a select party at dinner at their house in May Fair. **1874** H. C. PENNELL *(title)* The Muses of Mayfair: selections from *vers de société* of the nineteenth century. **1933** J. BUCHAN *Prince of Captivity* II. i. 146 Clothes slightly astray from the conventions of Mayfair. **1953** A. CHRISTIE *Pocket Full of Rye* i. 8 Miss Grosvenor..wailed in a voice whose accent was noticeably less Mayfair than usual.

c. *attrib.* and *Comb.*

1752 H. WALPOLE *Let.* 27 Feb. (1903) III. 85 They were married with a ring of the bed-curtain..at Mayfair chapel. **1843** CARLYLE *Past & Present* III. ix. 252 Patent-Digester, Spinning-Mule, Mayfair Clothes-Horse. **1866** M. MACKINTOSH *Stage Reminisc.* vi. 74 So elegant and comfortable that even luxurious west-enders might have fancied themselves at home in their own May-Fair drawing-rooms. **1940** N. MARSH *Surfeit of Lampreys* (1941) ii. 31 The twins were saying..that..the only thing..was for them to turn crooks and be another lot of Mayfair boys. **1943** I. BROWN *Just Another Word* 24 'She got terribly akimbo'..a species of Mayfair slang for what was earlier called 'high horse'. **1957** R. W. ZANDVOORT *Handbk. Eng. Gram.* v. ii. 225 It's such a bore, don't you know. In the..example (which really represents 'Mayfair' English) the tag practically ceases to be a question. **1962** J. D. SALINGER *Franny & Zooey* 155 He was still for a moment. Then, in an almost unintelligibly thick Mayfair accent: 'I'd rather like a word with you, Miss Glass.' **1967** K. GILES *Death in Diamonds* i. 21 He's insolent, smooth and tough, very hip in his talk. Like the Mayfair boys in the thirties. **1970** C. DRUMMOND *Stab in Back* iv. 88 They 'ad a saying when we were young about 'Mayfair Boys', meaning gentlemen crooks.

Hence ˈ**Mayfairish** *a.*, of the nature or character of Mayfair.

1938 G. ALLIGHAN *Sir John Reith* iv. 235 The B.B.C. organisation..is too isolated from the common people. There is a West End outlook, a Mayfairish idea of the elite, an everlasting implication of superiority. **1967** [see *ideal home*].

mayflower (ˈmeɪflaʊə(r)). [f. MAY *sb.*[3] + FLOWER *sb.* Cf. G. *maiblume*, Du. *meibloem* lily of the valley; so *may-blossom* (MAY *sb.*[3] 5 c).]

1. A flower that blooms in May: used locally as a specific name for various plants, as the Cowslip (*Primula veris*), the Lady's Smock (*Cardamine pratensis*); see Britten & Holland *Plant-n.*

1626 BACON *Sylva* §507 They are commonly of rancke and fulsome Smell; As May-Flowers, and White Lillies. [**1659** HOWELL *Prov.* 12/1 April showers bring forth May flowers.] **1688** R. HOLME *Armoury* II. 70 The Cowslip..we call it a May-flower. **1776** MICKLE tr. *Camoens' Lusiad* I. 24 May-flowers crouding o'er the daisy-lawn. **1817** KEATS *'I stood tiptoe'* 29 A bush of May-flowers with the bees about them. **1853** G. JOHNSTON *Bot. E. Bord.* 33 *Cardamine pratensis*... In Roxburghshire..it is called the May-flower.

fig. **1576** GASCOIGNE *Steele Glass* (Arb.) 119, I hope very shortly to see the May flowers of your fauour.

2. A variety of apple.

1664 EVELYN *Kal. Hort.* Aug. 72 Apples... Cushion Apple, Spicing, May-flower.

3. *N. America.* **a.** *Azalea nudiflora.* **b.** The trailing arbutus, *Epigæa repens.*

1838 LOUDON *Arboretum* II. 1140 *Rhododendron nudiflorum* Torr. (*Azalea nudiflora* L.)..the American Honeysuckle; May Flowers. **1853** W. H. BARTLETT *Pilgr. Fathers* iii. 182 The beautiful May-flower—with its delicate roseate blossom and delicious scent. **1882** *Garden* 13 May 323/1 The May-flower..is the emblem of Nova Scotia, with the motto, 'We bloom amid the snow'.

4. The West Indian *Dalbergia Brownei* and *Ecastaphyllum Brownei.*

1864 GRISEBACH *Flora W. Ind.* 785.

5. The South American *Lælia majalis.*

1894 WRIGHT & DEWAR *Johnson's Gard. Dict.*

ˈ**may-fly.** [f. MAY *sb.*[3] + FLY *sb.*]

1. An insect of the family *Ephemeridæ*; esp. as an angler's name for *Ephemera vulgata* and *E. dania* or an artificial fly made in imitation of either of these.

1651–3 T. BARKER *Art of Angling* 6 As for the May-Flie you shall have them alwayes playing at the River side. **1653** WALTON *Angler* iv. 115 First for a May-flie, you may make his body with greenish coloured crewel. **1769** G. WHITE *Selborne* (1789) 60 What time the may-fly haunts the pool or stream. **1856** 'STONEHENGE' *Brit. Rural Sports* §650 Caddies are the larvæ of the ephemera, or May-fly, as well as the stone-fly and the caddis-fly. **1867** F. FRANCIS *Angling* vi. (1880) 223 The May Fly or Green Drake, called in Wales the Cadow.

2. An insect of the family *Phryganeidæ* or *Sianidæ* (e.g. *Sialis lutaria*); the caddis-fly.

1816 KIRBY & SP. *Entomol.* ix. (1818) I. 282 *Phryganeæ* [in their imago state are called] may-flies (though this last denomination properly belongs only to the *Sialis lutaria*.. and *Ephemeræ*. *Ibid.* II. 295 [The larvæ] of the true may-fly (*Semblis lutaria*, F.)..use their legs in swimming.

†**3.** A dragon-fly. *Obs.*

1744 COLLINSON in *Phil. Trans.* XLIV. 329 The May Flies, a Species of Libella. **1750** *Ibid.* XLVI. 400 A further Account of the Libellæ or May-flies, from Mr. John Bartram of Pensylvania.

4. *attrib.*, as *may-fly season, tribe.*

1816 KIRBY & SP. *Entomol.* xxi. (1818) II. 240 The May-fly tribe (*Phryganea*, L., *Trichoptera*, K.). **1857** HUGHES *Tom Brown* I. ix, But now came on the may-fly season.

ˈ**May-game.** [MAY *sb.*[3]]

1. a. *pl.* The merrymaking and sports associated with the first of May. **b.** *sing.* A set performance or entertainment in the May-day festivities.

1549 COVERDALE, etc. *Erasm. Par. 1 Tim.* 8 In such maner of apparaill, as the commen sorte of vnfaithfull women are wonte to goe forth vnto weddynges and maygames. **1583** R. ROBINSON *Anc. Order Pr. Arthur* L 4 b, A May game was of Robyn-hood, and of his traine that time. **1589** GREENE *Menaphon* (Arb.) 56 He was chosen Lord of the May game, king of their sports, and ringleader of their reuils. **1641** HINDE *J. Bruen* iii. 12 The holy Sabbaths of the Lord were ..spent..in May-poles and May-games. **1888** CHILD *Eng. & Sc. Ball.* III. 46 Maid Marian is a personage in the May-game and morris.

2. *transf.* and *gen.* Merrymaking, sport, frolic, entertainment; foolish or extravagant action or performance, foolery.

1571 GOLDING *Calvin on Ps.* lxxiii. 1 He cryed out..that the endever of living well was but a Maygame. **1660** R. COKE *Power & Subj.* 50 It were a fine may-game to be a King, if Kings might make their Will the rule of their actions. **1768–74** TUCKER *Lt. Nat.* (1834) I. 357 The vulgar [have] their..coarse jokes, and may-games. **1843** CARLYLE *Past & Pr.* III. xiii, Life was never a May-game for men.

3. An object of sport, jest, or ridicule; a laughing-stock. Also in phr. *to make a May-game of.*

1569 J. SANFORD tr. *Agrippa's Van. Artes* 158 A manifest foolishnes, and a maie game to the multitude. **1583** FULKE *Defence* iv. 137 Whereas in one translation we vse the worde Generall for Catholike, you make a greate maygame of it. **1644** QUARLES *Barnabas & B.* 253 What is man but..the spoil of time, the may-game of fortune? *a* **1739** JARVIS *Quix.* I. III. xxv. (1885) 146 She..makes a jest and a may-game of everybody.

4. *attrib.*, as *May-game king, lord, morris, pastime*; also as adj. with the sense 'trivial'.

1586 J. HOOKER *Hist. Irel.* in *Holinshed* II. 79/2 This maigame lord, named indeed Peter (in scorne Perkin) Warbecke. **1602** I. R[HODES] *Answ. Rom. Rime* C 3, Your May-game pastimes. **1614** RALEIGH *Hist. World* IV. ii. §4. 148 In this sort came the Maygame-King into the field, incumbred with a most vnnecessary traine of Strumpets. **1653** DELL *Tryal Spirits* 86 School Doctors, that is, Trifling or May-game Doctors. **1888** CHILD *Eng. & Sc. Ball.* III. 45 The relation of Robin Hood, John, and the Friar to the May-game morris is obscure.

Hence †**Maygamester**, one who takes part in May-games.

c **1585** R. BROWNE *Answ. Cartwright* 37 Drunkardes, Maygamesters, blasphemers.

maygh(e, variant forms of MAUGH.

maygne, -gnelle, obs. ff. MEINIE, MANGONEL.

mayhap (meɪˈhæp, ˈmeɪhæp), *adv.* Now *arch.*, *rhetorical* and *dial.* Also 8 **mehap**, 8–9 **mayhaps**. [The phrase *(it) may hap* (see HAP *v.*), taken as one word.] Perhaps, perchance.

a **1536** *Interl. Beauty & Gd. Prop. Women* A v, May hap ye stomble Quod he on the trewth, as many one doth. **1575** *Gamm. Gurton* v. ii. (Manly), There is a thing you know not on, may hap. **1706** MRS. CENTLIVRE *Basset-Table* IV, Sir Richard, mehap a woman may not like me. **1718** MOTTEUX *Quix.* (1733) III. 67 I'll trust no longer to Rewards, that mayhaps may come late, and mayhaps not at all. **1840** DICKENS *Barn. Rudge* lxxii, Mayhap she's hungry. **1870** MORRIS *Earthly Par.* II. III. 37 Or hast thou mayhap wandered wide? **1900** HOPE in *Yorks. Arch. Jrnl.* XV. 300 Pins or hooks, mayhap for hanging curtains from.

mayhappen, *adv.* Now *arch.* and *dial.* Also **mappen**, etc. (see E.D.D.). [The phrase *(it) may happen* (see HAPPEN *v.*), taken as one word.] = prec.

c **1530** H. RHODES *Bk. Nurture* 747 in *Babees Bk.* 102 Another tyme may happen he may doe as much for thee. *a* **1843** SOUTHEY *Doctor* Interch. xxiv. (1847) VII. 83 Mappen they'll sarra us. **1887** W. MORRIS *Odyss.* x. 269 Let us..flee; if yet mayhappen we may 'scape our evil day.

mayhem (ˈmeɪhɛm), *sb. Old Law.* Forms: 5 **mahyme**, 5–7 **mayme**, 6 **mayom**, **maiheme**, **mayheme**, **mahym**, 6–7 **maime**, 6–8 **mayhim**, 7 **mahin**, 7–8 **maim**, 7–9 **maihem**, **mahim**, 7– **mayhem**. [a. AF. *mahem*, *mahaym*, *maiheme*, *maheyng*, etc.: see MAIM *sb.*] The crime of violently inflicting a bodily injury upon a person so as to make him less able to defend himself or annoy his adversary.

1472–3 *Rolls of Parlt.* VI. 54/2 For the punycion of the said murdre and maymes. **1503** *Ibid.* 550/1 The same Sir William, suyde Appele of Mayme ayenst the said Sir Edward. **1523** in W. H. Turner *Select. Rec. Oxford* (1880) 33 Morders, fellonyes, mayoms. **1529** S. FISH *Supplic. Beggers* (1871) 8 Robbery, trespas, maiheme, dette or eny other offence. **1620** J. WILKINSON *Coroners & Sherifes* 22 Mayhem is properly said where any member of a man is taken away. **1641** *Termes de la Ley* 198 The cutting off of an eare or nose, or breaking of the hinder teeth, or such like, is no Maihem. **1765** BLACKSTONE *Comm.* I. 130 Those members which may be useful to him in fight, and the loss of which only amounts to mayhem by the common law. **1802–12** BENTHAM *Ration. Judic. Evid.* (1827) V. 139 All imaginable crimes,—rape, robbery, burglary, mayhem, incendiarism. **1853** T. WHARTON *Digest Cases Pennsylv.* (ed. 6) 486 An indictment for maihem which does not contain the words 'lying in wait' is bad.

fig. **1868** LANIER *Jacquerie* II. 44 Thou felon, War, I do arraign thee now Of mayhem of the four main limbs of France. **1894** *Critic* (U.S.) 30 June 444/1 The literary mayhem becomes as inexplicable as it is unpardonable.

Hence **mayhem** *v. trans.*, to inflict mayhem on.

1534 *Act 26 Hen. VIII*, c. 11 Diuers..haue beaten, mayhimed..and somtimes murdered diuerse of the same pursuers. **1743** *Conn. Col. Rec.* (1874) VIII. 579 For that he ..did feloniously mayhem the body of one Thomas Allyn. **1879** TOURGEE *Fool's Err.* xxxix. (1883) 251 To buy, to sell, to task, to whip, to mayhem this race at will.

mayhime, mayhme, obs. forms of MAIM *v.*

mayht, obs. form of MIGHT *sb.*

Mayie, variant of MAYEY *a.*, *Obs.*

maying (ˈmeɪɪŋ), *vbl. sb.* [f. MAY *v.*[2]] The celebration of or participation in the festivities of May-day or the month of May. Chiefly in phr. *to go a maying*, † *to ride on maying.*

1470–85 MALORY *Arthur* XIX. i. 772 That erly vpon the morowe she wold ryde on mayeng in to woodes. **1598** STOW *Surv.* 74 These great Mayinges and Maygames were made by the gouernors..of the Citie. **1632** MILTON *L'Allegro* 20 Zephir with Aurora playing, As he met her once a Maying. **1674** PLAYFORD *Skill Mus.* I. 64 Now is the Month of Maying. **1712** BUDGELL *Spect.* No. 365 ¶ 10 Proserpine was out a Maying, when she met with that fatal Adventure. **1824** MISS MITFORD *Village* Ser. I. 81 A country Maying is a meeting of the lads and lasses of two or three parishes, who assemble in certain erections of green boughs called May-houses, to dance. **1899** 'Q.' *Ship of Stars* x. 79 It had been a grand Maying.

b. *attrib.* in **maying-party** *U.S.*, a party making an excursion for gathering flowers.

1853 W. H. BARTLETT *Pilgrim Fathers* iii. 182 It is a favourite pastime to make Maying parties in the woods.

mayl, obs. f. MAUL *sb.*[1]

mayl-: see MAIL-.

ˈ**May-lady.** *Obs.* exc. *Hist.* [MAY *sb.*[3]] A Queen of the May. Also, a puppet in a May-day game (see quot. 1802).

1560 BECON *Catech.* VI. Wks. 1564 I. 516 b, To be decked and trimmed like a Marelady [*sic: ? misprint for* Maie-], or the Quene of a game. *Ibid.* 533 As though they were mareladies [*sic*] or Popets in a game. **1619** FLETCHER *M. Thomas* II. ii, Or you must marry Malkyn the May Lady. **1621** BURTON *Anat. Mel.* III. ii. II. iii. 573 Some light huswife belike, that was dressed like a may lady, and as most of our gentlewomen are. **1802** AUDLEY *Comp. to Almanack* 21 The custom..of children having a figure dressed in a grotesque manner, called a May-lady; before which they set a table, having on it wine, &c. They also beg money of passengers,..their plea to obtain it is, 'Pray remember the poor May-lady'.

mayll easse, variant of MALEASE.

mayllet, obs. form of MALLET *sb.*[1]

ˈ**May-lord.** [See MAY *sb.*[3] and LORD *sb.* 14 a.] A young man chosen to preside over the festivities of May-day; *transf.* one whose authority is a matter of derision.

1599 NASHE *Lenten Stuffe* 9 Cerdicus..was the first may-lord, or captaine of the morris daunce that [etc.]. **1622** WITHER *Mistr. Philar.* in *Juvenilia* (1633) 741 Wealth and Titles would hereafter Subjects be for scorn or laughter, All that Courtly stiles affected Should a May-Lords honour have. **1633** P. FLETCHER *Purple Isl.* I. ii, The Shepherd-boys who with the Muses dwell Met in the plain their May-lords new to choose..to order well Their rural sports. **1639** SHIRLEY & CHAPMAN *Ball* III. iii, [I] blush within to think How much we are deceived; I may be even With this May-

Fig. 1.

or incorrect forms of a word to the complete information contained in its *main* entry. An alternative way of thinking about the function of the two types of entries is that the main entry collects all of the known variants of a word (broadly defined) and groups them, together with their history, under one main headword. The headword is usually the most recent form of a word in current use, or the most typical of the later forms of an obsolete word. Cross-reference entries (or 'subordinate' entries as they were referred to in the first edition) serve as links or pointers for the reader who may only be aware of a variant spelling of the main word.

When searching the Dictionary, readers also need to be aware of the implications of the statement that the *OED* contains 290,500 entries and 616,500 word forms. This means that in addition to the nearly three hundred thousand headwords, many combinations and derivatives which do not warrant an entry in their own right, are defined and/or illustrated in the main entry for their root or initial word, combining form, etc. For example, less important derivatives often appear within the entry for their root word as in the case of the adjective **Mayfairish** which is defined and illustrated in the last paragraph of the entry for **Mayfair** in Fig. 1. In the case of combinations, a definition and illustrative quotations for **television network** are found within the main entry for **television**, and the term **auto-immune** is defined under the entry for the combining form **auto-**. Within entries, these terms, which function as subordinate headwords, are identified by bold type (slightly smaller than the headword) or bold italic type. Note, however that some phrases and idiomatic expressions appear under their most important word. For instance, the proverbial phrase 'he that would go to sea for pleasure, would go to hell for a pastime' is found in the entry for **sea**. The important point to remember is that before concluding that a combination, phrase, derivative, or similar form is not in the Dictionary, one must be sure to check all possible entries.

A WORD ABOUT CROSS-REFERENCES

Special mention needs to be made of the role of **cross-references** in the *OED*. The Dictionary thus far has been presented as a collection of entities referred to as 'entries', although, as noted in the previous section, some of these entries function as cross-references directing the user to the comprehensive entry for a main word form.

The use of cross-reference entries, however, is only one of the ways in which linkages are made in the Dictionary. Entries themselves contain various forms of cross-references: some point to another section of the same entry; some direct the user to another entry; some to a particular element in another entry such as a sense or an individual quotation. The second edition's 580,000 cross-references are like an immense web tying together various components of the dictionary. It is little wonder that Elisabeth Murray chose to entitle her biography of her grandfather, James Murray (the principal editor of the first edition of the *OED*), *Caught in the Web of Words*.

Because cross-references vary considerably in form and because they are so universal, it is difficult to fit them into the structural description of a typical main entry. It was therefore decided to discuss cross-references within the context of the elements in which they appear, such as variant forms lists, etymologies, etymological notes, definitions, and definition notes. It is perhaps useful to mention, however, that in cases where the cross-reference is to another entry headword, the targeted headword is always printed in small roman capitals.

MAIN ENTRIES

WHAT IS A MAIN ENTRY?

Main entries provide the most comprehensive information about what has been identified as the *main form* of a meaningful unit of the language. 'Main form' usually means the most recent form in current use or, in the case of obsolete words, the most typical of its later forms. Main entry headwords include, in addition to single words and phrases:

- combinations
- important abbreviations and acronyms
- important affixes (prefixes or suffixes)
- combining forms
- letters of the alphabet
- proper names used attributively, allusively, or possessively
- proprietary names in widespread or generic use

STRUCTURE AND CONTENT OF A MAIN ENTRY

In the simplest terms, a main entry has two major components—a **headword section** and a **sense section**. The headword section contains information that applies to the entire entry. The sense section includes one or more units, or sub-sections, consisting of a **definition** and a **quotation paragraph** describing and illustrating the meaning(s) or sense(s) of the headword, and, optionally, those of its combinations and derivatives which do not warrant a main entry in their own right. These units, in turn, have elements of information that are identifiable not only by their content, but also by their typography and the order in which they appear.

How do these components translate into the reality of the printed text? Fig. 2, the entry for **marmalade**, is an example of the structure of a typical entry with several senses. The headword section (containing the headword, pronunciation, part of speech, variant forms, etymology, and etymological note) is followed by

Headword Section

marmalade ('mɑːməleɪd), *sb.* Forms: 6 **marmylate, -elad, -ilat, -ilade, mormelade, marmlet, mermelado,** 6–7 **marmelet(t, -alad, -alate,** 6–8 **marmalet, -elade,** 7 **marmilad, -ilitt, -alit, -alett, -ulade, -ulate, -ulet, -aled, -eleta, -elate, mermalade,** 8 **marmolet, mermelade,** 6– **marmalade.** [a. F. *marmelade*, in Cotgr. *mermelade*, a. Pg. *marmelada*, f. *marmelo* quince, repr. (with dissimilation of consonants) L. *melimēlum*, a. Gr. *μελίμηλον* ('honey-apple', f. *μέλι* honey + *μῆλον* apple) the name of some kind of apple which was grafted on a quince. From the Pg. word are also Sp. *marmelada*, It. *marmellata*, and (through Fr.) G., Du., Da. *marmelade*, Sw. *marmelad.*]

Sense 1.a.

1. a. A preserve or confection made by boiling fruits (orig. quinces, now usually Seville oranges) with sugar, so as to form a consistent mass.

Often with prefixed word, as ***apricot, lemon, orange, quince marmalade***; when there is no word prefixed, orange marmalade is now commonly meant.

[**1524** in *Lett. & Papers Hen. VIII* (1870) IV. I. 339 Presented by Hull of Exeter one box of marmalade.] **1533** ELYOT *Cast. Helthe* (1541) 44 b, A piece of a quynce rosted or in marmelade. *Ibid.* 79 b, Marmalade of quynces. **1580** LYLY *Euphues* (Arb.) 266 Therfore you must giue him leaue after euery meale to close his stomacke with Loue, as with Marmalade. **1621** BURTON *Anat. Mel.* II. ii. I. i, Marmalet of plummes, quinces &c. **1634** SIR T. HERBERT *Trav.* 168 A healing powder of Gall and Marmalate of Dates. **1767** MRS. GLASSE *Cookery* App. 353 Marmalade of cherries. Put the cherries into the sugar, and boil them pretty fast till it be a marmalade. **1769** MRS. RAFFALD *Eng. Housekpr.* (1778) 223 To make Orange Marmalade. Take the clearest Seville oranges you can get [etc.]. *Ibid.* 225 To make Apricot Marmalade. **1845** ELIZA ACTON *Mod. Cookery* 457 Marmalade for the [Apple] Charlotte. Weigh three pounds of good boiling apples . . let these stew over a gentle fire, until they form a perfectly smooth and dry marmalade. *Ibid.* 489 Very fine imperatrice-plum marmalade. **1862** ANSTED *Channel Isl.* IV. xxi. (ed. 2) 487 The fruit is without much flavour, . . though it is well adapted for marmalade.

Sense 1.b.

b. *Proverbial* and *fig.*

1592 G. HARVEY *New Letter* Wks. (Grosart) I. 280 Euery Periode of her stile carrieth marmalad and sucket in the mouth. **1607** WALKINGTON *Opt. Glass* 53 The marmalade and sucket of the Muses.

Sense 2.

2. The fruit of *Lucuma mammosa*; also, the tree itself. Also called ***natural marmalade***.

1797 *Encycl. Brit.* (ed. 3) I. 69/1 [*Achras mammosa.*] Fruit . . inclosing a thick pulp called *natural marmalade.* **1821–2** LINDLEY in *Trans. Horticult. Soc.* (1824) IV. 97 The Mammee Sapota . . is called Natural Marmalade. **1846** —— *Veg. Kingd.* 591 The Marmalade (*Achras mammosa*). **1866** *Treas. Bot.* 698/1 *Lucuma mammosum* . . is cultivated for the sake of its fruit, which is called Marmalade, or Natural Marmalade.

Sense **3.a.** and **b.** (Combinations)

3. a. *attrib.*: **marmalade box,** (*a*) a box for marmalade; (*b*) the fruit of *Genipa americana* = GENIPAP; †**marmalade-eater**, ? one daintily brought up; **marmalade fruit**, the fruit of the marmalade-tree; †**marmalade-madam**, a strumpet; **marmalade-plum**, the fruit of the marmalade-tree or the tree itself (J. Smith *Dict. Pop. Names Plants*, 1882); **marmalade-tree**, the mammee-sapota (see sense 2).

1624 *Althorp MS.* in Simpkinson *Washingtons* (1860) App. p. lviii, 6 galley potts and 12 *marmalett boxes for Mrs. Segrave. **1796** STEDMAN *Surinam* II. xxviii. 318 A singular kind of fruit, called here the marmalade box, . . the husk . . opens in halves like a walnut, when the pulp appears like that of a medlar. **1614** R. TAILOR *Hog hath lost Pearl* II. D, Th'art as witty a *marmaled eater as euer I conuerst with. **1840** SCHOMBURGK *Brit. Guiana* 100 The Pine-apple, the Guava, the *Marmalade fruit. **1674** JOSSELYN *Voy. New Eng.* 162 The Gallants a little before Sun-set walk with their *Marmalet-Madams, as we do in Morefields. **1717** E. WARD *Wks.* II. 351 More Marmulet Madams will be met strolling in the Fields, than Honest Women in the Streets. **1866** *Treas. Bot.* 722/2 *Marmalade-Tree, *Lucuma mammosum.*

†**b.** quasi-adj. = 'sweet'. *Obs.*

1629 MASSINGER *Picture* I. i, I cannot blame my ladies Vnwillingnesse to part with such marmulade lips.

Sense **3.c.**

c. quasi-*adj.*: of the colour of marmalade (so ***marmalade-coloured*** adj.).

1926 S. T. WARNER *Lolly Willowes* III. 184 Jim was . . a mottled marmalade cat. **1938** K. HALE (*title*) Orlando, the marmalade cat. **1951** 'C. CARNAC' *It's her own Funeral* iv. 38 James, the marmalade cat, was sitting disapprovingly outside. **1957** *Times Lit. Suppl.* 15 Nov. p. xvii/2 Miss White's account of how a fierce little Siamese and an unsnubbable marmalade kitten learnt to live amicably together. **1961** *Guardian* 20 Jan. 9/7 A magnificent dark marmalade-coloured Persian cat. **1965** G. MCINNES *Road to Gundagai* ii. 29, I faced a crowd of blonde giants with marmalade fuzz on their chests. **1972** J. AIKEN *Butterfly Picnic* iii. 55 The local marmalade-coloured rock. **1973** 'E. PETERS' *City of Gold & Shadows* iii. 47 A very austere dress in a dark russet-orange shade that touched off the marmalade lights in her eyes.

Derivatives

Hence '**marmalady** *a.*, resembling marmalade in sweetness, etc.; also *fig.*

1602 MIDDLETON *Blurt* III. i, The Frenchman you see has a soft mermaladie heart. **1920** JOYCE *Let.* 3 Jan. (1957) I. 135 *Nausikaa* is written in a namby-pamby jammy marmalady . . style. **1960** P. COLERIDGE *Running Footsteps* 59 A clipped marmaladey moustache.

Fig. 2

three senses, two of which are subdivided. Sense **1.a.** contains a definition and a series of chronologically ordered quotations illustrating the usage of the word. The definition of sense **1.b.** notes that the word, as defined in **1.a.**, is sometimes applied proverbially or figuratively, and offers two supporting quotations. Sense **2.** informs the reader that 'marmalade' may also refer to a specific type of tree or its fruit and, again, this use is illustrated by quotations. The last numbered sense (**3.**) contains three types of combinations formed with the word 'marmalade' as the first component. The first group (**3.a.**) consists of a list of alphabetically-arranged attributive combinations, each with a brief definition. The paragraph of supporting quotations that follows is arranged in the same order. Senses **3.b.** and **3.c.** note the word's use in a 'quasi-adjectival' sense, again with relevant quotations. Finally, there is an unnumbered paragraph containing a derivative, **marmalady**, also defined and illustrated.

While this entry is structurally quite typical, the reader will encounter both less complex entries (for example, for a word with only a single sense), or much more complex entries with numerous senses and sub-senses that require expansion of the hierarchical numbering and lettering scheme. Nevertheless, as will be seen in the following pages, the basic organizational principles first established by Sir James Murray are retained. It is to his great credit that he had the foresight to create a scheme which provides for both coherence and flexibility.

In order to clarify further the structure and content of main entries, the next section first discusses the individual elements of the headword section and then explains the elements of the sense section. Each of these sections can be thought of as a box containing a number of individual elements arranged in a more or less consistent order. Becoming familiar with these structural conventions and with the abbreviated form in which they are frequently presented requires only a small investment in time and can greatly enhance the reader's enjoyment of the Dictionary.

HEADWORD SECTION

The purpose of the headword section is to describe the subject of the entry as a linguistic unit, in terms of spelling, pronunciation, and grammatical form, and to trace its origin and evolution by documenting its earlier or alternative spellings (variant forms) and its derivation and form history (etymology). The headword may also be described with regard to any special status within the language (obsolete, non-naturalized, partially naturalized), or if it has specialized application in a particular subject. The headword section of the typical main entry is therefore made up of a number of elements which normally appear in the following order, although not all of them will necessarily be found in any one entry:

1. **Status symbol**
2. **Headword**
3. **Pronunciation**
4. **Part of speech**
5. **Homonym number**
6. **Label**
7. **Variant forms**
8. **Etymology and etymological note**

Fig. 3 illustrates examples of headword sections for the words **orange, palumbine, palus²**, **pericyclic, ranch, restaurant, romance, salad**, and **tedify** as they appear in the Dictionary text. Numbers, keyed to the above list, are used to identify the elements. As will be noted, the content and length of a headword section varies considerably, depending on how long the word has been in the language, the intricacy of its history, the amount that is known about it, or whether relevant information on its origin is found elsewhere, as in the case of compound words derived from two previously existing word forms. For instance, the etymology of the word **pericyclic** in Fig. 3 refers the reader to the combining form **peri-** and the word **cyclic**. This convention is one example of another element frequently found within the headword section—the **cross-reference**.

Cross-references, because of their function as user aids and editorial pointers to pertinent information, may occur within other elements in entries. In the case of the headword section, they are most frequently employed in the etymology or the etymological note, but may also be encountered in the variant forms list. Mention will therefore be made of their use within the explanations of the relevant headword section elements, rather than under a separate heading.

In the following pages, the above elements are discussed more fully, citing the headword sections illustrated in Fig. 3, as well as other examples.

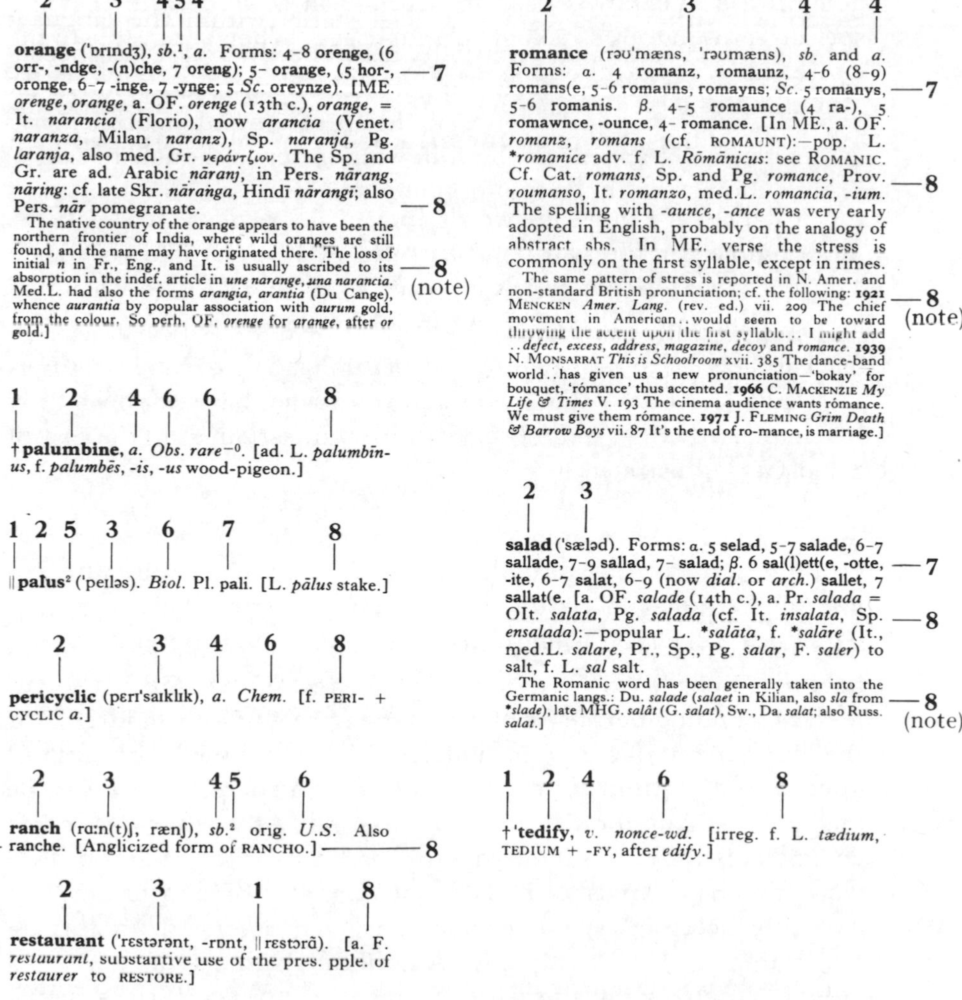

orange ('ɒrɪndʒ), *sb.*[1], *a.* Forms: 4–8 **orenge,** (6 **orr-, -ndge, -(n)che,** 7 **oreng**); 5– **orange,** (5 **hor-, oronge,** 6–7 **-inge,** 7 **-ynge**; 5 *Sc.* **oreynze**). [ME. *orenge, orange*, a. OF. *orenge* (13th c.), *orange*, = It. *narancia* (Florio), now *arancia* (Venet. *naranza*, Milan. *naranz*), Sp. *naranja*, Pg. *laranja*, also med. Gr. *νεράντζιον*. The Sp. and Gr. are ad. Arabic *nāranj*, in Pers. *nārang, nāring*: cf. late Skr. *nāraṅga*, Hindī *nārangī*; also Pers. *nār* pomegranate.

The native country of the orange appears to have been the northern frontier of India, where wild oranges are still found, and the name may have originated there. The loss of initial *n* in Fr., Eng., and It. is usually ascribed to its absorption in the indef. article in *une narange, una narancia*. Med.L. had also the forms *arangia, arantia* (Du Cange), whence *aurantia* by popular association with *aurum* gold, from the colour. So perh. OF. *orenge* for *arange*, after *or* gold.]

romance (rəʊ'mæns, 'rəʊmæns), *sb.* and *a.* Forms: α. 4 **romanz, romaunz,** 4–6 (8–9) **romans(e,** 5–6 **romauns, romayns;** *Sc.* 5 **romanys,** 5–6 **romanis.** β. 4–5 **romaunce** (4 **ra-**), 5 **romawnce, -ounce,** 4– **romance.** [In ME., a. OF. *romanz, romans* (cf. ROMAUNT):—pop. L. **romanice* adv. f. L. *Rōmānicus*: see ROMANIC. Cf. Cat. *romans*, Sp. and Pg. *romance*, Prov. *roumanso*, It. *romanzo*, med.L. *romancia, -ium*. The spelling with *-aunce, -ance* was very early adopted in English, probably on the analogy of abstract sbs. In ME. verse the stress is commonly on the first syllable, except in rimes.

The same pattern of stress is reported in N. Amer. and non-standard British pronunciation; cf. the following: **1921** MENCKEN *Amer. Lang.* (rev. ed.) vii. 209 The chief movement in American..would seem to be toward throwing the accent upon the first syllable... I might add ..*defect, excess, address, magazine, decoy* and *romance*. **1939** N. MONSARRAT *This is Schoolroom* xvii. 385 The dance-band world..has given us a new pronunciation—'bokay' for bouquet, 'rómance' thus accented. **1966** C. MACKENZIE *My Life & Times* V. 193 The cinema audience wants rómance. We must give them rómance. **1971** J. FLEMING *Grim Death & Barrow Boys* vii. 87 It's the end of ro-mance, is marriage.]

†**palumbine,** *a. Obs. rare*—0. [ad. L. *palumbīnus*, f. *palumbēs, -is, -us* wood-pigeon.]

salad ('sæləd). Forms: α. 5 **selad,** 5–7 **salade,** 6–7 **sallade,** 7–9 **sallad,** 7– **salad;** β. 6 **sal(l)ett(e, -otte, -ite,** 6–7 **salat,** 6–9 (now *dial.* or *arch.*) **sallet,** 7 **sallat(e.** [a. OF. *salade* (14th c.), a. Pr. *salada* = OIt. *salata*, Pg. *salada* (cf. It. *insalata*, Sp. *ensalada*):—popular L. **salāta*, f. **salāre* (It., med.L. *salare*, Pr., Sp., Pg. *salar*, F. *saler*) to salt, f. L. *sal* salt.

The Romanic word has been generally taken into the Germanic langs.: Du. *salade* (*salaet* in Kilian, also *sla* from **slade*), late MHG. *salât* (G. *salat*), Sw., Da. *salat*; also Russ. *salat*.]

‖**palus**[2] ('peɪləs). *Biol.* Pl. pali. [L. *pālus* stake.]

pericyclic (perɪ'saɪklɪk), *a. Chem.* [f. PERI- + CYCLIC *a.*]

†'**tedify,** *v. nonce-wd.* [irreg. f. L. *tædium*, TEDIUM + -FY, after *edify*.]

ranch (rɑːn(t)ʃ, ræntʃ), *sb.*[2] orig. *U.S.* Also ranche. [Anglicized form of RANCHO.]

restaurant ('rɛstərənt, -rɒnt, ‖rɛstɔrɑ̃). [a. F. *restaurant*, substantive use of the pres. pple. of *restaurer* to RESTORE.]

Fig. 3

1. Status symbol

The **status symbol** is used to distinguish a word form that has special status in the context of current usage. When applicable to the entire entry, the symbol *precedes* the headword; status symbols are also employed to identify the status of individual senses and for other special uses (see **pronunciation**). Two symbols are used with headwords:

(*a*) A dagger (†) precedes words judged to be obsolete, as in the example for the word **palumbine** in Fig. 3 (note that such entries are also typically supported by the label *obs.* (obsolete) as explained under the element **label** in this section).

(*b*) Parallels (‖) appear before non-naturalized or partially naturalized headwords—that is, foreign words that have not been fully anglicized either in their form or pronunciation, as in the case of **palus**², illustrated in Fig. 3.

2. Headword

The **headword** is the subject of a Dictionary entry and is printed in bold type in order to separate it from the rest of the entry. It serves both as a finding device for the reader and as a unique 'address' (or the first element of a unique 'address' when combined with **part of speech** and/or **homonym number**) to which references can be made. The main entry headword is normally the most current or common spelling of a modern word or, in the case of an obsolete word, the most typical of its later spellings. In some instances, two currently accepted spellings may be given as the main form—for example, the British and American spellings of the word **colour, color**, or the alternative forms **scallop, scollop**, as shown below.

colour, color (ˈkʌlə(r)), *sb.*¹ Forms: 3-6 colur, 4
scallop, scollop (ˈskɒləp, ˈskæləp), *sb.* Forms: *α.*

Superior (ˈ) and inferior (ˌ) stress marks are incorporated in some headwords and are explained under the element **pronunciation**, which follows.

Headwords are capitalized only where it is normal spelling to do so, as in the case of proper names, current proprietary terms, geographical names applied attributively, etc.

3. Pronunciation

In the context of a historical dictionary, **pronunciation** is 'the actual living form' of a word and, therefore, the latest fact in a word's history.

In the *OED*, pronunciation, when given, normally appears in round brackets immediately following the headword. Alternative pronunciations are included when two or more usages are common in spoken English (see **ranch, restaurant**, and **romance** in Fig. 3). Although, in general, pronunciation for native English words is given in accordance with educated standard southern British speech, alternatives may represent other British or non-British usage, as in the case of the verb **schedule** below. Note that the second pronunciation is preceded by a label *U.S.*, indicating its predominance in American speech.

schedule ('ʃɛdjuːl, 'ʃɛdəl; *U.S.* 'skɛdjuːl), *sb.*

For foreign words or phrases that have been only partially naturalized, alternative anglicized words and foreign pronunciations may be included, with the parallels symbol (‖) preceding the original pronunciation, as exemplified in the entry for **restaurant** (Fig. 3).

Older pronunciations, preceded by the word 'formerly', are also occasionally included, as illustrated below in the entry for **caffeine**.

caffeine ('kæfiːn, formerly 'kæfiːaɪn). *Chem.*

The phonetic system of symbols, consisting of letters and diacritics, used in the second edition, follows the principles of the International Phonetic Alphabet established by the International Phonetic Association. An explanation of the system is given in the introduction to the Dictionary (pp. xxxiii–xxxiv). A key to the pronunciation symbols is also printed in the front of the Dictionary. IPA pronunciation universally replaces the 'Murray pronunciation' system, devised by James Murray for the first edition of the *OED*.

Stress marks, showing the emphasis placed on syllables or words, are either incorporated as part of the bracketed IPA pronunciation, or where only stress is indicated, as part of the headword itself. These marks *precede* the stressed syllables or words (note that in the first edition stress marks *followed* the vowel in the stressed syllable). Main stress is indicated by a superior stress mark ('), as in the case of the alternative pronunciations for **romance** (Fig. 3), which emphasize either the first or second syllable. Where necessary, secondary stress is indicated by an inferior stress mark (ˌ), as in the entry for the multi-syllabic nonsense word **supercalifragilisticexpialidocious**:

Note, however, that the *OED* does not routinely show syllabification breaks except when relevant to pronunciation.

No pronunciation is given for several classes of headwords. Included are compound words and derivatives where pronunciation is considered to be self-evident because it follows that of the root or combining words involved. Stress, however, is indicated as, for example, in the entries for **May-game, May-lady**, and **May-lord** in Fig. 1, all of which are pronounced with the emphasis on the initial word, **May**. In addition, pronunciation is not generally given for obsolete or rare words for which no model of the spoken form exists, although stress may be shown.

Occasionally pronunciation information may also be included in the etymology to indicate a historical precedent, or in the body of an entry when a sense or derivative has a distinct pronunciation. Also, a historical explanation of the reason for a pronunciation may be included in an etymological note, as in the case of **romance**.

4. Part of speech

The **part of speech**, or grammatical designation, of the headword normally appears in italic type in abbreviated form immediately following the pronunciation (if given) as, for example, *v.* (verb), *a.* or *adj.* (adjective), *pple.* (participle). The treatment of nouns is an exception. In the first instance, a noun in the *OED* is always referred to as a 'substantive', abbreviated *sb.* However, it will be observed that many entries for nouns, in accordance with *OED* policy, omit the *sb.* designation; in general, it may be assumed that the headword is a noun when no part of speech is indicated. When the abbreviation *sb.* is used, its purpose is usually to avoid ambiguity as in the case of homographs (headwords with the same spelling but different parts of speech). For example, the entry for **marmalade** in Fig. 2 includes the designation *sb.* in order to differentiate the entry for the noun from the next entry for marmalade as a verb.

5. Homonym number

The **homonym number** is used to ensure that headwords with the same spelling and the same part of speech, but which warrant separate entries because of their distinct meanings and histories, are differentiated and given unique 'addresses'. In such cases, a superior number is either inserted following the part of speech (as in the case of **orange** in Fig. 3) or immediately after the headword (as in the entry for **palus**^{2}) if no part of speech is given. The latter practice is usual when the homonyms are nouns only.

The need for homonym numbers is especially evident in the case of a word such as **row**, which requires eighteen entries to cover its seven noun, two adjective, one adverb, and eight verb forms.

6. Label

A **label** identifies the usual context or status of a word (or sense). When it applies to the entire entry, it normally appears in the headword section in italic type following the **part of speech** (if given). The five major categories of labels are *status*, *regional*, *grammatical*, *semantic*, and *subject*:

(*a*) A *status* label indicates the frequency or register of a word. Status labels include *obs.* (obsolete), *rare*, *slang*, *colloq.* (colloquial), and *nonce-word* (a word used 'for the nonce' or for the occasion). An example of this type of label is found in the entries for **palumbine** and the obsolete nonce-word **tedify** in Fig. 3. Occasionally, as in the case of **palumbine**, the label *rare* is further defined by a superior number preceded by a dash ($^{-1}$) or ($^{-0}$) to indicate that only one or no contextual quotations were found. The '$^{-0}$' usually also implies that the word was only located as an entry in an earlier dictionary or similar reference book.

(*b*) A *regional* label indicates that a word originated or is used in a particular geographical area, such as *U.S.*, *Canad.* (Canada), *Austral.* (Australia), *Sc.* (Scottish), *south.* (southern), *north.* (northern), etc. The entry for **ranch**, for example, has the label 'orig. *U.S.*'.

(*c*) A *grammatical* label identifies a word's or a sense's syntactical function, over and above its part-of-speech role, and includes terms such as *pl.* (plural), *collect.* (collective), and *attrib.* (attributive).

(*d*) A *semantic* label is used to describe the type of meaning assigned to a word in a particular context, such as *fig.* (figurative), *spec.* (specific), or *transf.* (transferred).

(*e*) A *subject* label is employed when the headword is derived from, or used in, a specific discipline or subject area such as *Biol.* (Biology), *Chem.* (Chemistry), *Mus.* (Music), *Law*, as, for example, in the entries for **pericyclic** and **palus**[2] in Fig. 3.

Of the above five categories, *OED* editors are aware that the status label is the most open to debate. As Sir James Murray observed, there are many words that are 'alive to some speakers, and dead to others'. In a similar fashion, words considered objectionable or questionable by one generation are often accepted as part of everyday speech by the next generation.

7. Variant forms

Variant forms are current or earlier forms of the headword and may include irregular inflections, unusual plurals, or alternative spellings. They appear in light bold type, sometimes preceded by the words 'Forms' or 'also'. In the case of older words which have undergone many changes, variants are often listed chronologically; that is, the most commonly occurring spellings are listed by relevant centuries or century ranges. In order to compress the information, centuries are given in abbreviated form. For example, in the variant forms list of the entry for **orange** (Fig. 3), 4–8 is intended to be read as 14th to 18th centuries, 6–7 as 16th to 17th centuries, and so forth. The single number '1' that appears in some entries should be read as 'before 1100', the number '20' signifies the 20th century.

Some words, such as **romance** and **salad** illustrated in Fig. 3, develop two or more 'form branches'. In the case of **salad**, which is shown with its first sense and supporting quotations in Fig. 4, the branch with the forms selad, salade, sallade, etc. is obviously distinct from the branch with the spellings sal(l)ette, sal(l)otte, salat, sallet, etc. To distinguish the two groups, lower case italic Greek letters are used; the Greek letter alpha (α) appears before the first series of forms and beta (β) before the form '6 sal(l)ett(e)'. The same Greek letters are often used to identify a particular branch in subsequent etymologies or illustrative quotations in order to alert the reader that these sections are to be read in conjunction with one or the other of

(α)

salad ('sæləd). Forms: α. 5 **selad**, 5–7 **salade**, 6–7 **sallade**, 7–9 **sallad**, 7– **salad**; β. 6 **sal(l)ett(e**, **-otte**, **-ite**, 6–7 **salat**, 6–9 (now *dial.* or *arch.*) **sallet**, 7 **sallat(e**. [a. OF. *salade* (14th c.), a. Pr. *salada* = OIt. *salata*, Pg. *salada* (cf. It. *insalata*, Sp. *ensalada*):—popular L. **salāta*, f. **salāre* (It., med.L. *salare*, Pr., Sp., Pg. *salar*, F. *saler*) to salt, f. L. *sal* salt. — (β)

The Romanic word has been generally taken into the Germanic langs.: Du. *salade* (*salaet* in Kilian, also *sla* from **slade*), late MHG. *salât* (G. *salat*), Sw., Da. *salat*; also Russ. *salat*.]

1. a. A cold dish of herbs or vegetables (e.g. lettuce, endive), usually uncooked and chopped up or sliced, to which is often added sliced hard-boiled egg, cold meat, fish, etc., the whole being seasoned with salt, pepper, oil, and vinegar.

For an earlier wider use see quot. 1688 in β and cf. quot. 1687 s.v. SALADING.

α. **1481–90** *Howard Househ. Bks.* (Roxb.) 398 Item, for erbes for a selad j. d. **1533** ELYOT *Cast. Helthe* (1539) 41 Yonge men.. shell eate.. salades of cold herbes. **1578** LYTE *Dodoens* 125 This herbe.. is much vsed in meates and Salades with egges. **1601** HOLLAND *Pliny* II. 37 If you would make a delicate sallad of Cucumbers, boile them first, then pill from them their rind, serue them vp with oile, vinegre, and honey. **1699** DAMPIER *Voy.* II. I. 72 Purslain.. tis very sweet, and makes a good Salad for a hot Country. **1712** ARBUTHNOT *John Bull* I. xvi, She turned away one servant for putting too much oil in her sallad. **1726** SWIFT *Gulliver* IV. ii, Wholesome herbs, which I boiled, and eat as sallads with my bread. **1846** FORD *Gatherings from Spain* (1906) 147 The salad is the glory of every French dinner and the disgrace of most in England. **1855** DELAMER *Kitch. Gard.* (1861) 107 The most approved autumnal salads are those mainly composed of endive. — (α)

β. *c* **1390** *Forme of Cury* (1780) 41 Salat. Take persel, sawge, garlec [etc.].. waische hem clene.. and myng hem wel with rawe oile, lay on vyneger and salt, and serue it forth. **1550** J. COKE *Eng. & Fr. Heralds* §30 (1877) 64 Oyle olyve whiche was brought out of Espayne, very good for salettes. **1597** HOOKER *Eccl. Pol.* V. lxxvi. §8 A Sallet of greene herbes. **1629** PARKINSON *Paradis.* 468 Asparagus.. whose young shootes.. being boyled, are eaten with a little vinegar and butter, as a Sallet of great delight. **1660** PEPYS *Diary* 14 — (β)

Fig. 4

the word's form branches. For instance, the first paragraph of quotations for **salad** is preceded by *α* and the second paragraph by *β*, indicating that the citations are grouped to show examples of the two branches of spelling.

Within variant forms lists, status and regional labels may be encountered. For example, in the list for **orange**, the label *Sc.* for Scottish precedes the 15th-century variant 'oreynze', and the same label precedes the 15th-century form 'romanys' in the entry for **romance**. The *List of Abbreviations, Signs, etc.* at the front of the Dictionary is always useful for clarifying abbreviated forms.

In the case of verbs with very long and complex histories, variants of tenses and inflections may be discussed separately, each with illustrative quotations (for a further explanation of entries of exceptional length or complexity, see *lengthy entries* under the heading **special types of main entries**).

8. Etymology and etymological note

The **etymology** documents the headword's origin and history. Together with the optional **etymological note**, it is that part of the headword section enclosed in square brackets. Depending on availability and appropriateness, an etymology may contain a number of informational elements about the headword, including the following:

- its origin or derivation
- an explanation of, or commentary on, its variant forms
- an explanation of its phonetic descent
- its equivalence or similarity to other English word forms or those in other languages
- miscellaneous facts relating to the word's history, usage, pronunciation, etc.
- cross-references to other components of the same entry (for example, quotations, senses), or to headwords or other elements of other entries
- references to external sources, especially to foreign language dictionaries, for verification of the history or development of antecedent word forms.

Sometimes an etymology may contain little or no information about a word's origin, in which case, an explanation is usually offered by a phrase such as 'origin unknown', 'origin uncertain', or 'of obscure origin', frequently followed by an etymological note citing possible or erroneous assumptions about origins as suggested by other sources or popular opinion. The length of an etymology may, therefore, be as brief as a single word or very lengthy and complex; the longest etymology in the *OED* is for the word **church**, which runs to some 15 column-inches. Length is affected not only by the amount of information available, but also by whether the headword has a unique history of its own, or if it can be explained in terms of one or more of its constituent word forms, as is the case with many **derivatives** and **combinations**.

Although the Dictionary is known for its detailed etymologies, the *OED* was originally conceived as a history of the English language which would not attempt to duplicate the coverage of an etymological dictionary. Because the emphasis was placed on *history* related to *English*, the stated policy was that native words would be traced to their earliest known English form and, when possible, to their earliest Germanic form, and words of foreign origin to the language of the foreign word or elements that immediately preceded their introduction into the English language. The latter stipulation was extended to antecedent forms or component words when they helped to explain the history of the use of the words in English. In actual practice, however, this policy is often generously interpreted and many words are traced to antecedents—and even to a unitary language.

Etymologies can be the most problematic entry elements to understand. The difficulty is largely due to the many abbreviations and symbols used to present complex information as succinctly as possible. Like the variant forms list, an etymology becomes much more readable once its conventions are understood. Use of the *List of Abbreviations, Signs, etc.* at the front of the volume is usually essential until one becomes familiar with the Dictionary's terminology.

Broadly speaking, abbreviations and other conventions can be categorized as relating to **derivation, language forms**, and **references**. Obviously these categories overlap, but approaching them in this way may help to simplify not only the conventions, but the underlying concepts of linguistic development.

Derivation

Derivation deals with the ways in which word forms originate. Some understanding of the classification of English words and the means by which they enter the language is helpful before discussing specific abbreviations. In general, English words can be classed as:

(*a*) direct descendants of Old English words and hence belonging to the Germanic branch of Indo-European (the common root of most European languages, as well as Sanskrit), or

(*b*) 'borrowed' in the sense that they entered the English language indirectly through another language such as French, Italian, Latin, Greek, Arabic, etc.

In the first instance, the *OED* etymology attempts to trace the phonetic modifications, or changes in sound, that 'native' English words have undergone over the centuries. Whenever possible it notes that a word is directly descended phonetically from an Old English form (abbreviated as *OE.*) and then provides support for this statement by documenting its various modifications.

In the case of words derived from other languages, the process of borrowing is represented primarily by the use of two abbreviations; *a.* for *adopted*, *ad.* for *adapted*. These terms often introduce an etymology and refer to the language immediately preceding the headword's introduction into English. A third abbreviation, *f.* for *formed on* or *with*, is used when a word is derived from several native or foreign elements, or a combination of both. To a lesser extent *mod. f.* for *modern formation* will also be encountered. Finally, the symbol ':—', meaning 'normal development of' is sometimes used to introduce a word's phonetic descent. Further explanations of these terms are given below:

- As originally conceived by Sir James Murray, *adopted* (*a.*) referred to the informal and gradual integration of foreign ideas, things, names, etc. into the language. Words in this class include naturalized and partially naturalized terms. In the examples in Fig. 3, **restaurant** is a naturalized form of the French word brought into the language without a change in spelling. In the case of **salad**, earlier forms of the word were adopted from the Old French *salade* which, in turn, was adopted from the Provençal form *salada*. Note, however, that for non-naturalized words such as **palus**[2] it is usual to indicate simply the language of origin (in this case, Latin) and, sometimes, the meaning of the word in that language.

- *Adapted* (*ad.*), on the other hand, was seen by Murray as a more deliberate and formal process whereby a foreign word was altered in order to conform to English word structure. Numerous examples of adaptation can be found in scientific terminology directly derived from Greek or Latin stems with the addition of an English ending. Botanical and zoological terms also sometimes appear first in another language and are then altered to conform to English usage as in the case of words such as **palumbine**.

As will be understood, the distinction between adopted and adapted, as originally conceived, is not always entirely clear-cut. Therefore, for entries compiled after the first edition, these terms were redefined so as to be more intuitively logical. In general, in current *OED* lexicographical practice, 'adopted' is used to refer to words that have entered the language without change, while words which are altered in some way are considered to be 'adapted'.

- The third class, *formed on* or *with* (*f.*) is a process by which existing words or parts of words (either native or foreign, or both) are combined to produce a new word with its own distinct meaning. **Pericyclic** (Fig. 3), formed on the combining form **peri-** and the word **cyclic**, is an example of this type of word formation. In this case, the etymology notes the word forms used to construct **pericyclic** in small roman capitals, the convention used throughout the dictionary to signal a cross-reference to a headword. The abbreviation *f.* often appears *within* an etymology to indicate the earlier history of a word.
- The fourth, and less usual class of identification, is *modern formation* (*mod. f.*). This abbreviation is found in etymologies (mainly those compiled for the first edition) of words that appeared simultaneously in several modern languages with no clear indication of the language of origin. Many of the headwords so designated are early scientific or technical terms based on Greek or Latin forms.
- Finally, the use of the symbol ':—' is exemplified in the entry for **salad** in Fig. 3 to signify that the preceding Romance language forms represent an obvious phonetic development from the popular Latin form which, in turn, had its roots in the word for salt (sal).

Language forms

Numerous abbreviations are used for language forms, such as *F.* or *Fr.* (French), *OF.* or *OFr.* (Old French), *ONF.* (Old Northern French), *G.* or *Ger.* (German), *LG.* (Low German), *OHG.* (Old High German), *MHG.* (Middle High German), *WGmc.* (West Germanic), etc. Most of these can be found in the *List of Abbreviations, Signs, etc.* at the front of each volume. Occasionally, one may also encounter a language form prefaced by an asterisk (*), indicating a 'hypothetical' or reconstructed form—that is, it represents a word or form that is assumed to have existed, but which was not actually found. Examples of this usage occur in the etymology and etymological note of the entries for **salad** and **romance** in Fig. 3.

References

There are two major types of references in the etymologies (and in the Dictionary generally)—**cross-references** which refer to other elements *within* the Dictionary itself, and references to sources external to the *OED*. Several abbreviations are used in etymologies to suggest that the reader refer or compare the form under discussion to another similar or equivalent word form, either native or foreign. These include: 'Cf.' or 'cf.' (meaning 'confer' or 'compare'), '=' (equivalent to), 'cogn. w.' (cognate with), and 'see'.

- 'Cf' is used when the editor wishes to suggest that the reader compare the headword, or some form of it, to something else. The 'something else' might be a similar word in another language, an example of a similar word formation process in English, or another headword or a specific sense of another headword (in which case the headword as cross-reference appears in small roman capitals), as in the case of 'cf. ROMAUNT' in the entry for **romance** in Fig. 3.
- Similarly, the equals sign (=) is used to indicate that a form is the equivalent of a similar word form in English or another language. For example, the English expression *to be a good sailor* = the French expression *être bon marin*, or in Fig. 4, the Provençal form *salada* is equivalent to the Old Italian *salata* and Portuguese *salada*, which in turn should be compared with the Italian and Spanish forms, etc.
- *Cogn. w* also implies comparison since it tells the reader that the form under discussion is 'cognate with', or akin to, another word form, either native or foreign.
- A stronger type of cross-reference is the instruction to 'see' some other headword, sense, etc., sometimes in the form of 'see next' or 'see prec.', meaning refer to the next or preceding entry for etymological information. There is also a cross-reference version of 'f.' (formed on), as in 'f. prec.' (formed on the preceding), meaning that the reader should refer to the previous entry.

One further class of abbreviated reference which appears frequently in etymologies (as well as sometimes in definitions and quotations) may be especially puzzling since no interpretation is given in the *List of Abbreviations*. Two examples are *Florio* and *Du Cange* in the entry for **orange**. These citings of earlier foreign language dictionaries will be familiar to some scholars but may confuse the reader who does not have such specialized knowledge. In most cases, full bibliographical information can be found in the *Bibliography* at the end of the Dictionary if the reference is not included in the *List of Abbreviations*. *Florio* and *Du Cange*, for example, appear in the bibliography under the following entries:

FLORIO, John *Firste fruites. Also a perfect induction to the Italian, and English tongues* 1578
DU CANGE, Charles Dufresne, Sieur *Glossarium mediæ et infimæ Latinitatis* (1840–50; 1883–87)

Further reference to the *OED*'s use of earlier dictionaries will be found in the explanations of definitions and quotations in the **sense section** that follows.

This explanation by no means exhausts the kinds of references or cross-references found in etymologies, but in most cases such directions will be clear to the reader from the context. For example in the entry for **Sally Lunn** the etymology reads '[see quot. 1827]'. This quite clearly refers to a citation of that date within the quotation paragraph where it is suggested that the name of this kind of 'tea-cake' originated with a young woman in Bath who 'cried them'.

The **etymological note** is often used to provide supplementary information or to discuss popular or proposed theories of origin that the editors consider unsubstantiated or unproven. This type of note appears as part of the etymology (that is, within the square brackets) but as a separate paragraph in smaller print. An example of a typical note is found in the preceding entry for **orange** (Fig. 3) which supplies information about the orange's origins, as well as a possible association of its name with the Latin word (*aurum*) for gold. Other examples are found in the explanation of pronunciation in the entry for **romance** and the note about the usage of the word **salad** in Germanic languages.

Like the etymology, the etymological note may contain a number of language abbreviations and references to external dictionaries or other relevant works, most of which can either be found in the *List of Abbreviations, Signs, etc.* at the front of each volume or in the *Bibliography*.

Note that etymological information enclosed in square brackets may also occur within other sections of an entry, most frequently within individual senses when the information is relevant to that sense only.

SENSE SECTION

While the **headword section** describes the headword in terms of its form (that is, how it occurs in its written and spoken forms within the language), the **sense section** defines its meaning or 'signification'. In *OED* terms, a sense is an entity that, in its simplest form, consists of a definition and a series of chronologically arranged illustrative quotations. Some words have a single, readily definable meaning, but many, particularly those which have been in existence for several centuries, have acquired new or extended meanings. A word used in a literal sense may later be applied figuratively and develop its own history, or in other cases the entire meaning or significance of the word is altered. For example, the word **silly** first meant 'happy' or 'blessed', a **petticoat** was originally a man's short coat, the word **glamour** was a corruption of 'grammar' and also had an early meaning of 'magic' or 'witchcraft'. A major function of the *OED* is to trace the way in which such words evolved by illustrating their usage over time. Thus, for a complete understanding of a word's sense development, both the definitions and the quotations need to be read in full. Quotations also frequently illustrate the usage of variant spellings listed in the headword section, so that they support not only the senses, but the entry as a whole.

When a headword has more than one sense, the senses are listed in order of their development which in the majority of cases means that their arrangement is chronological as determined by the date of the first quotation supporting each sense. However, in some instances the chronological listing does not, in the lexicographer's judgement, reflect the order in which the senses are likely to have developed. Senses for some headwords are therefore arranged in 'logical' rather than chronological order. Readers should also be aware that the first quotation for any sense is the earliest example of literary use *located*; it is not claimed that it is the *first use* of the word and should not be interpreted as such, although in a number of cases evidence suggests this may be a reasonable conclusion.

The sense section of a typical main entry consists of a series of sense units made up of the following elements, although not all of them are necessarily found in any one entry. With the exception of the last two elements (**combinations** and **derivatives**) whose locations may vary, the elements are shown in the order in which they normally appear.

1. **Status symbol**
2. **Sense number**
3. **Label**
4. **Definition and definition note**
5. **Quotation paragraph**
   (*a*) date of publication
   (*b*) author
   (*c*) title
   (*d*) text of quotation
6. **Combinations**
7. **Derivatives**

In addition, an eighth element, the **cross-reference**, occurs, as it does in the headword section, within other elements of the sense section, notably—the definition, the definition note, quotation paragraph, and combinations. Examples of its usage are discussed as they arise within the explanations of those elements.

1. Status symbol

The **status symbol** preceding an individual sense performs the same function as it does with headwords that are so designated; that is, the dagger (†) indicates that the sense is obsolete and the parallels (‖) tell the reader that a particular sense is not fully naturalized. An example of the obsolete symbol attached to a sense is seen below in the entry for **palus**[1].

> **palus**[1]. Also 5 **palusche, palusshe**. [a. OF. *palus*, *paluz* (12th c. in Godef.), ad. L. *palūs* marsh.]
> † **1.** A marsh, a fen; an abyss. *Obs. rare.*
> **1471** CAXTON *Recuyell* (ed. Sommer) 390 In myddis of this palus was a grete lake or ponde. **1489** —— *Faytes of A.* I. xiv. 38 A place . . fer from eny palusche or mares grounde. **1490** —— *Eneydos* xi. 42 The depe palusshe infernalle.
> **2.** With capital initial and pronunc. (palys): a wine produced in the Palus region of Bordeaux in France. Also *attrib.*
> **1833** C. REDDING *Hist. Mod. Wines* v. 144 Bassens and Mondferrand grow the second class of Palus wines. **1861** MRS. BEETON *Bk. Househ. Managem.* 888 The genuine wines of Bordeaux are of great variety . . and the principal vineyards are those of Medoc, Palus, Graves, and Blanche. **1953** E. HYAMS *Vineyards in England* 90 Such *palus* wines are good enough of their kind. **1968** *New Statesman* 29 Nov. 744/2 How many little Palus and/or Bourg wines reach the market as Médoc, or even as St Julien?

A third status symbol (not used with headwords) may occasionally precede an individual sense. This is the catachrestic symbol (¶), which is the reverse of the paragraph symbol occasionally found within a citation in a quotation paragraph. When applied to a sense, it indicates a usage that, in the editor's view, is confused or erroneous. Normally the definition that follows includes an explanatory phrase such as *erroneous use* or *misused for*, as in the example below for **flota**, in which its use in the sense of 'a floating barrier' is questioned (?). Readers should compare this usage with the *spurious entry* discussed under the section **special types of main entries**.

flota (ˈfləʊtə). [a. Sp. *flota* fleet.]
1. The name given to the Spanish fleet which used to cross the Atlantic and bring back to Spain the products of America and the West Indies. Also *gen.*
1690 CHILD *Disc. Trade* Pref. B. iv b, The arrival of the Spanish Flota. *a* **1763** SHENSTONE *Elegies* xiv, What envy'd flota bore so fair a freight? **1796** NELSON 28 Sept. in Nicolas *Disp.* II. 284, I believe I can destroy their Flota.
¶**2.** ? *erroneous use.* A floating barrier (see quot.).
1777 WATSON *Philip II*, II. xix. 180 For the greater security of.. the work, a flota, one thousand two hundred feet long, was constructed of barks, bound together.. with ..beams pointed with iron, resembling a file of pikes.

2. Sense number

A **sense number** provides a unique location or 'address' for individual senses that can serve as a reference. In documenting a word's history, *OED* lexicographers study quotations, and sometimes other modern or early dictionaries, in order to distinguish steps in the development of the word's meaning. Once this not insignificant task is accomplished, the steps are identified by a hierarchical scheme of letters and numbers. The scheme adopted by the *OED* has two levels designed to serve two functions; to provide

- a means for listing individual senses and their subdivisions in the order of their development
- a framework for grouping *sets* of individual senses and sub-senses when simple linear ordering is not adequate to express a headword's history

Figs. 5, 6, 7, and 8, duplicating the entries for **whimsy-whamsy, whim-wham, whim, cardiac**, and **whimsy**, are used to illustrate the application of the numbering and lettering scheme. As an aid to understanding, a structural diagram accompanies each entry example.

In Fig. 5 **whimsy-whamsy** and **whim-wham** are typical simple entries, the first with only one sense, and the second with two senses.

whimsy-whamsy. [f. WHIMSY after next.] = next, 2. Also *attrib.*

1807 SOUTHEY *Lett. from England* III. lix. 109 An old Welsh baronet..chose some years ago to set up a heresy of his own... He himself called it Rational Whist; his friends, in a word of contemptuous fabrication, denominated it his *whimsy-whamsy.* **1871** CADDELL *Never Forgotten* ii, Maude always was obstinate when she had one of her religious whimsey whamseys in her head. **1900** 'ANTHONY HOPE' *Quisanté* v, The real reason..why the Dean hasn't risen higher is because he always has some whimsy-whamsy in his head. **1931** *Time & Tide* 26 Sept. 1118 Have we not whimsy-whamsy authors of our own without importing the too, too, quaint devices of foreign playwrights? **1945** S. LEWIS *Cass Timberlane* xl. 302 Sure, the jolly little playboy, and underneath his whimsy-whamsy, he's the coldest-hearted rich-man's lawyer. **1951** MCLUHAN *Mech. Bride* (1967) 101/1 It is not a laughter or comedy to be compared with the whimsy-whamsy article of James Thurber.

whim-wham ('hwɪmhwæm). Also 6–7 **whym wham,** 7 **whimwhom,** 8–9 **whimwam,** 9 **wimwam, whim-, wim-wom.** [A reduplication with vowel-variation, like *flim-flam, jim-jam, trim-tram,* all of which are similarly applied to trivial or frivolous things.

The history of the group of words of which WHIM *sb.*[1], WHIMSY, and this word are the chief members, is not clear. The existence in ON. of *hvima* to wander with the eyes as with the fugitive look of a frightened or silly person, and *hvimsa* to be taken aback or discomfited, suggests the possibility of an ultimate Scand. origin; but, seeing that *whim-wham* is the earliest recorded of the group (contemporaneously with the similar reduplicated forms mentioned above), an indigenous symbolic origin is more likely; in which case *whimsy* may be related to *whim-wham* as *flimsy* to *flim-flam.*]

1. A fanciful or fantastic object; *fig.* a trifle; in early use chiefly, a trifling ornament of dress, a trinket; later in various local uses (see quots.).

a **1529** SKELTON *E. Rummyng* 75 After the Sarasyns gyse, With a whym wham, Knyt with a trym tram, Vpon her brayne pan. **1602** DEKKER *Satirom.* F 2, Dost loue that mother Mumble-crust, dost thou? dost long for that whim-wham? **1621** J. TAYLOR (Water P.) *Superbiæ Flagellum* C 7 b, Whimwhams & whirligiggs to please Baboones. **1625** FLETCHER & SHIRLEY *Nt. Walker* I. i, They'll pull ye all to pieces, for your whim-whams, Your garters and your gloves. **1641** J. TAYLOR (Water P.) *Reply as true as Steel* (1877) 6 He caus'd some formes of flowers..'twixt the Beast legges be painted To hide his whim wham. **1659** TORRIANO, *Tencone,* ..a mans whim-wham. **1691** MRS. D'ANVERS *Academia* 17 The Yat's [= gate's] all hung about with whimwhoms, As Fishes Bones, and other thingums. **1721** RAMSAY *Scriblers Lash'd* 197 Dealers in small Ware, Clinks, Whim Whams. **1808** HAN. MORE *Cœlebs* (1809) II. 183, I have spent 700 pounds..for her to learn music and whim-whams. **1818** SCOTT *Br. Lamm.* xi, Florentine and flams—bacon, wi' reverence, and a' the sweet confections and whim-whams. *a* **1842** HAWTHORNE *Twice-told T.* (1851) I. ix. 163 So much for the commencement of this long whim-wham. **1854** MISS BAKER *Northampt. Gloss., Whim-wom,* a bird-boy's clackers for frightening birds from fruit or corn. **1860** *Slang Dict., Whim-wham,* an alliterative term, synonymous with fiddle-faddle, riff-raff, etc., denoting nonsense, rubbish, etc.

1.

2.

2. A fantastic notion, odd fancy; = WHIM *sb.*[1] 3.

1580 FULKE *Stapleton Confut.* II. viii. 117 Voluntarie pouertie in Augustine not found in the first planters of this newe trim tram. A matter worthie to be aunswered with a whim wham. **1588** J. HARVEY *Disc. Probl.* 40 Such blind vnreasonable whimwhams. **1621** FLETCHER *Wild-Goose Chase* III. i, Your studied Whim-whams; and your fine set faces. **1759** STERNE *Tr. Shandy* I. vii, Who..not only hit upon this dainty amendment, but coaxed many of the old-licensed matrons..to open their faculties afresh, in order to have this whim-wham of his inserted. **1807–8** W. IRVING *Salmag.* (1824) 123 He declared he would humour the weather no longer in its whim-whams. **1832** ROWL. HILL in *Life* (1834) 382 The pure and simple gospel of Christ, but not intermixed with the whim-whams of the present day. **1882** C. D. WARNER *W. Irving* iv. 50 The follies and 'whim-whams' of the metropolis.

Fig. 5

whim (hwɪm), *sb.*[1] Also 8 **whym.** [See WHIM-WHAM. The transference of meaning from branch I to branch II is similar to that in ENGINE and GIN *sb.*[1]]

I. †1. A pun or play on words; a double meaning. *Obs.*

1641 BROME *Jov. Crew* I. (1652) B 1 b, There was the whim, or double meaning on't. *Ibid.*, One told a Gentleman His son should be a man-killer, and hang'd for't; Who, after prov'd a great and rich Physician, And with great Fame ith' Universitie Hang'd up in Picture for a grave example. There was the whim of that. Quite contrary! *Ibid.* B 2 b, Shall Squire Oldrent's Daughters Weare old rents in their Garments? (there's a whim too).

2. †**a.** A fanciful or fantastic creation; a whimsical object. *Obs.*

1678 BUTLER *Hud.* III. i. 108 When he.. Had rifled all his Pokes and Fobs Of Gimcracks, Whims and Jiggumbobs. **1712–13** SWIFT *Jrnl. to Stella* 16 Jan., I came home at seven, and began a little whim, which just came into my head; and will make a threepenny pamphlet. **1731** CHENY *List Horse-Matches* 89 This Prize is call'd a Whim or whimsical Plate, because the Conditions of running for the same, are different from those of all other Prizes. **1752** HUME *Ess. & Treat.* (1777) I. 275 Were the testimony of history less positive.. such a Government [as that of Sparta] would appear a mere philosophical whim or fiction. **1821** CLARE *Vill. Minstrel* I. 111 Some may praise the grass-plat whims, Which the gard'ner weekly trims.

†**b.** A whimsical fellow. *Obs.*

1712 ADDISON *Spect.* No. 371 ¶2 That sort of Men who are called Whims and Humourists.

c. In ombre, the deciding on the trump suit by turning up the top card of the stock.

1874 H. H. GIBBS *Ombre* 41 *note*, Voltereta, though known in England (under the name of the Whim), was not appreciated there.

3. A capricious notion or fancy; a fantastic or freakish idea; an odd fancy.

1697 VANBRUGH *Prov. Wife* II. ii, Walking pretty late in the Park.. A Whim took me to sing Chevy-Chace. **1702** SAVERY *Miner's Friend* 80 Many such like Whims [as perpetual motion] are pretended to by Designing Men. **1713** HEARNE *Collect.* (O.H.S.) IV. 254 The New-Printing House just erected, w[ch] is (it seems, out of a Whim) to be called Typographeum Clarendonianum. **1781** COWPER *Truth* 89 See the sage hermit,.. Wearing out life in his religious whim, Till his religious whimsy wears out him. **1832** HT. MARTINEAU *Ella of Gar.* viii, The scheme was no whim of the moment. **1848** DICKENS *Dombey* xlii, Mrs. Dombey may be in earnest, or she may be pursuing a whim, or she may be opposing me. **1899** CONAN DOYLE *Duet, Confessions*, There are all.. degrees of love, some just the whim of a moment, and others the passion of a lifetime.

b. In generalized sense: Capricious humour or disposition of mind.

a **1721** PRIOR *Enigma*, '*Form'd half beneath*, etc.' 7 They [*sc.* skates] serve the poor for use, the rich for whim. **1728** POPE *Dunc.* III. 153 Sneering Goode, half malice and half whim. **1809** MALKIN *Gil Blas* XII. i. (Rtldg.) 423, I came up to pay my devotions; but whim, or perhaps revenge.. determined her to put on the stranger. **1884** STEVENSON *Mem. & Portraits* xvi. (1887) 275 Mr. Besant so genial,.. with so persuasive and humorous a vein of whim.

c. *Comb.*

1647 WARD *Simple Cobler* 25 These whimm' Crown'd shees, these fashion-fansying wits. **1786** BURNS *Bard's Epit.* i, Is there a whim-inspir'd fool, Owre fast for thought, owre hot for rule,.. Let him draw near.

II. 4. A machine, used esp. for raising ore or water from a mine, consisting of a vertical shaft carrying a large drum with one or more radiating arms or beams to which a horse or horses, etc. may be yoked and by which it may be turned, the rope being wound on the drum by the horse's motion. Also ***horse-whim***.

1738 *MSS. Dk. Portland* (Hist. MSS. Comm.) VI. 177 This Lord has destroyed the old ridiculous water works and whims that were then when made much in vogue. **1759** B. MARTIN *Nat. Hist.* I. *Cornwall* 11 A Wheel and Axle, (which they call a Whim). **1778** PRYCE *Min. Cornub.* 143 A proper working Shaft, upon which a Whym may be erected. **1859** H. KINGSLEY *G. Hamlyn* xxxvi, They above.. were rigging a rope to an old horse-whim. **1890** 'R. BOLDREWOOD' *Miner's Right* xliv, The whole plant, the whim, the tools,.. —every mortal thing down to a worn-out hide bucket—was sold.

b. *attrib.* and *Comb.*, as ***whim-driver***, ***-engine***, ***-gin***, ***-horse***, ***-house***, ***-kibble***, ***-rope***, ***-round***, ***-shaft***.

1757 BORLASE in *Phil. Trans.* L. 504 The whim-house shook so terribly, that a man there at work ran out of it, concluding it to be falling. **1778** PRYCE *Min. Cornub.* 144 A whym Shaft to draw the Deads and Ore from the Sump of the Mine. *Ibid.* 150 Two horses.. go round upon a platform named the Whym-round. *Ibid.* 165 In deep Mines, some whym ropes cost fifty or sixty pounds. *Ibid.* Gloss. s.v. *Kibbal*, A Whym-Kibbal is a larger [bucket], which.. serves to draw water with, or bring up the Ore to grass. **1789** BRAND *Hist. Newc.* II. 684 In a whim gin the ropes run upon two wheel pullies over the shaft. **1834** *2nd Rep. Cornwall Polytechn. Soc.* 41 The Steam Whim Engine. **1855** LEIFCHILD *Cornwall* 139 Shafts.. intended for the extraction of ores (called whim-shafts where horse-whims are employed for extracting the produce). **1881** *Instr. Census Clerks* (1885) 84 Whim Driver. **1896** J. HOCKING *Fields of Fair Renown* i, The boy who drove the 'whim horse' cracked his whip.

¶ In sense 4 a variant *whin* is found.

1838 SIMMS *Publ. Wks. Gt. Brit.* II. 3 Cutting the whin ropes nearly through. **1884** KNIGHT *Dict. Mech.* Suppl., *Whin* (Mining), a machine for raising ores and refuse. **1897** *Westm. Gaz.* 9 June 5/3 Rolling a large oak tree with a timber whin.

Hence **whimmed** *a.*, ? possessed with a whim or odd fancy; ˈ**whimmery**, a piece of whimsicality; ˈ**whimship**, mock title for a whimsical person.

1654 GAYTON *Pleas. Notes* I. viii. 29 Our Don (or if Sancho had the braines, for the Squires were *whim'd in the whiske) might very well from that encounter have stil'd himself a Knight of Millan. **1837** *Fraser's Mag.* XV. 333 Had not Mr. Pugin's attention been too exclusively engrossed by that architectural *whimmery. **1906** T. SINTON *Poetry of Lochaber* 182 We can imagine the swing of his bow with many a pause and twirl carrying through the whimeries of the rhyme. **1793** *Ann. Reg.*, *Projects* 337 You're sure to find his *Whimship there.

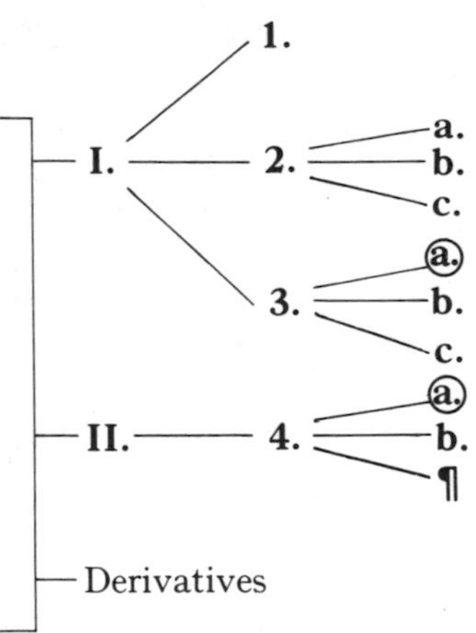

Fig. 6

cardiac ('kɑːdıæk), *a.* (and *sb.*) Forms: 5 cardiake, 7 -aque, -acke, 7–8 -ack, 8– cardiac. [a. F. *cardiaque* of the heart, ad. L. *cardiacus*, a. Gr. καρδιακός, f. καρδία heart.]

A. *adj.*

1. Of or pertaining to the heart, anatomically, physiologically, or pathologically. †***cardiac passion*** [L. *cardiaca passio*]: 'an old name for cardialgia or heartburn' (*Syd. Soc. Lex.*); but app. *orig.* palpitation of the heart. ***cardiac arrest***, sudden cessation of the heart's pumping action.

1601 HOLLAND *Pliny* II. 153 The Cardiacke passion, which is a feeblenesse and trembling of the heart. **1629** CHAPMAN *Juvenal* v. 65 His longing friend..blown in fume up with a cardiack fit. **1726** MONRO *Anat. Nerves* (1741) 74 The Cardiac Nerves. **1810** *Encycl. Brit.* (ed. 4) V. 177 Cardialgia..better known by the name of cardiac passion, or heartburn. **1835–6** TODD *Cycl. Anat.* I. 192/1 The cardiac arteries arise from the aorta close to its origin. **1883** *Nature* 15 Mar. 468 The cardiac action became stronger. **1950** *Ann. Surg.* CXXXII. 855 The sudden onset of ventricular fibrillation in 15 and cardiac arrest in two as observed in the continuous electrocardiographic image. **1961** *Lancet* 5 Aug. 293/2 The technique..has been used in all cases where the period of cardiac arrest was expected to exceed about 15 minutes. **1977** *Rolling Stone* 30 June 35/1 Jazz pianist Hampton Hawes died May 22nd in Los Angeles of a cardiac arrest following a cerebral hemorrhage. **1982** *Macmillan Guide Family Health* 388/1 If cardiac arrest happens when nobody else is present, it is fatal. **1983** *Oxf. Textbk. Med.* II. xiii. 90/1 Signs of cardiac arrest such as dilated pupils, apnoea, and absent heart sounds.

2. a. 'Applied to medicines supposed to invigorate the heart' (*Syd. Soc. Lex.*); cordial, strengthening.

1661 EVELYN *Fumifug.* Misc. III. (1805) 241 Strawberries, whose very leaves..emit a cardiaque & most refreshing halitus. **1718** QUINCY *Compl. Disp.* 77 Whatsoever raises the Spirits, and gives sudden Strength..is term'd Cardiack, or Cordial, as comforting the Heart. **1744** BERKELEY *Siris* §64 The stomachick, cardiack, and diuretick qualities of this fountain. **1807** in G. GREGORY *Dict. Arts.*

b. ***cardiac glycoside***, any of a group of steroid glycosides (as digoxin, ouabain) that occur in certain plants and are heart stimulants; similarly ***cardiac glucoside***, a glucoside of this group.

1927 *Jrnl. Biol. Chem.* LXXIV. 787 (*heading*) The relationship between the structure and the biological action of the cardiac glucosides. **1937** A. STOLL (*title*) The cardiac glycosides. **1951** A. GROLLMAN *Pharmacol. & Therapeutics* xviii. 332 The cardiac glycosides have been used from time immemorial principally because of their toxic effects. **1983** *Oxf. Textbk. Med.* II. XIII. 61/1 Many patients on maintenance cardiac glycosides do not require them, and in view of their potential danger the need for continued treatment should be reviewed frequently.

3. Pertaining to or affected with disease of the heart.

1748 tr. *Vegetius' Distemp. Horses* 50 Such [Horses] as have the Head-ach, or the Staggers, or are mad or are cardiac. **1856** KANE *Arct. Expl.* II. 30 We both suffered from cardiac symptoms.

4. *Anat.* Distinctive epithet of the upper orifice of the stomach; hence applied to the corresponding end or region of the stomach, or to some organ connected with it. Cf. CARDIA.

1843 J. WILKINSON tr. *Swedenborg's Anim. Kingd.* I. ii. 70 The cardiac orifice guards the stomach. **1866** HUXLEY *Phys.* vi. (1869) 166 Its [the stomach's] left end is produced into an enlargement which, because it is on the heart side of the body, is called the cardiac dilatation. The opening of the gullet into the stomach, termed the cardiac aperture.

5. Heart-shaped (in ***cardiac wheel*** = HEART-CAM).

1864 in WEBSTER.

B. *sb.*

†**1.** A disease or affection of the heart, or referred to the heart; ? = *cardiac passion* (see A. 1).

c **1450** *Destr. Jerus., Addit. MS.* 10036, f. 29 Suche joie Titus gan undretake, That him toke a cardiake. **1468** *Medulla* in *Cath. Angl.* 54 *Cardiaca; quidam morbus*, a cardyake. **1483** *Cath. Angl.* 54 A Cardiakylle or cardiake, *cardia, cardiaca.*

2. A medicine supposed to stimulate the heart, a cordial. Also *fig.*

1746 BERKELEY *2nd Let. Tar-water* §6 This medicine of tar-water worketh..as a..cardiac. **1803** *Man in Moon* (1804) 65 No. 9 How many cardiacs has the fertile invention of modern dramatists mixed up..to please an audience?

3. A person suffering from heart disease.

1934 in WEBSTER. **1957** *Amer. Heart Jrnl.* LIV. 352 These patients represent an important group of cardiacs who are often denied surgical relief. **1972** I. L. RUBIN et al. *Treatm. Heart Dis. Adult* (ed. 2) xviii. 445 All cardiacs should be watched carefully for fall in blood pressure.

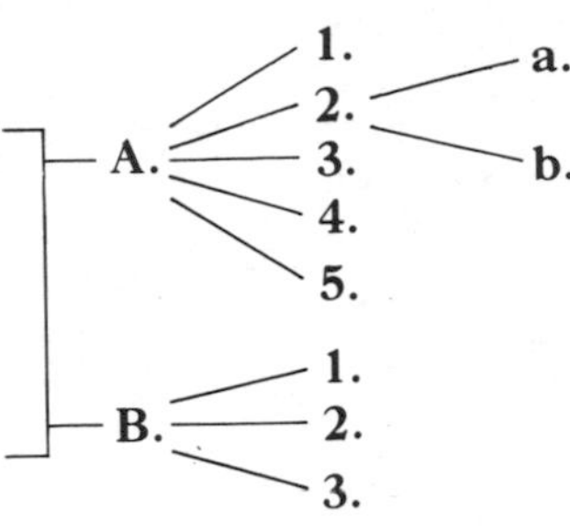

Fig. 7

whimsy, whimsey ('hwɪmzɪ), *sb.* (*a.*) Forms: 7 **whim-, whymzie, whimsee,** 7–8 **whimzy,** 8 **whymsey,** 7–9 **whimsie, whims(e)y.** [See WHIM-WHAM.]

A. *sb.* **I. † 1.** Dizziness, giddiness, vertigo. *Obs.*

16.. MIDDLETON, etc. *Old Law* III. ii, I ha' got the scotomy in my head already, The whimsey: you all turn round. **1656** BLOUNT *Glossogr.*, *Scotomatical*, that is troubled with such a whimsey in the head.

† 2. A wench. *Obs. rare.*

1614 B. JONSON *Barth. Fair* II. iv, And shall we ha' smockes Vrsla, and good whimsies, ha? *a* **1625** FLETCHER *Bloody Brother* IV. ii, You'l pick a bottle open, or a whimsey, As soon as the best of us.

3. a. = WHIM *sb.*[1] 3.

1605 B. JONSON *Volpone* III. i, I can feele A whimsey i' my bloud: (I know not how) Successe hath made me wanton. **1628** VENNER *Baths of Bathe* (1650) 365 Such as have their pates full of outlandish whimsies. **1646** J. HALL *Horæ Vac.* 31 That whimsey of Pythagoras of the transmigration of Soules. **1713** DERHAM *Phys.-Theol.* I. i. 7 *note*, Our Inability to live in too rare and light an Air may discourage those vain Attempts of Flying, and Whimsies of passing to the Moon. **1803** JEFFERSON *Writ.* (1830) III. 508 Plato, who only used the name of Socrates to cover the whimsies of his own brain. **1849** MACAULAY *Hist. Eng.* ii. I. 164 Both had what seemed extravagant whimsies about dress, diversions, and postures. **1891** BESANT *St. Katherine's* I. vi, Why, I was young once, and had my own whimsies like the rest.

b. = WHIM *sb.*[1] 3 b. *arch.*

a **1680** GLANVILL *Sadducismus* II. (1681) 50 All this is Whimsey and Fiction. **1709** SHAFTESB. *Charac.* (1711) II. 337 In One there are the Marks of Wisdom and Determination; in the other, of Whimsy and Conceit. **1775** WRAXALL *Tour N. Eur.* 121 It may just as well be called an European structure, where whimsy and caprice form the predominant character. **1881** BLACKMORE *Christowell* xlviii, They winnow my gatherings on every wind of whimsy.

4. = WHIM *sb.*[1] 2 a.

1712 *H. More's Antid. Ath.* III. ix. §2. Schol. 169 Engrav'd with Characters, and other Magical whimsies of this sort. **1785** J. COLLIER *Mus. Trav.* (ed. 4) 62 The Italian whimsies and tweedle-dums, that people played upon in these days. **1791** COWPER *Yardley Oak* 118 Thy root.. A quarry of stout spurs, and knotted fangs,.. crook'd into a thousand whimsies. **1860–1** D. COLERIDGE in *Phil. Soc. Trans.* 164 The proposed Dictionary.. must include many a mere whimsey and many a gross corruption. **1906** E. V. LUCAS *Wand. in Lond.* i. 14 The lodge in the garden of the Record Office. This little architectural whimsy might be the abode of an urban fairy or gnome.

II. † 5. A merry-go-round, roundabout. *Obs.*

1684 *Ballads illustr. Gt. Frost* (Percy Soc.) 4 There were Dutch whimsies turned swiftly round Faster then horses run on level ground.

6. a. = WHIM *sb.*[1] 4. *local.*

1789 J. WILLIAMS *Min. Kingd.* I. 430 This may be done.. with a small horse-gin or whimsy, instead of a windlass, for drawing the water and work in sinking. **1836** *Hull & Selby Railw. Act* 44 To make use of any gins, whimsies, tackling, ropes, machines. **1875** *Ure's Dict. Arts* III. 319 In Cornwall, a kibble, in which the ore is raised in the shafts, by machines called whims or whimseys.

b. (See quot.)

1867 SMYTH *Sailor's Word-bk.*, *Whimsey*, a small crane for hoisting goods to the upper stories of warehouses.

7. a. *Glass-making.* (See quot.)

1856 H. CHANCE in *Jrnl. Soc. Arts* IV. 224/2 Still whirling, the table [of crown glass], as it is now called, is carried off, laid flat upon a support called a whimsey, detached by shears from the ponty, [etc.].

b. A small object made by a glass-maker or potter for his own amusement.

1938 A. FLEMING *Scottish & Jacobite Glass* ix. 109 Dame Fashion.. seems to settle upon glass as a favourite and satisfactory medium of decoration. Other 'wimsies' are cheap little fantastic groups of figures, fruit and flowers delicately made from a tube modelled by a tool with infallible dexterity. **1976** *Canadian Collector* (Toronto) Mar.–Apr. 23/1 We were able to locate several more examples of the whimseys produced by the last potter.

B. *adj.* Whimsical.

1632 SHIRLEY *Hyde Park* II. ii, Ieere on, my whimsy Lady. **1867** LANIER *Strange Jokes* 7 Poems (1892) 217 Once in a whimsey mood he sat. **1913** MRS. STRATTON-PORTER *Laddie* xiv, Laddie studied the sky, a whimsy smile on his lips.

C. *attrib.* and *Comb.*, as ***whimsy-pate, -shaft***; ***whimsy-headed*** adj.; **† whimsy-board,** ? a board or table used in some game of chance, or on which different objects were carried about for sale.

a **1704** T. BROWN *Lett. Living to Dead* Wks. 1720 II. 19, I am sometimes a small Retainer to a Billiard-Table, and sometimes, when the Master on't is sick, earn a Penny by a *Whimsy-Board. **1708** W. KING *Art of Cookery* (1709) 99 Then Pippins did in Wheel-barrows abound, And Oranges in Whimsey-boards went round. **1710** *Lond. Gaz.* No. 4659/3 He frequents the Cock Pits and Gaming Houses, Whimsy Boards. **1698** E. WARD *Lond. Spy* III. (1706) 63 The first *Whimsie-headed Wretch of this Lunatick Family. **1682** WINYARD *Mercurius Menip.* 6 His *Whimsie-Meagrim must be an Ecstasie. **1654** GAYTON *Pleas. Notes* III. iv. 88 What a company.. doth this phantasticall *whimzy-pate gather. **1821** W. FORSTER *Section of Strata* (ed. 2) 331 *Whimsey Shafts may be sunk to the depth of ten .. fathoms.

Hence '**whimsily** *adv.*, '**whimsiness.**

1654 GAYTON *Pleas. Notes* IV. iii. 188, I love Toboso, and I know not why, Only I say, I love her (whimsyly). **1909** *Daily Chron.* 14 Sept. 5/3 To.. indulge his political whimsiness. **1980** P. MOYES *Angel Death* xviii. 237 The whimsily-drawn pamphlet which they gave to visitors.

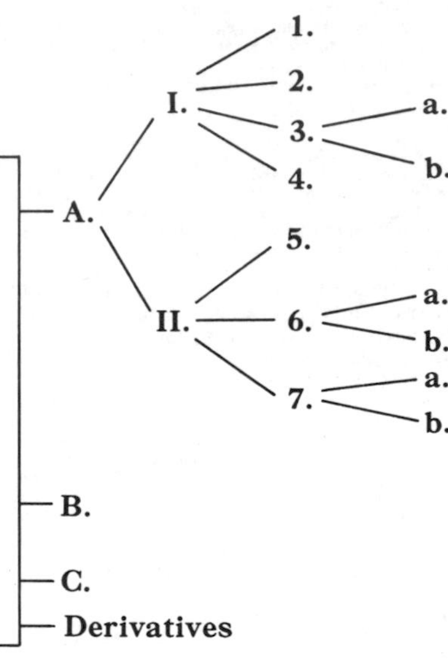

Fig. 8

Whim-wham represents the most basic form of the first level of the hierarchical scheme in which each sense is numbered consecutively (**1.**, **2.**, **3.** . . .). However, a single sense such as **whimsy-whamsy** is not usually numbered.

A slightly more complex type of entry results when the numbered senses are subdivided. The subdivisions represent separate aspects of a sense as in the case of the entry for **marmalade** shown in Fig. 2 and already discussed. Note that each time a higher level of numbering is reached, the ordering of the lower level (**a.**, **b.** . . .) begins again, as in the case of **whim** in Fig. 6. Sometimes, there is a need to subdivide further the lower level, in which case lower case bracketed italic letters—(*a*), (*b*), (*c*) . . .—or roman numerals—(i), (ii), (iii) . . .—are used. Thus, a 'sense' (the word is used inclusively to refer to either a main sense or a subdivision) may have an 'address' such as **1.** or **2.**; **1.b.** or **3.d.**; or **1.d.**(*a*), etc.

The second level of the numbering and lettering scheme is used when the lexicographer wishes to separate *groups* of numbered senses, either because the headword's sense development is not straightforwardly linear, or because it is an aid to comprehension to group senses syntactically or semantically. Upper case roman numerals (**I.**, **II.**, **III.** . . .) are employed to separate groups or branches of senses that developed simultaneously and/or divergently. An example of this usage is seen in the entry for **whim** in Fig. 6, in which branch **I.** senses relate to notions, fancy, etc., while the branch **II.** sense deals with the word's use as a type of machinery. Note, however, that the second branch does not interrupt the numerical sequence of the individual senses (**1.**, **2.**, **3.**, **4.**). In complex entries, where further grouping is required, an increasing series of asterisks (*, **, *** . . .) is used (application of this level is exemplified in the explanation of *lengthy entries* under the section **special types of main entries**).

Another form of grouping is needed when two grammatical forms of a word, such as noun and adjective, are included in one entry rather than creating two separate entries (this is often done when the two forms share a common etymology and history). In this case, the highest level of the hierarchical scheme, bold upper case letters (**A.**, **B.**, **C.** . . .), are used. In the entry for **cardiac** (Fig. 7), for example, adjectival senses are grouped under **A.** and noun senses under **B.** The senses within each section are treated as they would be in separate entries, that is, the linear sequence of individual senses (**1.**, **2.**, **3.** . . .) is reset for each grammatical grouping. In addition when a **cross-reference** is made to such an entry, each grammatical section is treated as a separate entry, i.e. the reference 'address' for Sense **1.** of section **A.** is '**cardiac**, *adj*. **1.**'.

When two or more grammatical forms of a word are included in one entry *and* the development of one or more of the forms is not simply linear, the **A.**, **B.**, **C.** . . . , and **I.**, **II.**, **III.** . . . levels are integrated. An example of this arrangement can be seen in the entry for **whimsy** in Fig. 8. In this case, the **A.** (noun) level is divided in two (**I.**, **II.**) branches. (Note that had there been several senses in either **B.** or **C.**, the arabic numerals (**1.**, **2.**, **3.** . . .) would have been reset in each case.)

It should be noted that all entries other than those with a single definition begin their sense sections with either **A.**, **I.**, or **1.**, although instances will be found where the initial-level letter or numeral is not printed, but rather, 'understood'. In the structural diagrams accompanying each of the examples, the numbers or letters which do not appear in the actual text are circled. For example, it is quite common to find the first sense numbered **1** only, rather than **1.a.** although the intent is evident when the following sense subdivision appears as **b.**

While the lettering/numbering scheme may seem intricate, it is intuitively logical, as will be seen if one scans a few Dictionary entries. Even though the second level grouping system is sometimes employed for purposes other than those described above (for example, the **A.**, **B.** . . . scheme might be used to group, first, a verb's inflectional forms and then its signification or senses, while the **I.**, **II.** . . . scheme might further group the signification under intransitive senses, transitive senses, senses with prepositions, senses with adverbs, etc.), such variations should not disturb the Dictionary user if the scheme is viewed as a logical means for presenting information in an orderly fashion within the context of an individual entry. The major problem *OED* users may encounter is in deciphering very long entries with several branches and many senses and sub-senses. In this case, it is often helpful to scan the entry first to acquaint oneself with the principal schematic divisions. As previously mentioned, lengthy entries are discussed further, with examples, under the section **special types of main entries**.

3. Label

Labels indicating status, region, grammatical function, semantic context, or subject are often attached to individual senses in place of, or in addition to, a label applying to the entire entry in the headword section. An individual sense of a word, for example, may have become obsolete, but the word could still be in common use in another sense. In addition, a word may have acquired special meaning within a certain subject field, or may be used in a slang expression. Subject labels, such as *Chem.*, *Nat. Hist.*, normally follow the sense number. Status and regional labels, on the other hand, often follow the definition, as in the case of the label *Obs.* in senses **I. 1.** and **2.** of **whim** in Fig. 6. (For a more complete explanation of label categories, refer to the discussion of this element in the **headword section.**)

4. Definition and definition note

The **definition** is a familiar feature of any dictionary and usually requires little explanation. *OED* definitions, however, are somewhat different, since they are designed to be read in conjunction with the quotations that form an integral part of the documentation of the meaning of a particular sense of a headword. In addition, at least three types of definitions may be encountered, either in combination or singly: explanatory, structural, and cross-reference.

An *explanatory* definition, that is, the traditional explanation of the meaning of a sense or word, may take several forms. For example, where appropriate, a word's relationship to another word may be noted as in the case of an adjective that is defined as 'of or pertaining to' its related noun form. The basic explanation may also be supplemented by a series of synonyms, and sometimes antonyms (usually italicized and preceded by 'opp.' for opposite), as an aid to understanding. Where a sense has developed its own history, an etymological comment in square brackets may be included. Occasionally, particularly in the case of obsolete or rare words located in earlier dictionaries, the entire text may consist of a quotation, followed by an abbreviation for the source. For example, the single capital letter 'J.' is often encountered. By referring to the *List of Abbreviations, Signs, etc.* in the front of the Dictionary, one learns that the definition quoted is taken from Dr Samuel Johnson's famous dictionary, first published in 1755. Sense **A. 2.a.** for **cardiac**, *adj.* (Fig. 7) is an instance of a quotation from another source forming part of the definition. In this case, the parenthetical source for the definition 'Applied to medicines supposed to invigorate the heart' is '(Syd. Soc. Lex.)', which, if one checks the *Bibliography* at the end of the Dictionary, is identified as the Sydenham Society's *Lexicon of Medicine and Allied Sciences*, published in various editions between 1879 and 1899.

A *structural* or functional definition is one that describes the use of the headword in terms of some grammatical or syntactical structure. Definition components may take the form of an italicized abbreviation such as *ellip.* (elliptically), *attrib.* (attributively), *comb.* (combined), or a comment regarding a special construction such as the use of a verb with a specific preposition, or the use of a noun without an article. These descriptions often depend on the quotations to illustrate the function in context. For example, the entry for **whimsy-whamsy** (Fig. 5) notes that the word is used 'Also *attrib.*'. This is illustrated in the 1951 quotation from Marshall McLuhan's *Mechanical Bride*, in which he refers to 'the whimsy-whamsy article of James Thurber'.

A *cross-reference* definition is one that contains, or consists entirely of, a **cross-reference** to another part of the same entry, to another headword, to a specific sense (or combination or derivative) within an entry, or to a quotation. The most common indicators of a cross-reference are '='(meaning equivalent to), 'see', and 'cf.' (compare with). There are a number of instances of cross-references in the examples in Figs. 5, 6, 7, and 8:

- **whimsy-whamsy** (Fig. 5) is defined as '=next, 2', referring the reader to Sense **2.** of the next entry for **whim-wham**. There, one finds the definition 'a fantastic notion, odd fancy', but once again the reader is referred to another entry; this time to **whim** *sb.*[1], Sense **3.** 'a capricious notion or fancy' (Fig. 6). Similarly, senses **I.3.a., I.3.b., I.4.**, and **II.6.a.** of **whimsy**, *sb.* (the **A.** branch of the entry) refer to senses of **whim**.

- Senses **II.6.b.** and **II.7.a.** of the substantive branch (**A.**) of **whimsy** are defined by quotations, '(See quot.)', which follow in the relevant quotation paragraphs. (Note that in the latter sense, '*Glass-making*' is a subject label, not a definition, since it appears in italics.) An alternative to the 'see quot.' cross-reference is 'cf. quot.', used when a quotation casts a slightly different light on a definition, or adds to it in some way.

- Sense **4.** of **cardiac**, *adj*. suggests the reader should compare (Cf.) this sense with the entry for **cardia**.
- Sense **5.** of **cardiac**, *adj*. contains a definition 'heart-shaped', followed by a somewhat confusing reference '(in *cardiac wheel*=HEART-CAM)'. Read in conjunction with the quotation that follows, it is unclear which term is referenced in the 1864 edition of *Webster's Dictionary*. In addition, since HEART-CAM is printed in small roman capitals, one might quite naturally assume the reference is to a headword. Instead it can be found in the list of combinations under sense **III.56.a.** of the entry for **heart**, and is defined by a quotation from an 1875 mechanical dictionary in the quotation paragraph that follows. This is an example of the occasional ambiguous or incomplete cross-reference that still remains to be corrected in the third edition of the dictionary.
- Sense **1.** of **cardiac**, *sb*. contains a definition '?=*cardiac passion* (see **A.1.**)'. In other words, the lexicographer is suggesting that this 'disease or affection of the heart' may be the same condition as that noted in the combination *cardiac passion*, mentioned in the first sense for the adjectival form of the word.

Many other variations of cross-references may be found, but their meaning should be quite clear from the context. For example, a cross-reference to a quotation ('cf. quot.') may be used within an explanatory definition to provide supplementary information. Regardless of the syntax, it is well to remember that a reference to another entry normally contains the relevant headword in small roman capitals, usually with its part of speech, homonym number, and sense number 'address'.

The **definition note** is used to provide explanatory information that adds historical or usage details over and above the conventional definition. For example, at the end of the definition for **marmalade 1.a.** (Fig. 2), a note in a separate paragraph in small print adds further comments about types of marmalade, with the observation that the word, unless otherwise specified, is usually interpreted as referring to orange marmalade.

5. Quotation paragraph

The nearly two and a half million quotations in the second edition are a major feature of the *OED*. Each sense of a headword is normally followed by a supporting **quotation paragraph** in smaller typeface. Occasionally, more than one paragraph supports a sense when it covers, for example, both the literal and figurative use of a word. The quotation paragraph consists of one or more quotations from literary works, including books, journals, newspapers, published letters, and diaries. The source of each quotation is cited with the information, where appropriate, appearing in the following order:

(*a*) date of publication
(*b*) author
(*c*) title of the work, together with details such as chapter, page number, etc.
(*d*) text of quotation

Fig. 9 illustrates typical quotation paragraphs from entries for **academia, after, palumbine, periderm, phlizz**, and **wranlons**; these examples will be referred to in the explanation which follows. As will be noted, the quotations are arranged chronologically with the earliest citation listed first (an exception to this policy is sometimes made in the case of **combinations**, as discussed under that element). In the first edition, an endeavour was made to include at least one quotation from each century for words which make up the core vocabulary of the English language. More recent words may have one or more per decade. The second edition, which integrates the first edition and the *Supplement*, added another 5,000 new words or new uses of old words. While the supplementary information updates many of the original entries, the reader will still encounter words and senses for which no recent quotations are given. Updating these entries will be one of the tasks of the third edition, already in progress.

The quotations, which are largely a result of an ongoing international reading programme, are carefully selected to illustrate how a word is used in context in a particular sense. They also help to define the meaning of a word or word sense, and in fact definitions (as noted in the earlier explanation of this element) sometimes consist of cross-references to quotations. Regardless of whether the quotation fills an illustrative and/or defining role, citations are essential to a complete understanding of the word or sense under consideration.

While most citations follow the structure indicated above, certain exceptions may be encountered that require explanation:

- one or more citations, but usually the first, are sometimes enclosed in square brackets. This convention is used when a quotation does not actually illustrate the word in context, but is relevant to its history. In the case of a borrowed or loan word, it may document its use in the language of origin. The entry for **periderm** (Fig. 9), for example, informs the reader that the word first appeared in German as *peridermis*, as noted both in the definition and the earliest quotation.

- in the first edition, when no examples were found of contemporary usage, illustrations were occasionally 'made up'. These are introduced by the word 'Mod.' for 'modern' and normally appear as the last quotation in a paragraph without a date (the date of the original fascicle in which the example was first given is sometimes used, especially when the modern quotation is no longer the most recent). In a few instances, portions of nursery rhymes or proverbs are quoted as examples of usage with no actual source, other than prefatory wording such as 'Nursery Rhyme' (or 'Rime'), 'Mod.Prov.' (Modern Proverb). The quotation paragraph from a section of the entry for the adverb **after** illustrates the usage of both 'Mod.' and 'Nursery Rhyme'.
- occasionally, only a date is given, followed by a **cross-reference** in square brackets to another entry where the quotation appears in full. In this way, the single quotation supports two headwords, but the text is given in only one entry.
- in the case of obsolete or rare words, a phrase such as 'in mod. Dicts.', 'in Johnson' (or some other dictionary) may be used in place of an actual citation, as evidence of the word's existence. The quotation paragraph for **palumbine** tells the reader that the word is found in Blount's 1656 glossary, as well as the 1658 edition of Phillips's dictionary. Occasionally, one will also encounter a phrase in square brackets, such as '[Not in Johnson 1755]' or '[Not in Phillips 1706]', indicating either that the word did not appear in those dictionaries and so was probably not in use until after that date, or that the word was recorded in an earlier source and its absence from Johnson, etc. is notable. As can be seen from the entry for the obsolete and rare word **wranlons**, a word may appear more frequently in dictionaries than in other contexts.

Certain conventions are also followed pertaining to the individual sub-elements that make up a citation, as explained below.

Date

The first element of a quotation citation is the **date**, which is printed in bold face. The date given is normally that of the first printing of

academia (ækəˈdiːmɪə). Also **Academia.** [mod.L.: see L. *Acadēmia* and -IA[1].] The academic world or community; scholastic life; = ACADEME 2.

1956 W. H. WHYTE *Organization Man* (1957) xvii. 217 Let's turn now from the corporation to academia... If the academic scientist is seduced, it cannot be explained away as ..the pressures of commercialism. **1967** MRS. L. B. JOHNSON *White House Diary* 9 Oct. (1970) 582 If I had to capsule these two days in Academia, how would I? **1969** R. NEUSTADT in A. King *Brit. Prime Minister* 137 'In-and-outers' from the law firms, banking, business, academia, foundations, or occasionally journalism. **1971** A. SAMPSON *New Anat. Brit.* viii. 156 Businessmen liked to adopt the language of academia, and any conference of second-rate salesmen is now liable to be called a seminar..and any report a thesis. **1983** *Times* 17 Jan. 8/8 Has the Falklands inquiry been his last lapse from Academia?

after (ˈɑːftə(r), æ-), *adv.* and *prep.* Forms: 1–3 **æfter**, 2–3 **eafter**, 2–4 **efter**, 3–9 **after**; occas. 4–6 **aftir, -yr, -ur, -re.** North. 4–7 **efter, -ir, -yr.** [OE. *æfter* cogn. w. OS. and OHG. *aftar, -er*, OFris. *efter* adv. and prep., ON. *aptr* adv., *eptir* prep., Goth. *aftra* back, *aftaro* from behind, adv.; Gr. ἀπωτέρω, Skr. *apatarām*. Orig. a compar. form of *af*, L. *ab*, Gr. ἀπό, Skr. *ápa*, with compar. suffix *-ter*, -THER; = 'farther off, at a greater distance from the front, or from a point in front'; and hence in the Teutonic languages 'more to the rear, behind, later.' Used in the oldest Eng. as a separable verbal particle capable of governing a case (dat. or acc.) in composition, whence, when detached from the vb., it appeared as *adv.* or *prep.* according to the absence or presence of an object.]

¶ As adv. or prep. in separable comp.

c **885** K. ÆLFRED *Oros.* I. x, Him æfter folȝiende wæron. *c* **1230** *Juliana* (R.MS.) (1872) 32 Ant hare fan..þat ham efter sohten [*Bodl. MS.* ferden ham efter].

A. *adv.*

1. Of place or order: In the rear, behind. (With *go, come, follow*, etc.)

c **1000** *O.E. Gosp.* Matt. xxi. 9 Ðæt folc þæt þar beforan ferde, and þæt þar æfter ferde. *c* **1160** *Hatton Gosp.* ibid., Ðæt folc þe þær before ferde, & þæt þe þær æfter ferde. **1205** LAYAMON 1572 Þe king sette to fleonne and al þa ferde eafter. *c* **1380** *Sir Ferumb.* 1001 & þay folȝeaþ after wiþ rendouns. **1611** BIBLE *Luke* xxiii. 55 And the women also..followed after, and beheld the Sepulchre. *Nursery Rhyme*, Jack fell down and broke his crown, And Jill came tumbling after. *Mod.* Put your own first, and let these come after.

2. Of time: Subsequently, at a later time; afterwards. Formerly used before the vb., now only at the end of a sentence or clause, and chiefly in phr. ***before or after***, or as in 2 b.

a **1000** *Beowulf* 24 Ðæm eafera wæs æfter cenned. *c* **1220** *Leg. St. Kath.* 1223 We mahen haue sikere bileaue to arisen alle after. **1375** BARBOUR *Bruce* I. 127 And wyst nocht quhat suld eftir tyd. *c* **1400** *Destr. Troy* IV. 1439 Gyf an end hade ben now, & neuer noyet efter. **1481** CAXTON *Reynard* (Arb.) 65 Men may wel lye whan it is nede and after amende it. **1594** PLAT *Jewell-ho.* II. 40 A..substance, which you may after cleanse by ablution. **1601** SHAKS. *Jul. Cæs.* I. ii. 76 If you know, That I do fawne on men..And after scandall them. *a* **1631** DONNE *Serm.* xcii. IV. 171 The very place where Solomon's Temple was after built. **1640** FULLER *Abel Rediv., Peter Martyr* (1867) I. 251 Our worthy Jewel, after bishop of Salisbury. **1756** BURKE *Subl. & B.* Wks. I. 256 All we do after is but a faint struggle. **1768** H. WALPOLE *Hist. Doubts* 5 The king smote the young prince on the face, and after his servants slew him. *Mod.* I never spoke to him after; I was never so treated either before or after.

†**palumbine**, *a. Obs. rare*$^{-0}$. [ad. L. *palumbīnus*, f. *palumbēs, -is, -us* wood-pigeon.] Belonging to the wood-pigeon or ring-dove.

1656 in BLOUNT *Glossogr.* **1658** in PHILLIPS.

periderm (ˈpɛrɪdɜːm). [mod. f. Gr. περί around + δέρμα skin: in mod.F. *péridерme*.]

1. *Zool.* A hard or tough covering investing the body in certain Hydrozoa.

1870 NICHOLSON *Man. Zool.* 77 It is invested by a strong corneous or chitinous covering, often termed the 'periderm'.

2. *Bot.* A name introduced (in Ger. *peridermis*) by von Mohl (1836), to designate the corky layers of plant-stems; subsequently extended to include the whole of the tissues formed from the cork-cambium of phellogen.

[**1839** LINDLEY *Introd. Bot.* (ed. 3) 89 The *Epiphlœum* of Link, *Phlœum* or *Peridermis* of Mohl, consisting of several layers of thin-sided tubular cells.] **1849** J. H. BALFOUR *Man. Bot.* § 85 After a certain period,..the corky portion becomes dead, and is thrown off.., leaving a layer of tabular cells or *periderm* below. **1875** BENNETT & DYER tr. *Sachs' Bot.* 81 The formation of cork is very frequently continuous, or is renewed with interruption; and when this occurs uniformly over the whole circumference, there arises a stratified cork-envelope, the Periderm, replacing the epidermis, which is in the meantime generally destroyed.

phlizz (flɪz). [Fanciful.] In Lewis Carroll's book *Sylvie and Bruno*, a fruit or flower that has no real substance; hence, allusively, anything without meaning or value, a mere name.

1889 'L. CARROLL' *Sylvie & Bruno* vi. 75 Bruno..picked a fruit... 'It hasn't got no taste at all!' he complained. 'It was a *Phlizz*,' Sylvie gravely replied. *Ibid.* xx. 294 They *will* be sorry when they find them [*sc.* flowers] gone!.. The nosegay was only a *Phlizz*. **1899** *Johnson Club Papers* 188 We crown the musicians with flowers that, like poor Bruno's in the fairy tale, are but a phlizz. **1926** GALSWORTHY *Silver Spoon* II. ix. 187 What was his image of her but a phlizz, but a fraud? *Ibid.* xii. 218 Was Foggartism a phlizz? **1931** —— *Maid in Waiting* iv. 20 The thing's a phlizz. Just a low type of Homo Sapiens.

†**wranlons.** *Obs. rare*$^{-1}$. [Of obscure origin. Cf. WRAGLAND 1.] *pl.* Unthriving trees that will never become timber.

1432-3 MARTIN in *Year-Book 11 Hen. VI* (1567) 1 b, Querkes qe sont appelles wranlons quel ne voet estre meresme, mes est suable bois, il nest aiuge wast. [Hence in Kitchin *Crt. Leet* (1580) *wranglans*, in translation (1651) *wrang-lands*, whence in Blount (1656), Skinner (1671), Coles (1677), etc.; also Bailey (1721) *wranglings*.]

Fig. 9

the work cited, although the quotation itself may be taken from a later printing or edition. Where a later text has been used, its date is given in parentheses after the title. Alternatively, if the text of a later revision was substantially revised and the word was not in the earlier edition(s), only the date of the actual edition used is cited in bold with the edition in brackets after the title, as, for example, '(ed. 3)', to indicate the third edition.

Dates that cannot be definitely established may be qualified by *a* (*ante*) meaning 'before' or 'not later than', or by *c* (*circa*) signifying 'around' or 'approximately'. A number of instances of this convention can be found in the quotation paragraphs from the entry for **after**. Alternatively, imprecise dating is sometimes indicated by replacing the last one or two or three digits by dots (. .), or by preceding an assumed date with a question mark (?).

Spoken words such as lectures and speeches are assigned the date of their first appearance *in print*, while the date of composition is used for quotations from letters, journals, etc. (note the reference under **academia** to the 1967 extract from Mrs L. B. Johnson's diary, published in 1970 as shown in brackets following the title). Occasionally, when a diary was actually 'written up' later, one may encounter a reference such as '**1666** Evelyn *Diary c.* 16 Nov., an. 1643' signifying that Evelyn actually wrote his account of the events of 16 November, 1643 in 1666. The date for posthumous publications is usually *ante* (*a*) the year of the author's death. Short stories and essays which are republished in a collection without change are given the date of their original publication, if known. If a quotation documents the first use of a word, the initial publication date is also given.

Author

The name of the **author**, when given, is usually the second element in a citation and is printed in large and small capitals. In general, 'author' means the personal name of the user of the quoted word. Normally this is straightforward, but occasionally an author's words may appear in a work compiled or edited by another. The secondary source is usually preceded by the word 'in', as in the case of the 1969 quotation by R. Neustadt (in the entry for **academia**) which appears on page 137 'in A. King *Brit. Prime Minister*'. In cases where the quotation taken from a secondary source was not verified by the *OED* editor (as quite frequently was the case in the first edition when quotations were extracted from earlier dictionaries), the secondary source appears in parentheses after the title. Note that references to other dictionaries are often cited simply by the author's surname. With some composite works, only the editor's name, preceded by the word 'in', is given. In all instances, secondary authors' or editors' names appear in the same upper and lower case typeface as the quotation text.

Translations are frequently cited by the translator's name (as the 'writer' of the text) with the possessive form of the original author's surname appearing before the title, as in '1953 G. E. M. Anscombe tr. *Wittgenstein's Philos. Investigations*'. Where the translator's name cannot be established, no author is given, as in '1922 tr. *Wittgenstein's Tractatus*'.

Names appear variously with surnames only, initials and surname, title and surname, first name (often abbreviated) and surname. In general, authors cited by surname only are well known and frequently quoted, such as Milton, Chaucer, or Scott. Shakespeare is, in most instances, abbreviated 'Shaks.'. However, the space-saving convention of surnames only is also used in referring to joint authors as exemplified in the 1875 quotation from 'Bennett & Dyer' in the entry for **periderm**. While the way in which authors are cited is normally quite consistent, variations will be found. For example, Sir Walter Scott is generally cited as 'Scott', but there are a few instances of 'Sir W. Scott' or 'W. Scott'. While such anomalies are of concern for computerized searching of the Dictionary, they should not cause difficulty for the user of the printed text. Authors with the same name can usually be distinguished by the date or the title of the work. Names of pseudonymous authors are enclosed in single quotation marks, as in the case of 'L. Carroll' in the entry for **phlizz**, with the exception of a few well-known pseudonyms, such as George Eliot, which appear without quotation marks.

In certain instances, the author's name is not given. For example, articles in periodicals and serials (journals, magazines, newspapers, etc.) are usually cited by title only, unless the quotation is assumed to contain the first use of the word. Corporate names, such as institutions or business firms, are not recognized as authors, but are included in parentheses at the end of the title. Anonymous works are cited by title, but may also appear under the author's name if identity has been established and generally recognized.

It should also be noted that quotations follow the normal bibliographical convention of using a double dash (——) in place of the author's name when the quotation is by the same author as the one immediately preceding it. If the quotation is also from the same work, *Ibid.* is used to replace any information that would otherwise be duplicated. Examples of both these conventions are found in the entry for **phlizz**.

Citations from the *Bible* are somewhat unusual. 'Bible' in large and small capitals (as author) usually refers to the 1611 King James version, as in the citation in Sense **1.** of **after**. Other translations are normally cited by the translator's name as author, for example, Tindale, Wyclif. The relevant book of the *Bible* then appears in italics as the title.

Title

Titles of publications appear in italics and are often shortened and/or abbreviated in order to conserve space. As has been noted, a number of works are cited by title only, including anonymous early works such as *Beowulf* and *Cursor Mundi*, as well as periodicals and serials. While many citations are straightforward, the liberal use of abbreviations and the many references to early or obscure titles may give the reader who wishes to trace the original source some difficulty. The abbreviations most frequently used in the titles can be found in the *List of Abbreviations, Signs, etc.* at the front of each volume, and in most instances, full bibliographical information (with the author's name and title in full, as well as publisher and place of publication) is given in the *Bibliography* at the end of the Dictionary. Readers should be aware, however, that not all cited works appear in the Bibliography, especially those which are cited infrequently. The considerable task of verifying quotations and checking them against the bibliography is a long-term goal of the *OED* editors.

In addition to the title, further information is supplied to help the reader locate the quotation in context. This includes specific references such as volume, section, chapter or page of a monograph; act, scene, line of a drama; canto, verse, line of a poem, depending on the information pertinent to the particular work. Like the sense letter/number system, these information divisions are distinguished by typeface with the upper level of information appearing in large roman capital numerals (I, II), followed by small roman capital numerals (I,II), then lower-case roman numerals (i,ii) and, finally, arabic numerals (1,2). Thus a citation to volume one, part two, chapter four, page eighty-five of a book appears as 'I.II.iv.85'. In the case of a play, act two, scene one, line (or page) twenty-five is designated II.i.25. Newspapers are cited by the day, month, section (if applicable), page and column number, as in the 17 January, 1983 citation from the *Times* under **academia** (note that the page number is given first followed by a diagonal slash and the column number, i.e. 8/8). Numerous examples of these conventions can be found in the illustrations in Fig. 9.

Quotation text

The **quotation text** is printed and *spelled* as it appears in the text and edition used as the source. Occasionally, a portion of the text is eliminated and the omission is indicated by two dots (. .), or three dots (. . .) if the elision includes a full stop. Less commonly, an explanatory word in square brackets may be inserted in the text, sometimes preceded by the abbreviation *sc.* (for *scilicet*, understand or supply), as in the first Lewis Carroll quotation for **phlizz**. If the text quoted appeared as a title, advertisement, heading, or other unusual source, this information is usually supplied in parentheses.

6. Combinations

A **combination** in the *OED* is any joining of simple words, whether separated, hyphenated, or combined as a single word, that functions as one grammatical category (noun, adjective, etc.). Examples of such combinations are **sea chest** (separated), **sea-gull** (hyphenated), and **seafood** (single word).

In the Dictionary, a combination may appear within the entry for its main (usually the first) word, or if it has become sufficiently unified and has developed its own etymology, meaning, or usage, it may be given an entry in its own right. The following explanation discusses combinations in the first category; word forms that are accorded main entry status are covered in the section **special types of main entries** under the heading *combinations and derivatives*.

'Combination', in this explanation, is applied generally to include specific terms such as 'compound' and 'collocation'. Theoretically, the *OED* refers to a noun joined to a noun as a combination (*Comb.*), and a noun joined to an adjective as a collocation. However, the latter usage is not consistently followed since the line between noun and adjective is often blurred. The term 'quasi-*adj.*' is also sometimes used to describe a noun performing an adjectival function in an 'understood' combination. For example, sense **3.c.** of the entry for **marmalade** (Fig. 2) illustrates the use of the headword in the 'understood' sense of 'marmalade-coloured' in the phrase 'the marmalade cat'. Verbs may also be used to form combinations as, for example, 'scatter-brain', 'drive-shaft', or 'feedback'. However, verbs used in phrases or combined with adverbs or prepositions in a special way are generally treated as separate senses (see *lengthy entries* in the section **special types of main entries** for a further explanation).

Combinations present a number of problems to lexicographers that are not always easily resolved. For example, should a combination be written as two words, hyphenated, or as one word? Usage, particularly in the case of newer combinations, is often not clearly established and can change over time. In such instances, editorial judgement must be based on factors such as usage and consistency with other similar forms.

The question of whether a combination should be included within the entry for its first element or given an entry of its own is sometimes compounded by the number of combinations formed on the main word, as in the case of the noun **sea**. Its main entry contains literally hundreds of combinations, but there are also over two hundred separate main entries for compounds beginning with the word 'sea' which have developed their own history and, indeed, have sometimes generated their own combinations.

Finally, there are several options regarding the treatment of a combination within an entry. Normally, combinations appear as the last numbered sense(s) of an entry, but, occasionally, in short entries with only one or two senses, or in entries for proper names, one may encounter combinations within the main definition text. The entry for the noun **sauna** in Fig. 10, in which the final statement in the definition text lists '*attrib.* and *Comb.*' forms, exemplifies this convention. In addition, the *OED* distinguishes types of combinations by the degree to which they are 'fixed' or established, and then accords them different treatment, both structurally and typographically:

- joinings of the main word to another word either attributively (*attrib.*) as a descriptor or as simple combinations (*Comb.* or *Combs.*) in which both words retain their own meaning and no further definition is

3. *attrib.* and *Comb.* **a.** In general uses, as ***television aerial, antenna, apparatus, box, channel, coverage, dealer, frequency, lounge, receiver, room, screen, service, set, signal, studio, supper, system, theatre, transmission, transmitter, van.***

1940 *Amateur Radio Handbk.* (ed. 2) 306/1 (Index), Television aerials. **1972** J. PORTER *Meddler & her Murderer* xi. 136 Rows of ugly little houses, their roofs buckling under a forest of television aerials. **1947** *Electronics* May 96/2

receiving television broadcasts from a local as well as a national transmitting station; **television satellite**, a satellite put into orbit round the earth to reflect back television signals; **television station**, a television broadcasting station (see STATION *sb.* 13 f); **television tube**, (*a*) = *picture tube* s.v. PICTURE *sb.* 6 d; (*b*) = *television camera tube* above.

1940 D. G. FINK *Princ. Television Engin.* i. 17 (*caption*) A typical television camera tube, the type 1849 iconoscope, now widely used in television broadcasting. **1974** *Encycl.*

b. Connected with, participating in, or transmitted as part of organized television broadcasting, as ***television announcer, audience, broadcast, broadcasting, commercial, crew, critic, discussion, drama, dramatist, film, interview, journalist, magazine, news, personality, play, producer, programme, public, pundit, reporter, serial, series, show, spot, star, version, viewer.***

1938 *Radio Times* 23 Dec. 36/1 It would be nice to say that the television announcers will hang up their stockings. **1972** J. MOSEDALE *Football* xi. 148 Gifford, then a television announcer, talked briefly with the coach. **1937** *Discovery* Nov. 331/2 Building up a television audience. **1959**

c. Special Combs. **television camera**: see CAMERA 3 c; **television camera tube**, an electron tube of the kind used in television cameras for converting a visual image into an electrical signal; **television engineer**, one who designs and maintains the mechanical and electrical processes involved in the transmission and reception of television signals; a television repairman; **television evangelist** orig. *U.S.* = TELEVANGELIST; also **television evangelism**; **television image** = *television picture* below; **television licence**, a licence to use a television set, renewable annually on payment of a fee; **television mast**, (*a*) a tall mast, usu. set up on high ground, carrying a television transmitting aerial; (*b*) = *television aerial*, sense 3 a above; **television network**, a system of television broadcasting stations; a television broadcasting organization or channel; **television picture**, the visual image received on a television screen; **television region**, a region of the country

sauna (ˈsɔːnə, ‖ˈsauna), *sb.* [Finn.] A bath-house or bathroom in which the Finnish steam bath is taken; the steam bath itself, taken in very hot steam produced by throwing water on to heated stones. Also *attrib.* and *Comb.*, as ***sauna bath, heat, stove, suite***; **sauna-like** *a.*, oppressively hot and steamy.

1881 P. D. DU CHAILLU *Land of Midnight Sun* II. xvii. 206 One of the most characteristic institutions of the country is the *Sauna* (bath-house), called *Badstuga* in Swedish. **1897** E. B. TWEEDIE *Through Finland in Carts* iii. 42 Every house in the country, however humble that house may be, boasts its *bastu*, or bath-house, called in Finnish *Sauna*. **1936** *Discovery* Apr. 110/1 A speciality of Finland which everyone who visits the country ought to try is the *Sauna*—the special steam-baths which Finnish people from time immemorial have been in the habit of taking. **1939** *Daily Tel.* 18 Dec. 1/5 The Finnish soldiers..continue to take their celebrated 'sauna' steam baths wherever they are stationed. **1957** A. BUCHWALD *I chose Caviar* 31 But in Finland a sauna is not just a bath—it is a way of life. A sauna is to a Finn what a pub is to a Britisher, what a café is to a Frenchman, what a television set is to an American. **1959** *Times* 2 Dec. 5/4 A move to make British business men sauna bath conscious begins next week with the opening of a Finnish-style sauna in the City of London... City Wall sauna, as it is called, has the requisite little wooden rooms with a stove containing a pile of heated stones on to which water is sprinkled to produce the sauna heat, and showers and rest cubicles. Bunches of leafy birch twigs will also be available, price 2s. 6d., for bathers to whisk up their circulation; the sauna itself costs 15s. **1971** *Country Life* 26 Aug. 512/3 It stands in six acres, with frontage to the river, and has a..sauna bath, stables, [etc.]. **1975** *N.Y. Times* 13 Apr. x. 1/2 The sauna, otherwise known as the Finnish bath, is a wood-lined room with benches built up toward the ceiling. A special sauna stove (today, usually electric) heats small rocks piled atop it and the rocks in turn radiate a dry heat. **1976** *Times* 22 July 4/4 The sauna-like conditions of the Oxford court during the [last] five weeks. **1978** *Morecambe Guardian* 14 Mar. 15/3 Preparing for the play involved the cast in a trip to the sauna suite at Lancaster Baths.

Fig. 10

necessary. Normally, a few examples of such usages, printed in heavy italics and defined only by illustrative quotations, are given.

- combinations, with somewhat more unified or specialized meanings, but which can still be defined in a few words. Such forms, together with brief definitions, are usually printed in bold type and listed alphabetically in a single paragraph followed by illustrative quotations arranged in the same order.

The decision as to whether combinations should be given special status (and thus appear in bold type), or whether they are straightforward examples of the way in which the headword may be combined with another word (and thus appear in bold italic type) can be difficult. Resolution is largely based on whether the combination is readily understood as a grammatical formation, or whether it requires further explanation by the lexicographer. In the entry for **sauna**, the decision to give a brief definition of **sauna-like** is understandable since the meaning is not immediately obvious. More complex examples of the two types of combinations are encountered in the entry for the headword **television**. Fig. 10 illustrates senses **3.a.**, **b.**, and **c.** of the word without their supporting quotations. Sense **3.a.** shows the way **television** can be combined attributively with a variety of other words as in *television aerial, television set*, etc. (note that these combinations are listed alphabetically). Sense **3.b.** gives examples of attributive use connected specifically with television broadcasting, as in *television commercial, television personality*, or *television viewer*. Finally, sense **3.c.** lists a number of **special combinations** that have acquired specific meaning and usage beyond simple attribution, such as **television camera, television network**. The difference between the italicized and bold type combinations is sometimes subtle, as for example between *television announcer* as attributive and **television engineer** as 'special'. Perhaps the simplest explanation is to note that *television announcer* is intuitively understood, while **television engineer** could be, and is, interpreted as relating to one of several specialized aspects of TV technology.

As will be seen from this example, combinations are usually listed in alphabetical sequence in one paragraph, with or without corresponding definitions. The supporting **quotation paragraph** frequently follows the same order. Where more than one quotation is given for a combination, they are grouped chronologically. In most cases, an asterisk precedes the first use of each combination in the quotation paragraph, as in the case of **marmalade, 3.a.** (Fig. 2). Alternatively, where the number of combinations and quotations is small, the citations may be listed in the normal chronological order as in the case of **whim, II.4.b.** (Fig. 6).

The use of the terms *attrib.* and *Comb.* in the *OED* is not always clear-cut. Variations and subcategories may be encountered, especially where a word has many combinations. For example, as in the entry for **television**, introductory phrases such as 'Special Combs.', 'Spec. Comb.', or 'In special collocations', may be used to distinguish defined combinations from undefined examples. Attributive uses may be subdivided by a general category called 'simple', 'obvious', or 'general', followed by uses within specific semantic or syntactic categories. For example, in the entry for the noun and adjective **ruby**, '*attrib.* and *Comb.*' uses are subdivided into 'attributive', 'similative' (as in *ruby-like*), 'Instrumental' (*ruby-circled*), 'In parasynthetic adjs.' (*ruby-berried, -budded, -coloured*), and 'In specific names of birds' (*ruby-crested, ruby-crowned*). Other variations of this kind may be noted, but normally they should not cause readers difficulty since the rationale for the alternative structure is usually evident and is designed to help the user.

Names of animals, birds, plants, etc. are special cases. The general rule is to include them within the entry for their generic name. For example, *sea anemone* is a type of anemone and therefore included in the main entry for the genus (**anemone**). On the other hand, the term **sea-canary**, a sailor's expression for a white whale or beluga, is found in the entry for the noun **sea** since it obviously does not refer to a type of canary. However, it will be observed that such terms sometimes appear under both the generic or species name and the defining word. The bird, **scarlet tanager**, for instance, is referred to under the entry for **tanager**, as well as under the entry for the first element of its name, **scarlet**.

7. Derivatives

A **derivative** is a word formed by the addition of a suffix to a dictionary main word (and, occasionally, by the alteration or removal of a suffix). Such additions often involve a change in grammatical category, for example, from a noun to an adjective. Common suffixes used to form derivatives include *-ly*, *-ness*, *-er* and the ubiquitous *-ize*. Some derivatives resemble combinations, such as the journalistic *-ville* (**Squaresville**), *-aholic* (**workaholic**), or the overworked *-wise* (**television-wise**). Others are closely related to inflections, both in their regularity and their form (*-ing, -ed*).

The *OED*'s policy is to treat the majority of recorded derivatives as main headwords in their own right, linked by cross-references to the word from which they are derived. However, derivatives that have only one or a few senses straightforwardly related to the root word are normally included in the entry for that word. This explanation discusses derivatives in the latter category. Those that are given main entry status are explained under the heading *combinations and derivatives* in the section **special types of main entries**.

Derivatives may appear in two locations within an entry, either as part of the definition text or as a last *unnumbered* paragraph following the numbered senses. As in the case of combinations, the decision as to location is often based on the length of the entry, that is, in an entry with only one or two senses, derivatives may be included in a final statement in the definition text. Like combinations, derivatives are supported by a quotation paragraph, usually arranged chronologically, although in cases where several derivatives are listed alphabetically, the illustrative quotations may occasionally follow the same order. Derivatives are normally printed in the same bold type as major combinations, and, whether they appear at the conclusion of a definition or as a concluding paragraph, are most often preceded by either the word 'hence' or 'so'. The choice of words may be significant, since in principle it indicates whether the derivative followed the root word ('hence') or preceded it ('so'), as documented by the supporting quotation paragraph.

The entries for **whim** (Fig. 6) and **whimsy** (Fig. 8) illustrate how derivatives are presented in a final unnumbered paragraph. Note that the paragraphs begin with the word 'Hence', and that slightly different conventions are followed in each case. **Whim** has three derivatives—'whimmed', 'whimmery', and 'whimship'—listed in alphabetical order and briefly defined. The quotation paragraph which follows is arranged in the same order, with an asterisk marking the first use of each form, although this convention is less frequently used in derivative quotation paragraphs than in lengthy paragraphs illustrating combinations in context. The derivatives for **whimsy**—'whimsily' and 'whimsiness'—are not defined, since their meaning is readily apparent and the quotations are listed in the more usual chronological order. However, in the case of the entry for **buttercupped** in Fig. 11, the decision was made to include the derivative 'buttercuppy' in a concluding paragraph prefixed by the word 'so', because the 1871 use of 'butter-cuppy' precedes the 1872 'buttercupped'.

The two entries for **boresome** and **academize**, also in Fig. 11, illustrate the inclusion of derivatives with the word 'so' as part of the main definition text. Note that in the case of **boresome**, the derivative 'boresomeness' was recorded in 1868 prior to 'boresome' in 1895. In the case of **academicize**, the 1968 quotation for the derivative, **academicized**, precedes its use as a transitive verb in the 1969 quotation, and the derivative **academizing** is recorded in the adjectival sense in 1972 prior to its verbal use in 1978. While 'hence' and 'so' are normally used to identify order of development, they are also occasionally used loosely as introductory words, as in the case of **bobber** in Fig. 11, where the noun clearly preceded the verbal noun 'bobbing'.

Although derivatives *within* entries typically involve the addition of a suffix, as in the above examples, instances will also be found of the inclusion of simple shifts in grammatical form in a final 'hence' paragraph. For example, in the entry for the noun **mayhem** illustrated in Fig. 1, the transitive verb **mayhem** is included in a final paragraph preceded by the word 'hence'. As previously noted, the more usual practice for handling different grammatical forms with the same spelling within the same entry is to give them equal importance by employing the upper level of the hierarchical numbering scheme (**A.**, **B.**, **C.** . . .). This convention is explained under the **sense number**, the second element of this section.

Finally, the rationale for certain derivative forms may not always be clear to users, especially in the case of participial adjectives ending in *-ed* and *-ing*, and verbal nouns ending in *-ing*. An explanation of how these forms are distinguished from inflections is given under *combinations and derivatives* in the section **special types of main entries**.

SPECIAL TYPES OF MAIN ENTRIES

There are several types of main entries that may be considered 'special'. For example, entries for letters of the alphabet, for

academicize (ækə'dɛmɪsaɪz), *v.* [f. ACADEMIC *a.* + -IZE.] *trans.* To render academic (sometimes with the implication of losing touch with the everyday world). So **aca'demicized, aca'demicizing** *ppl. adjs.*

1968 S. ROSEN in *Man & World* Feb. 80 The logicist ideology leads so quickly to boredom that it is easily absorbed by the ideology of the academicized marketplace. **1969** NAIRN & SINGH-SANDHU in Cockburn & Blackburn *Student Power* 109 They [*sc.* art colleges] have been academicized in the way described. **1972** P. COVENEY *Geo. Eliot's Felix Holt* 20 The question of the correct dating of 'five-and-thirty years ago' is no academicizing quibble. **1978** *Fortune* Dec. 50 The modern corporation, wrongly thinking that larger size and rapid change require special managerial methods, now runs the risk of academicizing and ruining itself.

bobber[6] ('bɒbə(r)). [perh. f. BOB *sb.*[8] (see quot. 1921).] In full ***fish bobber***: a workman who unloads fish from trawlers and drifters to the quay. So **'bobbing** *vbl. sb.*[3], working as a 'bobber'.

1921 *Dict. Occup. Terms* (1927) §745 ***Bobber, fish bobber*** (East Coast term which originated when fish porters were paid 1s. per hour). **1934** 'TAFFRAIL' *Seventy North* ix. §1. 185 Men called 'bobbers', hired by the owners, unloaded all the fish in baskets. **1959** *Times* 20 Jan. 6/3 The fish bobbers —men who unload trawlers. *Ibid.*, The bobbers are members of the General and Municipal Workers' Union. **1962** J. TUNSTALL *Fishermen* iii. 81 Bobbing..can easily be done by men in their fifties.

boresome ('bɔəsəm), *a.* [f. BORE *sb.*[2] + -SOME.] Tending to be a bore, boring. So **'boresomeness.**

1868 LD. R. GOWER *Rec. & Remin.* (1903) 150 So little real enjoyment to make up for so much loss of time and boresomeness. **1895** *Nineteenth Cent.* Sept. 474, I spent a boresome fortnight at Aden. **1905** E. GLYN *Viciss. Evangeline* 152 They were all casual and indifferent to their poor wives! and boresome, and bored!! **1925** P. A. SCHOLES *Second Bk. Gramophone Rec.* p. xii, There is..a degree of boresomeness in some of Beethoven's compositions.

buttercupped ('bʌtəkʌpt), *a.* [f. BUTTERCUP + -ED[2].] Abounding in or covered with buttercups.

1872 C. S. CALVERLEY *Fly Leaves* 89 Looking far over buttercupped leas. **1888** MRS. H. WARD *R. Elsmere* xliv, A wavering rainy light played..over the buttercupped river meadows. **1924** *Public Opinion* 9 May 400/1 Banks all buttercup'd and burning.

So **buttercuppy** ('bʌtəkʌpɪ), *a.*

1871 W. MORRIS in Mackail *Life* (1899) I. 237 The fields are all butter-cuppy. **1958** BETJEMAN *Coll. Poems* 259 That burning buttercuppy day.

Fig. 11

acronyms and abbreviations, and for affixes and combining forms require somewhat different treatment from 'normal' headwords because of their form. Similarly, the numerous proper and proprietary names included in the Dictionary reflect policy decisions which it may be helpful to clarify. Combinations and derivatives that warrant main entries, while handled in much the same fashion as their root words, require an understanding of several grammatical categories which some readers may find it useful to review. In addition, a small group of words referred to as 'spurious' will be encountered from time to time in the Dictionary. These may puzzle the reader unfamiliar with the usage of the first edition of the *OED* and call for an explanation. Finally, entries for words which have been in the language for many centuries and which have acquired a number of senses present special problems for both the lexicographer and the reader because of their length and complexity; a typical example of such an entry is discussed in detail and its structure is analysed step by step.

While most of these entries deal with somewhat unusual information, the Dictionary user will find that the contents are structured and numbered (or lettered) in much the same fashion as other *OED* entries which have been discussed. Once again, keeping in mind that this structural system is an organizational tool, the user should have no difficulty in following the logic of the way in which the contents are presented. However, for readers who are interested in knowing more about any of these special categories, explanations are presented in the following order:

1. **Letters of the alphabet**
2. **Initialisms, acronyms, and abbreviations**
3. **Affixes and combining forms**
4. **Proper and proprietary names**
5. **Combinations and derivatives**
6. **Spurious words**
7. **Lengthy entries**

1. Letters of the alphabet

Entries for letters of the alphabet (**A, B, C . . .**) appear, as one would expect, as the first entry within the relevant alphabetical sequence of headwords. Fig. 12 reproduces the first two columns of the relatively

D (di:), the fourth letter of the Roman alphabet, corresponding in position and power to the Phœnician and Hebrew *Daleth*, and Greek *Delta*, *Δ*, whence also its form was derived by rounding one angle of the triangular form. It represents the sonant dental mute, or point-voice stop consonant, which in English is alveolar rather than dental. The plural has been written D's, Ds, de's.

The phonetic value of D in English is constant, except that in past participles the earlier full spelling *-ed* is retained where the pronunciation after a breath-consonant is now *t*, as in *looked*, *dipped*, *fished*, *passed*. The spelling *-ed* is now even extended to words in which OE. had *t*, as in *wished*, *puffed*, *kissed*, OE. *wyscte*, *pyfte*, *cyste*.

c **1000** ÆLFRIC *Gram.* iii. (Z.) 6 *B*, *c*, *d*, *g*, *p*, *t*, ȝeendiað on *e*. **1673** WYCHERLEY *Gentl. Dancing-Master* v. i, His desperate deadly daunting dagger:—there are your d's for you! **1726** LEONI *Alberti's Archit.* I. 67b, The Walls..of Memphis [were] built in the shape of a D. **1879** MISS BRADDON *Vixen* III. 168 This..must end in darkness, desolation, despair—everything dreadful beginning with *d*.

2. a. Used in reference to the shape of the letter, as ***D block***, ***D-front***, ***D link***, ***D trap***, ***D valve***, etc.; ***D-shaped***, ***D-fronted*** adjs. See also DEE.

1794 *Rigging & Seamanship* I. 156 *D-Blocks* are lumps of oak in the shape of a D..bolted to the ship's side, in the channels. **1827** FAREY *Steam Eng.* 707 Sliding valves..called D valves. **1849** E. E. NAPIER *Excurs. S. Africa* I. 161 The saddle..should be abundantly studded..with iron loops: or as they are—from their shape—termed in Colonial phraseology, D's. [See DEE *sb.*] *Ibid.* 163 Append to one of the D's of the said saddle, a leathern bottle. **1883** W. S. GRESLEY *Gloss. Coal-m.* 72 *D link*, a flat iron bar attached to chains, and suspended from a hemp rope to a windlass at surface. It is a loop in which one man is lowered and raised in an engine-pit. **1890** W. J. GORDON *Foundry* 135 A closed crucible with a D-shaped opening in one of its sides. **1892** T. B. F. EMERSON *Epid. Pneumonia* 11 The catch-pit was covered in by a D trap. **1895** *Westm. Gaz.* 22 Nov. 5/3 D-shaped and oval tubes. **1908** *Ibid.* 16 Nov. 4/2 A D-front limousine. *Ibid.* 19 Nov. 5/2 A 'D'-fronted landaulette.

b. *Billiards*, etc. A semi-circle marked on the baulk side of the baulk-line from within which a player must strike the cue-ball when in hand; the area bounded by this semi-circle.

1873 J. BENNETT *Billiards* ii. 18 The diameter of the D varies from 21 in. on championship tables to 23 in. on ordinary tables. **1904** J. P. MANNOCK *Billiards Expounded* I. ii. 53 What I want you to do is, following your losing hazard in the corner pocket, to then take your ball to the D, and play in again off the red from there. ?**1968** *Billiards & Snooker* ('Know the Game' Ser.) 12/1 A player, whenever 'in hand'..must play out of the 'D' from some point within it. **1981** G. BRANDRETH *Everyman's Indoor Games* 240 On the baulk line there is a semi-circle known as the 'D'.

3. Used euphemistically for *damn* (often printed d——), etc. Cf. DEE *v.*

1861 DICKENS *Gt. Expect.* xi, He flung out in his violent way, and said, with a D, 'Then do as you like'. **1877** GILBERT *Com. Opera, H.M.S. Pinafore* 1, Though 'bother it' I may Occasionally say, I never use a big, big D——.

II. 1. a. Used like the other letters of the alphabet to denote serial order, with the value of *fourth*; applied, *e.g.*, to the fourth quire or sheet of a book, a group or section in classification, etc.

1886 *Oxford Univ. Statutes* (1890) 109 The examination in the above-mentioned Group D shall be under the direction of the Board of the Faculty of Theology.

b. In typical or hypothetical examples of any argumentation, D is put for a fourth person or thing. (Cf. A, II. 4.)

1858 KINGSLEY *Let. to J. Ludlow* in *Life* xvii. (1879) II. 78 How worthless opinions of the Press are. For if A, B, C, D, flatly contradict each other, one or more must be wrong, eh? **1864** BOWEN *Logic* 208 If A is B, C is D. **1887** *Times* (Weekly Ed.) 21 Oct. 3/2 This or that understanding between Mr. A, Mr. B, Mr. C, and Mr. D.

c. ***D-layer***, ***-region***: the lowest stratum of the ionosphere, occurring between 25 and 50 miles above the earth's surface, below the Heaviside or E-layer.

1930 APPLETON & RATCLIFFE in *Proc. R. Soc.* A. CXXVIII. 155 We therefore attribute the result of the small variation of the reflection coefficient with distance, to the influence of an absorbing zone (D region) of ionisation situated below the region (E region) in which the main bending takes place. *Ibid.*, Rays which travel to the more distant receiving stations have a longer path through the D region. **1935** *Nature* 8 June 953/2 Besides these two main regions [F and E], the existence of a so-called D or absorbing layer has been suggested. *Ibid.*, The appearance of echoes from the D layer is closely connected with the weakening of echoes from the E layer. **1955** *Sci. Amer.* Sept. 128/2 The lowest stratum of the ionosphere is called the D layer. Its electron density has not been measured accurately but is known to be low, because the layer does not reflect radio waves of one megacycle per second or higher frequency. **1968** G. M. B. DOBSON *Explor. Atmos.* (ed. 2) viii. 151 These radio waves will be absorbed as they come down through the *D* region.

2. *spec.* in *Music*. The name of the second note of the 'natural' major scale. (In Italy and France called *re*.) Also, the scale or key which has that note for its tonic.

1596 SHAKS. *Tam. Shr.* III. i. 77 *D sol re*, one Cliffe, two notes haue I. **1880** GROVE *Dict. Mus.* II. 269/2 A Concerto of Bach in D minor.

3. In *Algebra*: see A, II. 5. In the higher mathematics, *d* is the sign of differentiation, and *D* of derivation; *D* is also used to denote the deficiency of a curve.

1852 SALMON *Higher Plane Curves* ii. (1879) 30 We call the deficiency of a curve the number D, by which its number of double points is short of the maximum. **1873** B. WILLIAMSON *Diff. Calc.* (ed. 2) §5 When the increment is supposed infinitely small, it is called a *differential*, and represented by *dx*.

4. ***D notice***, short for *Defence notice* (see quot. 1967). Hence ***D list***, a list of D notices currently in force.

The Services, Press and Broadcasting Committee was set up in 1912 as the 'Admiralty, War Office and Press Committee'. Its main function is to give guidance to the press, etc., about matters which, in the interests of national security, should not be publicly disclosed.

1940 GRAVES & HODGE *Long Week-End* xxvi. 450 The Prime Minister authorized a 'D' notice to be sent round to the newspapers, warning them not to print it. **1961** *Times* 12 May 20/4 Mr. Lipton..asked the Prime Minister which Minister was responsible for preparing the D-list... *Mr. Macmillan* Ministerial responsibility for D-notices rests on the Minister responsible for the subject covered by the notice. **1964** 'C. E. MAINE' *Never let Up* v. 41 No names were mentioned... The story had probably been put out with a 'D' notice, which meant that editors were asked to toe the security line. **1967** *Rep. Comm. Privy Counsellors* (Cmnd. 3309) 1, A 'D' notice is a formal letter of warning or request, signed by the Secretary of a Committee known as the Services, Press and Broadcasting Committee, and addressed to newspaper editors, to news editors in sound broadcasting and television, [etc.]... Their purpose is to request a ban on the publication of certain subjects, indicated in the notices, which bear upon defence or national security.

III. Abbreviations, etc.

1. *d* stands for L. *denarius* and so for 'penny', 'pence'; as 1*d.* = one penny, £. *s. d.* = pounds, shillings and pence. †Formerly also, *d.* = one half (L. *dimidium*, also contracted *di.*, *dim.*); D. = dollar (in *U.S.*; now $).

1387 *E.E. Wills* 2 Y be-quethe to the werkes of poulys vj s. viij d. **1488** *Nottingham Rec.* III. 269 For d. a quarter of pepur. *c* **1500** *Debate Carpenter's Tools* in Halliwell *Nugae Poet.* 15 Fore some dey he wyll vij.ᵈ drynke. **1588** SHAKS. *L.L.L.* III. i. 140 What's the price of this yncle? i.d. **1791** JEFFERSON in *Harper's Mag.* (1885) Mar. 535/1 A pound of tea..costs 2 D. **1866** CRUMP *Banking* 233 Pence or halfpence are not legal tender for more than 12*d.*, or farthings for more than 6*d.*

2. D, the sign for 500 in Roman numerals, as MDCCCXCIII = 1893. [Understood to be the half of CIↃ, earlier form of M = 1,000.]

(Formerly occasionally written Dᶜ.)

1459 *Inv.* in *Paston Lett.* I 469 Summa, DCCCC lxv. unces. *Ibid.* 471 Summa, Dᶜ unces. **1569** GRAFTON *Chron.* 16 This Thurston obteyned the rule of the Abbey agaîne for the price of D. pound.

3. (Abbreviations cited here with full stops are frequently used without them.) **a. D.** = various proper names, as Daniel, David; **D**, 'in the *Complete Book*, means dead or deserted' (Adm. Smyth); **D.**, Deputy; **D.**, detective (*slang*); **D.**, Dictionary; **D.**, dimensional, as *3-D*, *3 D*, three-dimensional; **D.**, Distinguished; **D.**, District; **D.** = Doctor (in *academical degrees*, as a Lat. word following, and as English preceding, other initials), as ***D.D.*** (*Divinitatis Doctor*), Doctor of Divinity, ***LL.D.*** (*Legum Doctor*), Doctor of Laws, ***M.D.*** Doctor of Medicine, ***Ph.D.***, Doctor of Philosophy, ***D.C.L.***, Doctor of Civil Law, ***D.Lit.***, ***Lit.D.***, Doctor of Literature, ***D.Phil.***, Doctor of Philosophy, ***D.Sc.***, Doctor of Science; †**D.** = Duke; ***d*** (in dental formulæ) = deciduous, as ***dc.***, deciduous canine, ***di.***, deciduous incisor; **d.**, decent, esp. in ***jolly d.***; †**d.** = degree (of angular measure); **d.**, ***d.*** (usually before a date) = died; **d** or **D** (*Anat.*) = dorsal; **d.** (in a ship's log) = drizzling; **D.A.**, Dictionary of Americanisms; **D.A.**, District Attorney (*U.S.*); **D.A.**, duck's arse (style of haircut); **D.A.A.G.**, Deputy Assistant Adjutant General; **D.A.E.**, Dictionary of American English; **D.A.G.**, Deputy Adjutant General; **D. and C.**, dilatation and curettage; **D. and P.**, **d and p**, developing and printing; **D.A.Q.M.G.**, Deputy

Fig. 12

short entry for the letter **D** (the entry is complete except for the full abbreviations list and the quotations covering the abbreviations). Note that, as with other types of entries, each usage is illustrated with quotations.

Normally, as in the example, the only information given in the headword section is the pronunciation in brackets. This is immediately followed by an explanation of the letter's origin, its equivalents in other languages, the history of its use and pronunciation, and any other information relevant to its place in the language. Usually, with a few exceptions, this explanation, which varies considerably in length (the history of the letter **J**, for instance, runs to two and a half columns), is understood to be the first numbered (**1.** or **I.**) 'sense' in the entry. Note, for instance, that although the explanation for the letter **D** is not actually designated by a number, the section that follows it is numbered **2.a.**

In addition to the historical information, the entry may contain the following:

- comments on 'the letter and its sound', with quotations referring to the sound.
- illustrations of the 'literary use' of the letter—that is, examples of the way the letter itself is referred to in the written language. In the case of **D**, this information is contained in the first section, but may also appear as a separate sense.
- illustrations of the way in which the shape of the letter is used attributively, as in the case of **T**, **S**, etc., or **D** in sense **2.a.**
- illustrations of the way in which the serial order of the letter (as the second, third, fourth, etc. letter of the alphabet) leads to its use as a symbol within one or more subject areas.
- other symbolic uses of the letter within various subject areas, such as chemistry or physics.
- abbreviations in which the letter under discussion appears as the initial letter. These are, as in the case of sense **III.3.** in Fig. 12, normally listed in alphabetical order (letter by letter, ignoring punctuation), followed by a quotation paragraph, also arranged alphabetically, illustrating usage of the abbreviations in context. As in the entry for **D**, abbreviations are usually found in the final section of initial letter entries (in this instance, in sense **III.3.**). The first usage of each abbreviation is marked with an asterisk (*) in the quotation section (not shown); and

where there is more than one quotation for an abbreviation they are listed chronologically.

In most initial letter entries, large roman numerals (**I., II., III. . . .**) are employed for major components, with subdivisions designated by the appropriate arabic numerals and lower case letters, in the same fashion as for senses in conventional main entries. This pattern varies according to editorial judgement of what is an appropriate organizational scheme for the individual letter.

The fact that most initial letter entries contain extensive lists of abbreviations is an important point to remember. As will be seen in the next section, some important initialisms, acronyms, and abbreviations are given entries of their own, but one should always remember to check the initial letter entry before concluding that a particular form does not appear in the Dictionary.

Some readers may also find it interesting to explore the group of miscellaneous main entries for initial single letters, or combinations of letters, covering such anomalies as earlier spellings, 'clipped' forms, assimilated forms, or ways in which English represents some foreign sounds or letters. For example, the entries for **ry-**, **cn-**, and **ou-** explain and illustrate, with quotations, the history of earlier word beginnings where '*ri-*', '*kn-*', and '*ov-*' are now used. Similarly, the entry for **th-** illustrates a 'clipped' or shortened form used in older or dialectical elisions, often before vowels or the silent 'h', as in 'thands' for 'the hands' or 'thelder' for 'the elder', or even 'thman in th'moon'. In the same category are entries for shortened or apocopate forms such as **o'** or **a'** as in 'for a' that'. Examples of entries for assimilated forms include word beginnings such as **af-**, **ag-**, and **ap-**, which are altered forms of the original Latin '*ad-*'. In the last category are entries for word beginnings such as **dh-** and **dj-**, which are an attempt to represent the Indian dental sonant-aspirate and the Arabic 'j', respectively, within the limitations of the English language.

2. Initialisms, acronyms, and abbreviations

Some of the more familiar and important initialisms (for example, **B.B.C.**, **V.I.P.**, **P.S.**) and acronyms (for example, **AIDS**, **N.A.T.O.**) are covered in main entries, although the majority of these forms appear, as noted in the previous section, within the entries for their initial letter. When such forms are given a separate entry, punctuation, capitalization and spaces are ignored, and the headword appears in the normal letter-by-letter alphabetical sequence; thus **V.I.P.** is found between **viosterol** and **viparious**, as if it were a word 'vip'.

When a main entry is considered to be warranted, pronunciation, part of speech, and labels, if appropriate, and variants, if any, are given. Either the etymology or the definition contains an explanation of what the letters stand for, as well as any other useful information. The usual conventions for other main entries are followed, together with illustrative citations. For example, in the entry for **B.B.C.** in Fig. 13, the definition explains the meaning of the letters and the corporation's origins are briefly described. This is followed by a 'hence' statement, noting the combination **B.B.C. English**, and, resulting from that, the expression *B.B.C. pronunciation*. In the case of **P.S.** (Fig. 13), a cross-reference is made to an entry for **post-script**, indicated by the small roman capitals in which the word appears. The final paragraph includes two extensions of the form, also with appropriate quotations. The etymology (in square brackets) of the entry for the acronym **N.A.T.O.** (and its alternative forms, **NATO** and **Nato**) tells the reader that the term is 'formed on' (f.) the initials of the North Atlantic Treaty Organization set up in 1949. The definition further explains the acronym's origins, and includes two derivatives, **Nato-ish** and **Natoism**. Examples of the use of all three terms are given in the concluding chronologically arranged quotation paragraph.

Also in Fig. 13 are two examples of entries for the common abbreviations, **flu** (or **'flu**) and **sci-fi**. In each case, a cross-reference is given to the entries for the full forms of the words (**influenza** and **science fiction**). Variant forms for each term are listed (for example, the 19th-century spelling 'flue'). The quotation paragraphs contain citations that illustrate use of the abbreviated form.

Note that although this explanation differentiates between initialisms (first letters pronounced separately) and abbreviations (in the sense of shortening), the *OED* often uses the term 'abbreviation' to cover both forms as, for example, in the entry for **P.S.**, which is referred to as 'a common abbreviation'.

3. Affixes and combining forms

There are approximately 2,500 main entries for elements that can be attached to the beginning or end of words or word stems to qualify

B.B.C. (bi:bi:'si:). Initial letters of *British Broadcasting Corporation*, a public corporation orig. having the monopoly of broadcasting in Gt. Britain, financed by a grant-in-aid from Parliament; established 1927 by royal charter to carry on work previously performed by the British Broadcasting Company, hence **B.B.C. English**, standard English as maintained by B.B.C. announcers; so ***B.B.C. pronunciation***, etc.

1923 *Radio Times* 28 Sept. 12/1 It seems to me that the B.B.C. are mainly catering for the 'listeners' who own expensive sets. **1925** *Punch* 22 Apr. 440/1 The daily wireless programme of the B.B.C. **1926** *Encycl. Brit.* Suppl. I. 454/2 The 'B.B.C.' is constituted as a limited company, the shareholders being wireless manufacturers and traders. **1928** *Times* 13 Jan. 8/5 B.B.C. English. Mr. Lawrence omits from his list of solecisms in pronunciation perpetrated by the B.B.C.'s 'Advisory Committee on Spoken English' the crowning horror. **1932** *Listener* 13 Jan. 45/1 Critics who enjoy making fun of what they are pleased to call 'B.B.C. English' might with profit pay occasional visits to the other side of the Atlantic, in order to hear examples of our language as broadcast where there are no official 'recommendations to announcers'. **1936** W. Holtby *South Riding* i. 18 She talked B.B.C. English to her employer.. and Yorkshire dialect to old milkmen. **1938** P. Thoresby Jones *Welsh Border Country* viii. 95 The educated and older local (as opposed to the 'board-school' and B.B.C.) pronunciation of the town's name is *Shrozebury*, not Shroozbury. **1944** *Penguin New Writing* XXII. 47 Her accent was impeccably B.B.C. **1956** A. Wilson *Anglo-Saxon Attitudes* II. ii. 338 B.B.C. officials—programme planners, features-producers, poetry readers.

P.S., a common abbreviation of L. *post scriptum*, POSTSCRIPT, often pronounced as written ('pi:'ɛs).

1616 T. Roe *Let.* 30 Nov. in *Embassy to Court of Gt. Mogul* (1899) II. 359 P.S.—I humbly desire your Honor to doe me the fauour to thanck Sir Thomas Smyth in my behalfe. **1757** J. Lind *Lett. Navy* ii. 62 This defect is remedied by a law mentioned in the P.S. **1771** J. Wedgwood *Let.* 11 May (1965) 108 PS The letter to which this is a ps I did not like to send by the post. **1842** Orderson *Creol.* xviii. 221 As a little P.S... we will here note. **1842** Dickens *Let.* 1 May (1974) III. 228 Look over leaf for the PS. **1853** Mrs. Gaskell *Cranford* ix. 163 So she ended her letter; but in a P.S. she added, she thought she might as well tell me what was the peculiar attraction to Cranford just now. *a* **1909** *Mod.* (At end of a letter.) P.S. Since writing the above I have received your telegram, and am relieved to know that the missing luggage has turned up. Good-bye! **1969** *Listener* 15 May 682/3 PS. These are only hints. Please do not repeat verbatim.

Similarly **P.P.S.**, **P.P.P.S.**, (*post*) *post post scriptum*.

1841 Dickens *Let.* 9 July (1969) II. 325 P.S. Half asleep... P.P.S. They speak Gaelic here. **1900** G. B. Shaw *Let.* 30 Dec. (1972) II. 216 PPS I have been reading 'Herod' (I never go to the theatre now). *c* **1921** E. E. Cummings *Sel. Lett.* (1969) 81 P.S. am waiting for you... P.P.S. Elaine writes your painting is awfully good... P.P.P.S. Enjoyed the Krazy [Kat] you sent B. **1967** *Listener* 21 Dec. 814/2 PS: There'll be a special Christmas edition of *Round the Horne*. PPS: The new series of *Round the Horne* starts in February. PPPS: No advertising.

N.A.T.O., NATO, Nato ('neɪtəʊ). [Acronym f. the initials of *N*orth *A*tlantic *T*reaty *O*rganization, set up in 1949.] A military alliance of the United States and Canada with certain European nations. So '**Nato-ish** *a.*, supporting N.A.T.O.; '**Natoism**, adherence to N.A.T.O.; '**Natoist**, a supporter of N.A.T.O.

1950 *Newsweek* 14 Aug. 40/3 Nato is the newest synthetic word in the international gobbledygook and stands for the North Atlantic treaty organization. **1962** H. O. Beecheno *Introd. Business Stud.* i. 5 Britain had also put her military forces under a unified command in NATO (the North Atlantic Treaty Organization). **1965** *Economist* 28 Aug. 770/3 The Socialist People's party has accused Labour of being too capitalistic and too Nato-ish. **1965** *New Statesman* 24 Dec. 992/2 De Gaulle will not budge on his slightly neutralist type of Natoism. **1966** *Ibid.* 18 Mar. 366/2 The opposition.. includes a lot of outright Natoists (Mollet and even Mitterrand also support Nato, with reservations). **1975** *Guardian* 5 Dec. 3/1 Britain is interested in buying several of the aircraft provided that other European NATO countries also join in.

flu, 'flu (flu:), *sb. colloq.* Also 9 **flue**. Short for INFLUENZA.

1839 Southey *Lett.* (1856) IV. 574, I have had a pretty fair share of the Flue. **1893** *Mod. Let.*, I've a bad attack of the flu. **1911** *Chambers's Jrnl.* Apr. 239/2 We naturally ask ourselves what season—the 'flu' season, or was it the festive season? **1935** G. Barker *Janus* 151 She's in bed; she's got the 'flu. **1951** Auden *Nones* (1952) 28 Little birds with scarlet legs, Sitting on their speckled eggs, Eye each flu-infected city. **1957** *Times Lit. Suppl.* 15 Nov. p. ii/3 When the place is snowbound and the staff laid low with flu, the girls take over.

sci-fi (saɪ faɪ). Also **scifi, sci fi**. Colloq. abbrev. of SCIENCE FICTION.

1955 *Britannica Bk. of Year* 490/1 The popularity of science fiction was reflected in the contracted form Scifi. **1957** *MD Medical Newsmag.* June 62/1 Modern sci-fi writers follow an honorable tradition. **1961** B. Wells *Day Earth caught Fire* viii. 123 'I'm not up on my sci-fi,' hesitantly. 'So we're orbiting to the sun.' **1974** *Observer* 27 Oct. 1/7 The SF fan world abounds in language.. that can baffle the novice... Most important of all, you must not say 'sci fi'—it's always SF. **1978** *N.Y. Times* 30 Mar. c 22/3 A 10-part series based on what Mr. Kotlowitz called 'speculative fiction', stories that go beyond sci fi and deal with 'ethical and moral demands' made in new worlds to come. **1980** *Verbatim* Autumn 10/1 'Sci fi' is a term used to describe bad Hollywood science fiction movies, trashy science fiction novels, and bad science fiction written by mundane writers. **1981** 'D. Jordan' *Double Red* xiv. 61 There was a sci-fi film we didn't watch.

Fig. 13

their meaning and to form combinations, derivatives, or sometimes compounds. These word-forming elements appear in the Dictionary primarily with the part-of-speech labels *prefix* or *suffix* (collectively referred to as affixes), or they are described as 'combining forms', often abbreviated 'comb. form'. However, other descriptive terms may be encountered, such as 'stem of', 'final element of', 'second element of', or 'terminal ending'. Figs. 14 and 15 contain a number of examples of entries for word-forming elements.

In the *OED*, the distinction between what is termed a 'combining form' and an affix is usually that the combining form, as its name implies, represents the form in which an intrinsically meaningful word element (in English or the language of origin) is combined with another word element to produce a new word. Typically, the combining element undergoes some alteration in the process. For example, in Fig. 14, the combining form **chiro-**, **chir-** represents the Greek word for hand, while the terminals **-plegia** and **-ectomy** represent the Greek words for 'blow' or 'stroke', and 'excision'. Note that, with a few exceptions, such as **-ectomy**, the term 'combining form' is applied to the *first* element of a word.

Affixes, on the other hand, normally parallel a grammatical word or a grammatical form. For example, in Fig. 15 the suffix **-atic** is an adaptation of a particular instance of a Latin suffix, the prefix **con-** is derived from the Latin preposition *com*, the suffix **-dom** comes from the Old English word (later a suffix) used to imply a state or position, and the prefix **juxta-** represents a Latin adverb and preposition meaning 'near' or 'by the side of'. In principle, both affixes and combining forms can be added to individual words or other combining forms, but, unlike combining forms, an affix cannot normally be joined to another affix. The reader should be aware, however, that while these definitions and conventions generally hold true, seeming inconsistencies in the use of terms will occasionally be encountered. Decisions regarding terminology must, of necessity, be somewhat arbitrary since many word formation elements do not fit neatly into one or the other of the affixation or combining form categories. This is compounded by the fact that the terminology of word formation may be interpreted differently according to whether one is a linguist, a grammarian, or a lexicographer.

It is also difficult to generalize on the structure of main entries for combining elements, since they vary greatly in length (the entry for the common prefix **pre-**, for example, runs to eight pages) and

chiro-, chir-, = Gr. *χειρο-* combining form of *χείρ* hand, appearing in Greek in a very large number of words; several of these were adopted in Latin with the spelling *chiro-*, e.g. *chīrographum*, *chīromantia*, *chīronomia*, *chīrothēca*, *chīrūrgia*, and have thus passed into the modern langs.; many more have been taken by these directly from Greek, e.g. *chirocracy*, *chiroscopy*, *chirosophy*, *chirotechny*, or formed from Greek elements and on Greek analogies, as *chiropodist*, *chirosopher*. In modern technical terms, esp. those of botany and zoology, the spelling is often *cheir-*, e.g. *cheiranthus*, *cheiroptera*, *cheirotherium*.

In words thoroughly naturalized in Latin, CH was treated as C, and had in Romanic the phonetic history of *c* before *i*: hence such medL. forms as *cirographum*, *cirogryllus*, *cirotheca*, *ciromancia*, *cirurgianus*, also written *cyro-*, and It. and OF. and Eng. forms in *ciro-*, *cyro-*. But, in most words, modern scholarship has restored the *ch-* spelling and *k* pronunciation: see however CHIRURGEON, SURGEON.

The more important of these derivatives follow in their alphabetical order; a few trivial ones are given here: ˌ**chirocos'metics** *sb. pl.* [Gr. *κοσμητικός*; see COSMETIC], the art of adorning the hands. † '**chirogram** [see -GRAM], used by Bulwer for a diagram illustrating chironomy. **chiro-'gymnast** [Gr. *γυμναστής*; see GYMNAST], an apparatus for exercising the fingers for pianoforte playing. '**chiromys, cheiromys** [Gr. *μῦς* mouse], the AYE-AYE of Madagascar. '**chiroplast** [Gr. *πλάστης* moulder, modeller], an apparatus devised by J. B. Logier in 1814 for keeping the hands in a correct position in pianoforte playing; hence '**chiroplastic** *a.* ˌ**chiropoi'etic** *a.* [Gr. *ποιητικός* making, f. *ποιεῖν* to make, do], ? surgical. † **chi'roponal** *a.* [Gr. *πόνος* toil + -AL[1]], pertaining to or involving manual labour (*obs.*). † **chiro'scopical** *a.* [Gr. *-σκοπος* inspector, examiner], pertaining to palmistry.

1819 COLERIDGE in *Lit. Rem.* (1836) II. 119 Gloves of chicken skin..were at one time a main article in chirocosmetics. **1644** BULWER *Chirol. & Chiron.* 26 Types and Chirograms whereby this Art might be better illustrated then by words. **1845** *Mag. Sc.* VI. 137 The Chirogymnast.. ought..to cause the different parts of the hand to acquire.. dexterity. **1882** *Pop. Sc. Monthly Mag.* XX. 423 The chiromys..may be regarded as the last survivor. **1842** S. LOVER *Handy Andy* i. 9 As for the horse, his legs stuck through the bridge, as though he had been put in a chiroplast. *Ibid.*, The horse's first lesson in chiroplastic exercise. **1864** SPOHR *Autobiog.* II. 98 His [Logier's] chiroplast, a machine by means of which the children get accustomed to a good position of the arms and hands. **1866** *Athenæum* No. 2025. 215/2 Logier with his 'cheiroplast'. **1823** H. H. WILSON *Ess.* (1864) I. 391 Operations of the chiropoietic art..as extraction of the stone in the bladder. **1651** BIGGS *New Disp.* 16 ¶44 Chiroponall pyrotechny. **1652** GAULE *Magastrom.* 187 What a chyroscopical horoscope..of jugling, legerdemain, and superstitious imposture!

analytico-, combining form of Gr. *ἀναλυτικό-ς* analytic, prefixed to an adj. to denote **a.** 'pertaining to analytical...' as *analytico-chemical*; **b.** 'analytical and ...', as *analytico-synthetic*.

1920 T. P. NUNN *Education* xiii. 173 Thus the function of the nervous system is never purely integrative nor purely analytic, but always analytico-synthetic. **1938** R. W. LAWSON tr. *Hevesy & Paneth's Man. Radioactivity* (ed. 2) xxiii. 230 This analytico-chemical difference. **1961** T. LANDAU *Encycl. Librarianship* (ed. 2) 81/2 Attempts have been made..to build up classification schemes inductively from certain fundamental concepts which may be combined in various ways to form a synthesized concept for a whole book. Then groups of books in these analytico-synthetic schemes may be arranged into classes.

-ectomy, a combining form representing Gr. *ἐκτομή* excision, used to form words denoting a surgical operation for the removal of a part, as *appendicectomy*, *colectomy*, *hysterectomy*, *lobectomy*.

-plegia, formative element, f. Gr. *πληγ-ή* blow, stroke (f. *πλήσσειν* to strike) + -IA[1], used with the sense 'paralysis', as in HEMIPLEGIA, PARAPLEGIA, *iridoplegia* s.v. IRIDO-.

Fig. 14

con- *prefix*, of Latin origin. The form assumed by the Latin preposition *com* (in classical L., as a separate word, *cum*) before all consonants except the labials, *h*, *r*, and (in later times) *l*, as *concutĕre*, *condōnāre*, *confluĕre*, *congruĕre*, *conjūrāre*, *conquīrĕre*, *consistĕre*, *conspīrāre*, *constāre*, *contrahĕre*, *convincĕre*. In earlier times it was also used before *l*-, as *conloquium*; but here it was in later times always assimilated, as *colloquium*, and so in the modern langs. On the other hand it was not used in classical L. before *n* (e.g. *cōnātus*, *cōnubium*, etc.), but has been introduced subsequently, as *connātus*, *connubium*, and this spelling is followed in English. For meaning, see COM-.

Con- occurs in compounds formed in Latin, and that have come into English through French, or (in later times) directly. Also, in words formed on the analogy of these, and sometimes in casual combinations, as *conspecies*, where, however, CO- is the usual prefix: hybrids, frequent in *co-*, are rare with *con-*: cf. *con-brethren*, *con-truth*.

In OF. *con-* before *v* was often reduced to *co-*, *cu-*, *cou-*, as in *covenable*, *covenant*, *covent*, *coveiter*, *coveitus*, etc., in which form these words were taken into English. Following later French, some of these were afterwards altered back to *con-*, as *convenable*, *convent* (but *Covent Garden*, F. *couvent*); others retain *co-*, as *covenant*, *covet*, *covetous*, against mod.F. *convenant*, *convoiter*, *convoiteux*.

juxta- (dʒʌkstə), *prefix*, repr. L. *juxtā* adv. and prep. 'near, by the side of, according to', used in recent formations, in which it stands in prepositional relation to the sb. represented in the second element. **juxta-am'pullary** *a.*, situated by the side of an ampulla; **juxta-ar'ticular** *a. Anat.*, situated near a joint; **juxta-ma'rine** *a.*, situated by the sea; **juxta-'spinal** *a.*, situated by the side of the (or a) spine; **juxta-'tabular** *a.*, *Rom. Law*, according to a testament or written document.

1897 *Allbutt's Syst. Med.* III. 721 *Juxta-ampullary or peri-ampullary carcinoma. **1900** *Juxta-articular in DORLAND *Med. Dict.* **1910** CASTELLANI & CHALMERS *Man. Trop. Med.* lviii. 1137 (*heading*) Juxta-articular nodules. **1940** *Q. Bull. Northwestern Univ. Med. Sch.* XIV. 270/1 Juxta-articular nodes are non-inflammatory, painless, fibrous, subcutaneous growths. **1899** *Westm. Gaz.* 14 Mar. 3/3 Caves that are subterranean and *juxta-marine. **1876** *Trans. Clin. Soc.* IX. 190 There was no loss of lung-note between the scapulæ nor in the *juxta-spinal regions. **1875** POSTE *Gaius* II. (ed. 2) §148 *Juxta-tabular [= *secundum tabulas*] possession . . if defeasible by an adverse claimant, is ineffective.

-atic, *suffix*, forming adjs., (= Fr. *-atique*) ad. L. *-āticus*, a particular case of the suffix *-ic-us*, 'of, of the kind of' (see -IC), appended to pa. ppl. stems of verbs; as in *errā-re* to wander, *errāt-um*, *errātic-us* of wandering nature, *volātic-us* of flying kind, *vēnātic-us* of hunting kind; also used with sbs., e.g. *aqua* water, *aquāt-us* watered, watery, *aquātic-us* of watery kind, *Asiātic-us*, *fānātic-us* (*fānum* temple), *silvātic-us* (*silva* wood), *umbrātic-us* (*umbra* shade). Thence also neuter sbs. as *viāticum* 'what belongs to the way (*via*).' In late L. and Romanic, the subst. use received great extension: it survives phonetically in the Fr. and Eng. -AGE, in *umbrage*, *vantage*, *breakage*. The adjectives in *-atic*, as *aquatic*, *Asiatic*, *fanatic*, *lunatic*, *lymphatic*, are all of modern introduction; they are to be distinguished from words in which the suffix is *-ic* only, as *dramat-ic*, *hepat-ic*, *muriat-ic*, *pirat-ic*, *pneumat-ic*, *prelat-ic*.

-dom, *suffix*. [OE. *-dóm* = OS. *-dóm*, MDu. *-doem*, Du. *-dom*, OHG., MHG. *-tuom*, G. *-tum*.] Abstract suffix of state, which has grown out of an independent sb., orig. putting, setting, position, statute, OHG. *tuom*, position, condition, dignity, in OE. *dóm*, statute, judgement, jurisdiction, f. stem *dô-* of DO *v.* + abstract suffix *-moz*, OE. *-m*, as in *hel-m*, *sea-m*, *strea-m*, etc. Frequent already in OE. as a suffix to sbs. and adjs., as *biscopdóm* the dignity of a bishop, *cyningdóm*, *cynedóm*, royal or kingly dominion, kingdom, *ealdordóm* the position or jurisdiction of an elder or lord; *þeowdóm*, the condition of a þeow or slave; *fréodóm*, *háliȝdóm*, *wisdóm* the condition or fact of being free, holy, or wise. The number of these derivatives has increased in later times, and *-dom* is now a living suffix, freely employed to form nonce-derivatives, not only with the sense of 'condition, state, dignity', but also with that of 'domain, realm' (*fig.*). See in their alphabetical places *alderdom*, *Anglo-Saxondom*, *boredom*, *Christendom*, *cuckoldom*, *dukedom*, *earldom*, *freedom*, *kingdom*, *martyrdom*, *popedom*, *sheriffdom*, *thraldom*, *wisdom*, etc. Examples of nonce-words appear in the quotations.

1885 H. PEARSON *R. Browning* 8 Pomona . . to express all appledom and peardom. **1882** H. C. MERIVALE *Faucit of B.* I. I. iv. 58 Entitled him to all the honours of B.A. dom. **1887** *St. Louis Globe Democrat* 2 Feb., A real, live Dakota man . . fresh from Blizzardom. **1880** *New Virginians* I. 237 Meanwhile curdom flourishes. **1889** *Pall Mall G.* 3 Aug. 2/2 To test . . the good-sailordom of the spectators. *Ibid.* 7 Oct. 2/1 Imagine Manchesterdom Protectionist. **1894** *Times* 27 Sept. 7/4 Says Mr. Labouchere, 'Liberal officialdom has wet-blanketted it.' *Ibid* 6 June 11/3 The ranks of old fogeydom. **1894** HENTY *Dorothy's Double* I. 91 A . . specimen of English squiredom. **1889** *Pall Mall G.* 26 Dec. 1/3 The classic pile which . . divides clubland from theatredom. **1890** *Spectator* 18 Jan., A pervading atmosphere of topsy-turveydom.

Fig. 15

content. However, most entries for affixes consist of brief descriptions of the derivation and history of the forms with examples of the original or current use in italics, as in the case of the entries for **con-**, **-atic**, and **-dom**. Less common is the entry for **juxta-**, which defines several combinations, printed in bold type and arranged alphabetically, with their usage illustrated by citations listed in the same order. The latter structure is much more common with combining forms, as can be seen in the entry for **chiro-**, **chir-**, which begins with the usual descriptive and historical statement and the equivalent of a definition note (in small type) incorporating supplementary information on spelling and pronunciation, with cross-references to the entries for **chirurgeon** and **surgeon**. The important combinations are then listed alphabetically in bold type, followed by a supporting quotation paragraph in the same order. Note that brief etymological information (in square brackets), as well as a definition, follows each derivative.

Very long entries often require the use of the hierarchical numbering scheme employed in other main entries. In the case of the eight-page entry for **pre-** (not illustrated), the upper level hierarchical divisions (**A.**, **B.**; **I.**, **II.**) are used. Under **A.**, combinations in which **pre-** qualifies the word form to which it is attached adverbially or adjectivally are listed, while the **B.** section deals with combinations in which the prefix is prepositional. Large roman numerals (**I.**, **II.**) within each major section subdivide by semantic usage, while arabic numerals (**1.**, **2.**) further subdivide each branch into applications with various grammatical forms (adjective, substantive, etc.). The lower level division (**a.**, **b.**) is employed to separate groups of specialized combinations such as those used with proper names or for names of early geological formations. Supporting quotations are provided in each section.

Occasionally second or final elements of compound words are also given separate main entries. Compound words are formed by combining two independent English words to form a new word (for example, by the addition of common words such as **worthy**, **proof**, **hand**, etc. to another word). Sometimes, this type of usage is covered in the main entry for the terminal word in question. For example, Sense **1.b.** of the entry for the adjective **proof** notes its use as a second element, with examples cited in a quotation paragraph. On the other hand, a few compounding words such as the adjective **-worthy**, which has a long and complex history, and the more recent **-happy** and **-buster** are given entries of their own. Another variant, as in the case of **-wise**, is to include the compounding form as a cross-reference entry, directing the reader to the main entry for the noun **wise**. Once again, these forms, especially in the case of very old words, often overlap with affixes or may even have lost, in some instances, a clear-cut affixial function (for example, **-man** may be considered borderline).

4. Proper and proprietary names

The *OED* is not an encyclopaedic dictionary and therefore does not attempt to be comprehensive in its coverage of personal, geographical, and other proper names. Nevertheless, the Dictionary contains numerous entries for these forms, or their derivatives, where their use has been recorded either attributively, figuratively, allusively, or possessively. Such entries are normally capitalized, unless the word is widely employed in a generic sense, and/or sometimes, in the case of a proprietary name, if it is no longer registered as a trade name, for example, **aspirin**.

Figs. 16 and 17 illustrate some of the entries which are discussed in the following explanations. As will be seen, their structure is similar to other main entries, except that the entry usually incorporates the phrase 'the name of', either in the etymology in the case of derivatives, or in the definition text when the name is used possessively or in combinations.

It is important to remember the criteria governing such entries when searching the Dictionary, since seeming omissions might sometimes be puzzling. For example, there are no entries for the personal names of Freud, Hegel, Shaw, or Marx, but there are entries for the attributive forms of these surnames (**Freudian, Hegelian,** and **Shavian**). In the case of Marx, there are two entries for **Marxian** (one covering the attributive use of Karl Marx's name and the other based on references to the Marx Brothers), as well as separate entries for **Marxisant, Marxism, Marxite,** and **Marxize**. On the other hand, when a personal name is employed possessively, or attributively in its simple form, the surname often appears as the main entry. For example, **Einstein** is a headword because it is used possessively in terms such as 'Einstein's law', and attributively in phrases such 'the Einstein theory' and 'the Einstein effect'. In this instance, there are also entries for **Einstein-Bose,**

Marxian ('mɑːksɪən), *a.*[1] and *sb.*[1] [f. the name of Karl *Marx* (1818–83), German-born socialist writer + -IAN.] **A.** *adj.* Of or pertaining to the socialist doctrines or theories of Karl Marx. Also ***Marxian-Soviet*** adj., of or pertaining to the type of socialism found in the U.S.S.R.

1887 G. B. SHAW *Let.* 17 May (1965) 169 Your notion that he is getting the best is a Marxian illusion. **1896** B. RUSSELL *German Social Democracy* 71 The 'honourable' Social Democrats, as they called themselves, the party of thorough-going Marxian Communism. **1902** B. KIDD *Princ. Western Civilisation* 87 [Spencer] really has in view, like the Marxian socialists, a state of society in which [etc.]. **1919** J. SPARGO *Psychol. Bolshevism* iii. 12 Only an infinitesimal minority of those who call themselves Marxian Socialists have ever studied Marx at first hand. **1920** M. BEER *Hist. Brit. Socialism* II. III. i. 21 He [*sc.* Harney] stood much nearer to O'Brien and Louis Blanc than to the Marxian policy. **1930** T. OKEY *Basketful of Memories* vii. 61 The Marxian revolutionary social teaching was slow in penetrating this country. *Ibid.*, Indications were obvious.. that the Marxian bible..had begun to leaven English democratic thought. **1948** J. TOWSTER *Political Power in U.S.S.R.* i. 4 (*heading*) The Marxian-Soviet view of state and law. **1949** KOESTLER *Promise & Fulfilment* II. v. 281 The marxian dictum that man is a product of his environment. **1959** C. MACKENZIE *Lunatic Republic* xi. 190 We also regard revisionism as treachery to Marxian ideology. **1966** E. A. CARLSON *Gene* ix. 95 'Morganism', to this rival school, represented 'reactionary' and 'idealistic' tendencies which ran counter to the 'materialist' attitudes expressed by Marxian and Leninist (later Stalinist) outlooks on science. **1966** P. HEATH tr. *Wetter's Soviet Ideology Today* III. x. 294 The Marxian theory of value and surplus value has encountered its most serious troubles over the question of the average rate of profit. **1971** Z. A. JORDAN *Karl Marx* 20 Recent contributions concerning the concept of alienation.. follow the Hegelian rather than the Marxian path.

B. *sb.* One who holds or supports Marxian views; a follower of Marx. Cf. MARXIST *sb.*[1]

1896 B. RUSSELL *German Social Democracy* 89 Although this programme showed, on the whole, a victory of the Marxians, Marx protested against it. **1918** E. B. BAX *Reminisc.* 138 The question of Internationalism was indeed one of the great bones of contention between them and the Marxians. **1923** E. A. ROSS *Russ. Soviet Republic* 394 Even though it fell in partly with the program of the extreme Marxians, the expropriation of the landlords and capitalists was not really a thing planned. **1935** D. FAHEY *Mystical Body Christ* ix. 199 Marxians will take account of circumstances, in order to get their programme accepted.

Hence '**Marxianism**, adherence to Marxian doctrines or theories. Cf. MARXISM[1].

1896 B. RUSSELL *German Social Democracy* 93 The new philosophy of life which Marxianism had introduced. **1905** J. R. MACDONALD *Socialism & Society* iv. 99 Marxianism, however, is a product of German thought during the second and third decades of the nineteenth century. **1912** *Eng. Rev.* June 413 The British workman will never take up the theoretics of orthodox Marxianism. **1926** *Spectator* 22 May 871/2 It was Western Europe which gave Marxianism to Russia.

Marxian ('mɑːksɪən), *a.*[2] and *sb.*[2] [f. the name of the *Marx* Brothers (Chico, Harpo, Groucho and Zeppo), American comedians + -IAN.] **A.** *adj.* Of or pertaining to the Marx Brothers. **B.** *sb.* An admirer of the Marx Brothers. So '**Marxism**[2], (*a*) the type of comedy performed by the Marx Brothers; (*b*) a witticism typical of the Marx Brothers. Also '**Marxist** *a.*[2] and *sb.*[2]

1933 *Cherwell* 25 Feb. 131/2 No one who disliked *Monkey Business* will be converted to Marxism by *Horse Feathers*. **1940** G. MARX *Groucho Lett.* (1967) 47 Don't come out bluntly and say, 'How much dough have you got?' That wouldn't be the Marxian way. **1946** *Times* 6 July 5/4 There will be something like mourning among Marxists in London next week. **1951** K. CRICHTON *Marx Brothers* xv. 196 They opened on Thursday night and closed on Saturday. The post-mortem was short and typically Marxian. They had gambled, they had lost, and there would be no lamentations. **1962** *Sunday Times* 1 Apr. 32/8 Dr McCabe asked Groucho for a few words. The resultant Marxism is very much to the point. **1962** *Oxford Mail* 21 July 6/2 There are only one or two Marx Brothers comedies left in circulation now, so I recommend this..to Marxians. **1965** *Oxf. Mag.* 29 Apr. 303/2 We might not have been so much amused if there had not been a grain of zany probability—almost Marxist, in the Bros. sense—in it. **1966** A. EYLES *Marx Brothers* xvii. 156 'It made sages out of screwballs and accused wise men of being fools.' A perfect description of comedy's Marxism. We could be in *Duck Soup*, but this was American politics. **1969** *New Yorker* 25 Jan. 104/3 *The Marx Brothers at the Movies*. .. The book is the work of dedicated Marx fans, and its ideal readers are the nation's equally dedicated Marxists.

Einstein ('aɪnʃtaɪn, -staɪn). The name of Albert *Einstein* (1879–1955), German physicist and mathematician, used *attrib.* or in the possessive to designate certain theories and principles enunciated by him or arising out of his work.

1922 GLAZEBROOK *Dict. Appl. Physics* II. 359/2 According to Einstein's theory all energy possesses mass. *Ibid.* 595/1 Richardson has shown that Einstein's equation may be derived by thermodynamic and statistical methods. **1923** J. M. MURRY *Pencillings* 68 To some the Einstein theory may show the way of reconciliation. **1927** A. S. EDDINGTON *Stars & Atoms* 52 The Einstein effect is proportional to the mass divided by the radius of the star. **1934** WEBSTER, *Einstein shift*, the difference in wave-length..between light emitted by a source of a definite nature in the sun..and that emitted by a like source on the earth. **1958** *Listener* 11 Dec. 973/1 Eddington remained faithful to this idea that the universe evolved from the static but unstable Einstein universe. **1967** *Handbk. Chem. & Physics* (Chem. Rubber Co.) (ed. 48) F-69, *Einstein theory for mass-energy equivalence*, the equivalence of a quantity of mass m and a quantity of energy E by the formula $E = mc^2$. The conversion factor c^2 is the square of the velocity of light.

Einstein-Bose ('aɪnʃtaɪn'bəʊs, -'bəʊz, -st-). *Physics.* [The names of Albert *Einstein* (see prec.) and S.N. *Bose* (see BOSON).] A designation used as an alternative to BOSE-EINSTEIN, as ***Einstein-Bose particle***, ***statistics***, etc.

[**1929** DIRAC in *Proc. Cambr. Philos. Soc.* XXV. 62 The so-called 'statistics' of Einstein-Bose or Fermi applies only to an assembly of actual systems which could interact with each other.] **1931** *Physical Rev.* XXXVII. 333 We..justify the assumption that the clusters satisfy the Einstein-Bose or Fermi-Dirac statistics according to whether the number of particles in each cluster is even or odd. **1938** *Proc. R. Soc.* A. CLXVI. 127 (*heading*) Quantum theory of Einstein-Bose particles and nuclear interaction. **1955** R. D. EVANS *Atomic Nucleus* iv. 178 Photons and α particles obey Einstein-Bose statistics.

Einsteinian (aɪnʃ'taɪnɪən, -st-), *a.* [f. the name of Albert *Einstein* + -IAN.] Pertaining to or characteristic of Einstein or his theories.

1925 C. E. M. JOAD *Mind & Matter* 46 In an Einsteinian universe the velocity of light is the greatest velocity possible. **1928** *Observer* 25 Mar. 9/4 Einsteinian physics. **1937** *Mind* XLVI. 101 He rejects the view which would confine the importance of the Einsteinian relativity theory to scientific method. **1941** D. L. SAYERS *Mind of Maker* iii. 33 We may say..that Einsteinian physics has superseded Newtonian physics. **1959** *Encounter* Dec. 64/2, I confused Bergsonian time with Einsteinian time. **1968** E. MCGIRR *Lead-Lined Coffin* ii. 55 Once in every few years one of these thousands of men shows he has a brain of Einsteinian capacity.

einsteinium (aɪnʃ'taɪnɪəm, -st-). *Chem.* [f. the name of Albert *Einstein* + -IUM.] An artifically produced radioactive element. Symbol Es. Atomic number 99. Atomic mass of isotope 253 (1967) 253·0847.

1955 [see FERMIUM]. **1958** *Times* 29 Aug. 6/3 The following 10 [transuranic elements] were known.. einsteinium (99), fermium (100). **1967** *New Scientist* 6 July 22/2 Oak Ridge National Laboratory says it has succeeded in separating roughly one ten millionth of an ounce of einsteinium, the transuranic element first discovered in 1954.

Fig. 16

Waterloo (ˌwɔːtəˈluː). The name given to the battle fought outside the village of Waterloo, near Brussels, on June 18, 1815, in which Napoleon was decisively and finally defeated. Hence **a.** (with *a*, *his*): Something which is a 'settler'; a decisive and final contest; chiefly in the phrase ***to meet one's Waterloo***.

1816 BYRON *To Moore* 5 Dec., It [Armenian] is..a Waterloo of an Alphabet. **1842** J. AITON *Domest. Econ.* (1857) 68 If there must be a Waterloo, let it be a conflict for all the minister's rights, so that he may never require to go to law in his lifetime again. **1859** W. PHILLIPS *Lesson of Hour* 11 Every man meets his Waterloo at last. **1887** *Times* (weekly ed.) 24 June 9/3 He will have fought and lost his Waterloo. **1905** A. CONAN DOYLE *Return of Sherlock Holmes* 356 We have not yet met our Waterloo, Watson, but this is our Marengo. **1961** C. MCCULLERS *Clock without Hands* iii. 67, I felt right then and there I had met my Waterloo. **1982** *Times* 20 Oct. 19/6 The main fount of the economic nightmare now engulfing the world has met with its Waterloo.

b. The name of a bright blue tint (see quots.).

1823 MOORE *Country Dance & Quadrille* 84 Eyes of blue (Eyes of that bright, victorious tint, Which English maids call 'Waterloo'). **1871** MRS. H. WOOD *Dene Hollow* xxxviii, The frock..was of that dark bright blue colour called Waterloo, after the somewhat recent battle of Waterloo.

c. *attrib.*: **Waterloo ball**, a frivolous entertainment preceding a serious occurrence (with reference to a ball given in Brussels by the Duchess of Richmond on the eve of the Battle of Waterloo); †**Waterloo bang-up**, = *Waterloo cracker*; **Waterloo blue** (cf. b. above); **Waterloo church** (see quots. 1938, 1961); **Waterloo cracker**, a kind of firework (cf. CRACKER 6); **Waterloo Cup**, in Coursing, a race held annually at Altcar, near Liverpool; †**Waterloo fly**, an

Marengo (mæˈrɛŋgəʊ). [See def.] The name of a village in northern Italy, the scene of Napoleon's victory over the Austrians in 1800, used in the name of the dish ***chicken***, ***fowl***, ***poulet à la Marengo***, said to have been served to Napoleon after the battle of Marengo.

1861 MRS. BEETON *Bk. Househ. Managem.* 464 (*heading*) Poulet à la Marengo... Fowl à la Marengo. **1877** E. S. DALLAS *Kettner's Bk. of Table* 121 (*heading*) *Chicken à la Marengo*,—the chicken..is fried in oil. **1959** *Good Food Guide* 169 Chicken Marengo and tournedos.

Dr. Pepper (ˌdɒktə ˈpɛpə(r)). orig. and chiefly *U.S.* [f. the name of Charles *Pepper*, U.S. physician: see quot. 1986.] A proprietary name for a brand of aerated soft drinks; a bottle, can, or drink of this.

1906 *Official Gaz.* (U.S. Patent Office) 30 Jan. 1464/1 *Dr. Pepper*. Aerated tonic beverages and syrups for the same. The Dr. Pepper Co., Dallas, Tex. **1947** *Fortune* Oct. 108/1 Dr. Pepper..is a soft drink, colored ruby red, and variously described by Southerners who have been drinking it some sixty-three years as tasting like: (1) cherry, (2) almond, (3) raspberry, (4) prune juice. **1975** *Business Week* 10 Feb. 34/2 The success of Dr. Pepper, a cherry-flavored soft drink favorite of the South that went national in 1966.., could hardly go unnoticed. **1984** *Trade Marks Jrnl.* 14 Nov. 2977/2 (figure), Dr Pepper... 1,146,477. Non-alcoholic drinks and preparations for making such drinks... Dr. Pepper Company, 5523 Mockingbird Lane, Dallas, Texas, United States..Manufacturers and Merchants. **1985** *Toronto Life* Sept. 76/2 Upstairs in the second-floor common room, he pops a Dr. Pepper. **1986** *Time* 3 Mar. 67/1 Morrison,..hoping to curry favor with his beloved's father [Charles Pepper], named the new pop Dr Pepper.

Martini[2] (mɑːˈtiːnɪ). [f. the name of *Martini* and Rossi, Italian wine-makers.] The proprietary name of a type of vermouth; a cocktail consisting of gin and vermouth; ***dry Martini***, such a cocktail containing more gin than vermouth, sometimes with the addition of orange bitters. Also *attrib.*

1894 *Puck* (U.S.) 28 Nov. 238/2 (Advt.), The Club Cocktails Manhattan, Martini, Whisky, [etc.]. **1896** *Crescent* (Brooklyn, N.Y.) 1 Aug. 11/2 As he sipped his martini and inhaled its seductive bouquet, a far-away look came into his baby-blue eyes. **1903** ADE *People you Know* 20 It was an actual mystery to him that any one could dally with a Dry Martini while there was a Hydrant on every Corner. **1906** *Mrs. Beeton's Bk. Househ. Managem.* xlix. 1511 Martini cocktail. **1909** [see BRONX 1]. **1919** C. MACKENZIE *Sylvia & Michael* v. 203 What are you going to have? Ordered a Martini here the other day. **1930** WODEHOUSE *Very Good, Jeeves!* ii. 57 A nicely-balanced meal, preceded by a couple of dry Martinis, washed down with half a bot. **1953** D. A. EMBURY *Fine Art of Mixing Drinks* 36 Martinis, Manhattans, and other cocktails containing wine can be stirred with a rod or long spoon. *Ibid.* 106, I have already referred to the Martini as the most perfect of apéritif cocktails. **1958** *Times Lit. Suppl.* 19 Dec. 733/4 The sham, artificial life of all-night martini parties. **1962** 'E. MCBAIN' *Like Love* (1964) vii. 100 A tray with a Martini shaker and two iced Martini glasses. **1967** A. LICHINE *Encycl. Wines* 542/1 The Italian Cinzano may be red or white, sweet or fairly dry—as also may Martini and Gancia. **1968** [see GIBSON[2]]. **1972** J. MOSEDALE *Football* vii. 100 People tend to think of us professionals as guys who spend all their time around the swimming pool with a blonde in one hand and a martini in the other... A lot of us don't like martinis.

Guinness (ˈgɪnɪs). [Family name.] The proprietary name of a brand of stout manufactured by the firm of Guinness; a bottle or glass of this. Also *Comb.*, as ***Guinness-coloured*** adj.

1836 DICKENS *Sk. Boz* I. 190 A large hamper of Guinness's stout. *Ibid.* 191 Taking..a draught of Guinness. **1842** BARHAM *Ingol. Leg.* 2nd Ser. 79 With a three-corner'd Sandwich, and *soupçon* of 'Guinness's'. **1897** *Sat. Rev.* 2 Jan. 2/1 An Irishman drinking his Guinness with uncharacteristic quietude in a London 'pub'. **1922** G. SAINTSBURY *Scrap Bk.* viii. 33 You can't see the stones for the Guinness-coloured foam. **1928** H. JENKINS *Stiffsons* iv. 118 Oh! for some fish and chips and a bottle of Guinness. **1930** [see *black velvet*, BLACK *a.* 19].

Fig. 17

Einsteinian, and **einsteinium**, although often less important derivatives are included within the same entry. This can be seen by contrasting the two entries (not illustrated) for the surname **Parkinson**, one citing James Parkinson, whose name is used in the disorder *Parkinson's disease*, and one referring to Cyril Northcote Parkinson in the context of the widely quoted *Parkinson's law*. In the case of *Parkinson's disease*, two derivatives, **Parkinsonian** and **Parkinsonism**, are covered in separate main entries. However, the same forms, derived in this case from Cyril Parkinson's theory, are included in a final 'hence' paragraph within the main entry for his surname. Such decisions, discussed under the elements *Combinations* and *Derivatives* in the **sense section**, depend on the lexicographer's judgement as to whether the secondary terms warrant separate entries because of their importance or history.

Entries for geographical names follow similar criteria to those governing personal names. The place and battle name **Waterloo** is allocated an entry primarily because of its allusive or symbolic use in phrases such as 'to meet one's Waterloo', as well as its attributive use in various combinations. **Marengo**, on the other hand, receives a main entry not because of its fame as a battle, but because the name has been applied to a chicken dish which Napoleon's chef is said to have served the emperor after the battle.

The selection of proprietary names (the common umbrella term used in the *OED* for trade marks, trade names, etc.) is based on a similar policy, as well as on how widespread their usage is in a literary context. For example, some proprietary names such as **Kleenex** and **Band-Aid** are so well known that they are sometimes used as generic terms. Other trade names, while not necessarily accorded such common usage, are familiar to most people and often alluded to in books or articles—for example, **Guinness, Pabst, Martini, Coke** (Fig. 17). Note, however, that a proper name applied to a product is entered under the product's, *not* the individual's name. For instance, the soft drink, **Dr. Pepper**, appears in that form as an entry headword (alphabetically between **droyl** and **drub**), not under the surname 'Pepper' (for Charles Pepper, the US physician after whom the product was named).

As is usual with derivatives, some proprietary names are listed within other entries. This is often the case when a proprietary name is identical to and derived from a previously existing word. The trade name *Penguin*, as applied to paperback books, for example, is found under the entry for the noun **penguin**, the bird, and the proprietary name *Caterpillar*, applied to tractors or other earth-moving equipment, appears in the general entry for the noun, **caterpillar**. Names or derivatives which form the second element of combinations are usually included in the entry for the initial word form. Thus, the McDonald's proprietary name, *Big Mac*, is found under a list of combinations in the entry for the adjective **big**, where reference is made to its figurative use and its use as a nickname for the Municipal Assistance Corporation of New York City.

5. Combinations and derivatives

It is the policy of the *OED* to include recorded derivatives either as main entries in their own right or within the entries for their root words. The coverage of combinations is similarly comprehensive and, depending on a term's importance and history, it may appear either as a separate main entry in its alphabetical order, or under the word constituting, in most instances, its first element. For more information on these terms and the way in which they are incorporated *within* entries for root or first element words, refer to the explanation of **combinations** and **derivatives** in the **sense section** of this guide.

Main entries for combinations and derivatives are similar in construction to conventional main entries. The most noticeable difference for the reader is that the headword sections tend to be brief since the words, or part words, from which the combinations or derivatives are formed normally contain the major etymological information. Therefore, etymologies in most instances consist of **cross-references** (indicated by small roman type) to the main entries for the constituent word forms.

The major problem for the Dictionary user may be understanding the criteria for classifying certain words as main entries. The following explanation will therefore centre on this issue rather than on an analysis of the entry structure.

Combinations are normally made up of words or parts of words that are joined because of a semantic relationship. In most cases, the individual elements retain their meaning and spelling, although established compounds often develop a history and senses that are unique. Derivatives, on the other hand, are usually the result of the more grammatically-based addition of a suffix to a main word. Common examples are the formation of adverbs by the addition of **-ly** to an adjective, or of nouns by the addition of **-er** or **-ness**. Less clear-cut are word endings such as **-ville**, which fall somewhere between combinations and derivatives. Probably most confusing are derivatives ending in **-ing** and **-ed** that closely resemble inflectional forms of verbs.

Two parts of speech used in the *OED*, the participial adjective (usually abbreviated as *ppl. a.*) and the verbal substantive (*vbl. sb.*) or verbal noun, are most likely to cause confusion because of the terminology and because of their resemblance to present and past participles of a verb. Participial adjectives are usually formed on, or from (abbreviated as 'f.' in etymologies), a verb by the addition of **-ed** or **-ing** and are used to qualify nouns. Verbal nouns are also formed from verbs by adding **-ing**, but in this instance they act as nouns. Fig. 18 gives examples of entries for several derivatives from the verb **petition**: a noun, **petitionee**; a verbal substantive or noun, **petitioning**; and a participial adjective in the same form, **petitioning**. Note, however, that the editorial decision was made to include one participial adjective, **petitioned**, in a final 'hence' paragraph in accordance with the convention used for derivatives within entries for their root word.

If one studies these entries, the rationale for the part-of-speech designators is readily apparent. In general, verbal substantives and participial adjectives can be distinguished from inflectional forms, and from each other, by substituting another noun or adjective for the word in question. For example, if one substitutes the plural noun 'requests' for 'petitioning' in the last citation from Macaulay in the entry for the verbal substantive, the sentence 'James .. had treated modest requests as a crime', is still perfectly logical. Similarly, in the case of the entry for **petitioning** as a participial adjective, the substitution of the adjective 'hungry' in the last citation from Eastwick ('a pony standing on his hind legs like a hungry poodle') also makes good sense. The participial adjective **petitioned**, which is included in the entry for **petition**, *v.* is slightly less clear; however, if 'petitioned' is considered as describing an agent or individual (that is, those who were petitioned) the adjectival function becomes apparent.

Fig. 19 illustrates a selection of main entries formed on the noun **school**, consisting of both derivatives and combinations. These

petition (pɪˈtɪʃən), *v.* [f. PETITION *sb.*: cf. mod.F. *pétitionner* (1792 in Hatz.-Darm.).]

1. *trans.* To address or present a petition to; to make a humble request or supplication to; *spec.* to address a formal written petition to (a sovereign, a legislative body, person in authority, or court).

1607 SHAKS. *Cor.* II. i. 187 You haue, I know, petition'd All the Gods for my prosperitie. **1637** *Documents agst. Prynne* (Camden) 72 Sondaie last the parishieners petitiond his Majestie that their church might not be pulld downe. **1765** BLACKSTONE *Comm.* I. i. 143 There still remains a fourth subordinate right, appertaining to every individual, namely, the right of petitioning the king, or either house of parliament, for the redress of grievances. **1818** CRUISE *Digest* (ed. 2) V. 161 Lord Pembroke petitioned the House of Lords for a bill to set aside an amendment made in a fine, levied in the Court of Great Sessions in Wales. **1845** SARAH AUSTIN *Ranke's Hist. Ref.* II. 273 To petition the emperor to hold an ecclesiastical council in the German nation. **1857-8** SEARS *Athan.* II. ii. 186 They petition Pilate for a guard.

b. To solicit, ask, beg for (a thing).

1631 HEYLIN *St. George* 86 The picture of some state or Country, petitioning..the ayde and helping-hand of so great a Saint. **1812** CRABBE *Tales* XVI. *Confidant*, All that I hope, petition, or expect.

2. *absol.* or *intr.* To address or present a petition, to make petition, to make a humble request or entreaty, to ask humbly (*for* something).

1634 HEYWOOD *Maidenhead Lost* I. Wks. 1874 IV. 108 You petition heere For Men and Money! **1751** LABELYE *Westm. Br.* 25 Westminster Bridge was petitioned for. **1766** ENTICK *London* IV. 71 The method of gaining admission into this hospital is by petitioning to the committee. **1838** LYTTON *Alice* IV. v, The Colonel petitioned for three days consideration. **1847** TENNYSON *Princ.* VI. 300 Then Violet.. Petition'd too for him.

Hence **petitioned** (pɪˈtɪʃənd) *ppl. a.*

1894 H. HUNT in *Daily News* 11 June 8/2 That the petitioned should not misunderstand us.

petitionee (pɪˌtɪʃəˈniː). *U.S. Law.* [f. PETITION *v.* + -EE.] The person or party against whom a petition is filed, and who is required to answer and defend.

1764 *Conn. Col. Rec.* (1881) XII. 262 Unless the petitioner would..execute notes of hand to the petitionee for the whole added together. **1767** *Ibid.* 618 Under the circumstances the petitioner ought not in equity to be holden to answer the same to the petitionee. **1828-32** WEBSTER, *Petitionee*, a person cited to defend against a petition. **1895** in *Funk's Stand. Dict.*

peˈtitioning, *vbl. sb.* [f. PETITION *v.* + -ING[1].] The action of making or presenting a petition.

a **1649** DRUMM. OF HAWTH. *Declar.*, etc. Wks. (1711) 210 They could not be induced..to acknowledge the smallest error, either in the matter of their petition or in the manner of their petitioning. **1769** BLACKSTONE *Comm.* IV. 147 Nearly related to this head of riots is the offence of tumultuous petitioning. **1849** MACAULAY *Hist. Eng.* v. II. 658 James..had treated modest petitioning as a crime.

peˈtitioning, *ppl. a.* [f. as prec. + -ING[2].] That petitions; supplicating, humbly begging.

petitioning creditor, one who applies for an adjudication in bankruptcy against his debtor (*Wharton*).

1615 BRATHWAIT *Strappado* (1878) 111 This priuiledge and Knightly honour; Which hauing got by long petitioning suite. **1649** MILTON *Eikon.* iv. Wks. 1851 III. 361 Unarm'd and Petitioning People. **1845** POLSON *Eng. Law* in *Encycl. Metrop.* II. 835/1 Proof being given before them [commissioners of the Court of Bankruptcy] of the petitioning creditor's debt..and of the act of bankruptcy, the trader is declared a bankrupt. **1849** E. B. EASTWICK *Dry Leaves* 4 A pony standing on his hind legs like a petitioning poodle.

Fig. 18

schoolable (ˈskuːləb(ə)l), *a. rare.* [f. SCHOOL *sb.*[1] + -ABLE.]

†**1.** Capable of being schooled or trained. *Obs.*

1594 CAREW *Huarte's Exam. Wits* iv. (1596) 38 Amongst beasts of one kind, he which is most Schooleable and skilfull is such because he hath his braine better tempered.

2. Of proper age to attend school.

1846 *Eng. Rev.* VI. 138 In 1831 the number of children between the ages of 7 and 14, the approved schoolable period, was 2,043,030. **1869** *Echo* 15 Mar., 250,000 children of 'schoolable' age. **1888** *Rep. U.S. Commissioner Educ.* 1886–87, 59 Each tax-payer..would have a far less burden to bear in the work of getting all the 'schoolable' children within the schools.

school board. [BOARD *sb.* 8 b.]

1. In England and Wales from 1870 to 1902, and in Scotland from 1872 to 1918, a body of persons elected by the rate-payers of a 'school district', and charged by statute with the provision and maintenance of sufficient accommodation in public elementary schools for all the children of the district.

schoolboy (ˈskuːlbɔɪ). [f. SCHOOL *sb.*[1] + BOY.]

1. a. A boy attending or belonging to a school.

1588 SHAKS. *L.L.L.* v. ii. 403 O! neuer will I trust to speeches pen'd, Nor to the motion of a Schoole-boies tongue. **1599** B. JONSON *Cynthia's Rev.* IV. v, Death, what talke you of his Learning? he vnderstands no more then a schoole-Boy. **1600** SHAKS. *A.Y.L.* II. vii. 145. **1788** BURKE *Sp. agst. W. Hastings* Wks. XIII. 37 School-boys without tutors, minors without guardians. **1813** SOUTHEY in *Croker Papers* (1884) I. 49, I should go to the task like a schoolboy. **1881** CROWEST *Phases Mus. Eng.* 164 The merest schoolboy, it would be thought, could have detected the absurdity of such a musical passage.

b. In phr. ***every schoolboy knows***, referring to a matter of factual information, supposed to be elementary and generally known.

1654 JER. TAYLOR *Real Pres.* 80 Every Schole-boy knows it. **1721** SWIFT *Poems* (1958) I. 281 How haughtily he lifts his Nose, To tell what ev'ry School Boy knows. **1840** MACAULAY in *Edin. Rev.* Jan. 295 Every schoolboy knows who imprisoned Montezuma, and who strangled Atahualpa. **1966** *Listener* 8 Sept. 365/3 Tallis's motet *Spem in alium nunquam habui* was for years more often written about than heard. A *tour-de-force* in forty voice-parts. so much every schoolboy knew. **1977** *Times* 15 Oct. 2/8 Every schoolboy knows that the No. 3 bus from Piccadilly Circus comes to Valley Fields, Wodehouses's familiar pseudonym for Dulwich.

schoolboyish (ˈskuːlbɔɪɪʃ), *a.* [f. SCHOOLBOY + -ISH.] Schoolboy-like. Hence **ˈschoolboyishly** *adv.*, in the manner of a schoolboy; **ˈschoolboyishness**, the conduct or manner of a schoolboy.

1831 *Fraser's Mag.* IV. 278 All this being not particularly new, and rather schoolboyish withal. **1888** *Academy* 18 Feb. 112 An eminently schoolboyish story. **1898** G. B. SHAW *Let.* ? 2 May (1972) II. 39 Irving & I are too eminent to indulge in such schoolboyishness in public. **1901** W. J. LOCKE *Usurper* xviii. 247 He..was so schoolboyishly happy the next morning on starting for his holiday. **1972** J. POTTER *Going West* 159 His step was jaunty and his manner schoolboyishly affable. **1976** *Daily Tel.* 9 Sept. 13/1 As an example of the schoolboyishness, I would cite the fact that Ransome and a friend..had coded signals which they displayed on their respective houses..to give notice when they were going fishing.

schoolday (ˈskuːldeɪ). [f. SCHOOL *sb.*[1] + DAY.]

1. *pl.* The days or period (of one's life) at which one is at school.

1590 SHAKS. *Mids. N.* III. ii. 202 O, is all forgot? All schooledaies friendship, child-hood innocence? **1594** —— *Rich. III*, IV. iv. 169 Tetchy and wayward was thy Infancie. Thy School-daies frightfull,..Thy prime of Manhood, daring. **1798** LAMB *Old Familiar Faces* i, In my joyful school-days. **1885** LD. BLACKBURN in *Law Rep. 10 App. Cases* 388 In his schooldays or in his grown up days

attrib. **1844** DISRAELI *Coningsby* VII. ii, When two school-day friends..meet at the close of their college careers.

2. A day on which there is school.

1852 WALCOT *William of Wykeham* 233 On whole school-days, morning school lasts from 7 till 8 A.M.; middle school from 9 until noon; evening school begins at 2, and ends at 6. **1857** HUGHES *Tom Brown* II. v, It is a whole school-day. **1873** *Routledge's Young Gentl. Mag.* Dec. 101/1 During the holidays, or on a school-day.

schooldom (ˈskuːldəm). [f. SCHOOL *sb.*[1] + -DOM.] The domain or world of school or schools; the persons, things, and conditions concerned in the affairs of schools.

1826 MISS MITFORD *My Godfather* in *Lit. Souvenir* 393 A young girl, just freed from the trammels of schooldom. **1854** MARION HARLAND *Alone* iv, A summons to 'the study' was an event of rare occurrence..in the annals of schooldom. **1902** *Spectator* 26 July 110 The sense of injustice in this particular has permeated the ranks of schooldom.

-schooler (ˈskuːlə(r)). *U.S.* [f. SCHOOL *sb.*[1] + -ER[1].] As the second element in Combinations, designating a pupil at a specified type of school, or stage of school-life, as ***grade, high schooler***. See also PRE-SCHOOLER.

1971 *Sci. Amer.* Dec. 114/3 Martin Gardner's well-known learning and mathematical depth are worn lightly in this friendly, comical book for grade schoolers. **1972** *Newsweek* 25 Sept. 106/2 (*caption*) Harvard tutor..and high schoolers. **1973** *Black World* June 44/1 Ronald and Wayne are high schoolers. **1977** *Rolling Stone* 30 June 60/2 High schoolers will dye their hair gray, and buy iron-on wrinkles, and yearn for the day when their bodies begin to sag.

schoolful (ˈskuːlfʊl). [f. SCHOOL *sb.*[1] + -FUL.] As much or as many as a school will hold.

1881 *Academy* 22 Oct. 307 Such a monster may perchance exist,..but surely not a whole schoolful of them. **1900** *Daily News* 16 Aug. 6/7 We enjoyed it like a schoolful of children.

Fig. 19

include the adjective **schoolable**; a noun combination consisting of two words, **school board**; two single word noun combinations or compounds, **schoolboy** and **schoolday**; two noun derivatives, **schooldom** and **schoolful**, and a final element, **-schooler**. Note also the entry for **schoolboyish**, which illustrates a main entry for a derivative of a combination that, in turn, has its own adverbial and noun derivatives, *schoolboyishly* and *schoolboyishness*. Except for the brevity of the history, these headwords follow the normal entry structure, with senses itemized in a linear fashion, supported by quotation paragraphs.

6. Spurious words

Although there are fewer than 400 main entries for spurious words in the Dictionary, some explanation for their rationale may be helpful to the reader who chances upon such a rarity. The term 'spurious' is applied to words that are considered to be erroneous in their form, or in the meaning attached to them. Thus, the spurious entry is similar in intent to the catachrestic mark employed *within* entries and discussed under **status symbols** in the **sense section** of this guide.

All main entries of this type were written for the first edition, and are largely the result of the use of earlier dictionaries as one of the *OED*'s sources. It was discovered that certain copyists' or translators' errors, misprints, or misreadings tended to be perpetuated by dictionaries, and the *OED* editors endeavoured to correct such misapprehensions by checking original sources, alternative editions, etc.

Spurious words are readily identifiable because the entire entry is enclosed in square brackets, as illustrated by the sample entries in Fig. 20. Many spurious entries are very brief and merely note, in a similar format to cross-reference entries for obsolete words, that the word is an erroneous form or misspelling of another dictionary headword (as in the case of **cone and key**). Some entries offer further explanations for the error and give examples of the spurious usage; the entry for **David's staff** is one of the longest entries of the explanatory type.

Spurious entries tend to be somewhat idiosyncratic since they are in effect an editorial comment bringing to the reader's attention a 'blunder' (as in the entry for **ennation**) or a 'grotesque misreading' [**beast**, *v*. 'To hunt for beasts,' which modern dictionaries have inserted each from its predecessor, is a figment founded on a grotesque misreading of Spenser's *Amoretti* Epigr. ii.:

With that [i.e. Dian's dart] Love wounded my Loves hart,
But Diane [wounded] beasts with Cupids dart.]

[**cone and key**, misreading of *cove and key*: see COVE.]

[**David's staff**. Originally an error of Pietro della Valle's, who gave *Dauidstoff* as the English name of an instrument for taking the altitude of the sun. This was reproduced by his translator, Havers, as *David's Staff*, which was copied by Blount and Phillips, and is repeated in some modern Dicts. So also *David's quadrant* (= BACK-STAFF) in Phillips (ed. 1696), corrected in Kersey's ed. (1706) to *Davis's quadrant*: see QUADRANT *sb*.[1], quot. 1696.

1623 PIETRO DELLA VALLE *Viaggi* Let. i. 22 Mar. (1663) IV. 16 Con diuersi altri strumenti: e con vno in particolare, che mi dissero, da poco tempo in quà, essere stato inventato da vn tal Dauid, che dal suo nome l'haueua chiamato *Dauidstoff*, che in lingua Inglese vale à dir legno di Dauid. **1664** G. HAVERS *translation*, One [instrument] invented by one *David*, and from his name call'd *David's Staff*. **1674** BLOUNT *Glossogr*., *Davids-staff*, is an instrument in Navigation, consisting of two Triangles united together, one longer then the other, both having their base arched, and between them in the circle of their bases, containing an entire Quadrant of ninety degrees. *Valle's Travels*.]

[**dog-ray, -reie**. Explained in some mod. Dicts. as: Dog-fish. App. error arising from misreading *dorrey* (see quot.), var. of DORY.

[**1577** HARRISON *England* III. x. 110/1 in Holinshed *Chron*. I, Of the first [sort of fish, the flat] are the Plaice, the Butte, the Turbut, Dorrey, Dabbe, &c.]]

[**ennation, enneation**, 'the ninth segment in insects', for which mod. Dicts. cite 'Maunder', is a blunder for *ennaton* (a. ἔνvατον late spelling of Gr. ἔνατον ninth) which appears in Maunder's *Treas. Nat. Hist*. 1848–54, but not in later editions. We have no evidence that the word was ever in Eng. use.]

[**expediate**, *v*. Error for EXPEDITE in an imperfect and unauthorized edition of Sandys' *Relation of the State of Religion*, reproduced by Cockeram, copied by Todd, 1818; hence in later Dicts.

1605 SANDYS *Rel. State Relig*. K 3, Some great alterations in some kinde of marchandise..which may serve for that present instant to expediate [*MS. correction by author and ed*. 1629 expedite] their businesse. **1623** COCKERAM, *Expediate*, to dispatch, or make ready.]

[**lingerly**, *adv*., given in Dicts., appears to be a misprint in the later edd. of C. Bronte's *Jane Eyre* iii; ed. 1 (1847) has *lingeringly*.]

[**phantomnation**. Explained as: Appearance of a phantom; illusion. Error for *phantom nation*.

[**1725** POPE *Odyss*. x. 627 The Phantome-nations of the dead.] Entered as one word in **1820** JODRELL, in accordance with his method of writing compounds: *Phantomnation*, a multitude of spectres. Hence the following entries: **1860** WORCESTER, *Phantomnation*, illusion. *Pope*. **1864** WEBSTER, *Phantomnation*, appearance as of a phantom; illusion. (*Obs. and rare*.) *Pope*. So in OGILVIE (Annandale) and *Cassell's Encycl. Dict*.]

[**tendsome**, *a*. Explained as: Requiring much attendance. Known only in the following Dict. entries.

1847 WEBSTER, *Tendsome*, requiring much attendance; as, a *tendsome* child... *Tensome*, see Tendsome. So **1850** OGILVIE, adding (*Obs*. or *fam*.). **1864** WEBSTER, adding (Written also *tensome*). **1891** *Century Dict*.]

[**zimme**, spurious word; being the OE. *ȝimm* gem, with the *ȝ* taken for a *z*.

1848 LYTTON *Harold* II. iii, Taking from his own neck a collar of zimmes..of great price. *Ibid*. III. ii, His diadem, with the three zimmes shaped into a triple trefoil.]

Fig. 20

(as the error in interpreting **beast** in a line from Edmund Spenser's *Amoretti* is called). However, in the case of the rather amusing entry for **phantomnation** the reader is left to apply his or her own description to the perpetuated error.

Most entries are self-explanatory, although there are many references to source literary texts and dictionaries, such as Worcester, Webster, Ogilvie, Cockeram, and Todd. Full bibliographical details for such references can, in most cases, be found in the *Bibliography* at the end of the Dictionary.

7. Lengthy entries

The *OED* contains a number of very long and complex entries, primarily for core words that have developed many variant forms and senses over a number of centuries. Frequently such entries appear formidable and the reader may be discouraged from attempting to search for a specific meaning. However, if one examines a typical lengthy entry, paying particular attention to the structure, the task becomes much less daunting.

The verb **run** is a good example of the way in which the Dictionary's hierarchical lettering and numbering scheme is employed to document a verb whose history, in its multiple forms, can be traced to its Germanic roots. The entry not only contains numerous variant forms, but also eighty-two main senses with over 350 sub-senses, requiring, in total, sixteen pages of densely printed text.

If one wishes to study such an entry or locate a particular sense, the first step is to scan it quickly to identify its main components and its overall organization. Figs. 21 and 22 contain extracts from the entry for **run**, showing the beginning of the entry and each of its sections and parts. The upper level of the hierarchical system is used to divide the entry into two main sections, **A.** and **B**. The **A.** section covers the variants of inflectional forms of the verb. The introductory words of the etymology state that **run** is 'a verb of complicated history in Eng. representing two forms originally distinct (a strong transitive and a weak intransitive), each of which was subject to metathesis'. The first section reflects this statement by a further subdivision into two parts (**I.** and **II.**) covering 'Forms with Metathesis' and 'Forms without Metathesis' (metathesis is the transposition of sounds or letters in a word as, for example, *arn* instead of

run (rʌn), *v.* Forms: (see below). Pa. t. **ran.** Pa. pple. **run.** [A verb of complicated history in Eng., representing two forms originally distinct (a strong intransitive and a weak transitive), each of which was subject to metathesis; the forms are thus to some extent parallel to those of BURN *v.*[1] The strong intr. verb is represented by OE. *rinnan* (*ran*, **runnon*, [*ʒerunnen*]), = OFris. *rinna*, *renna*, *runna* (*ran*, pa. pple. *runnen*, *ronnen*), mod.WFris. *rinne*, *ronne* (*roan*, pa. pple. *roun*), NFris. *ren* (*ruan*, *ronen*), *run*, etc., MDu. *rinnen* (*ran*, *geronnen*); OS. *rinnan* (*ran*, *runnun*, ——), MLG. *rinnen* (*ran*); OHG. *rinnan* (*ran*, *runnun*, *girunnan*), G. *rinnen* (*rann*, *rannen*, *geronnen*); ON. *rinna*, later (also mod.Icel., Fær., Norw.) *renna* (*rann*, *runnu*, *runninn*), MSw. *rinna* (also mod.Sw.), *rynna* (*ran*, *runno*, *runnin*), MDa. *rinde* (*rand*, *runde*, *runden*), Da. *rinde* (*randt*); Goth. *rinnan* (*rann*, *runnun*, *runnans*). Of this type, however, very few examples occur in OE. texts (four or five in all of the simple verb, chiefly in verse, and a similar number of the pa. pple. from the compound **ʒerinnan*). The prevailing form in all dialects appears to have been that with metathesis, *irnan*, *iernan*, *yrnan* (*arn* or *orn*, *urnon*, *urnen*): for the later history of this see the forms below. The weak causative verb, of which the original form was **rannjan*, is represented in the cognate languages by OFris. *renna* (p. p. *rent*), MDu. *rennen* (*rende*, *rande*, *gerent*, *gerant*; Du. *rennen*), OS. *rennian*, MLG. *rennen* (*rende*, *rande*, etc.), OHG. *rennan*, (*ranta*, *girant*), MHG. and G. *rennen* (*rannte*, *gerannt* and *rennte*, *gerennt*), ON. (also Icel., Fær., Norw.) *renna* (*renndi*, *renndr*), MSw. and Sw. *ränna* (*rände*, *ränt*), MDa. and Da. *rende* (*rende*, *rendt*). In OE. it appears only in the metathetic form *ærnan*, *earnan* (usually in the sense of 'to ride').

The extreme rarity of OE. *rinnan*, and the entire absence of an OE. **rennan*, render it probable that ME. *rinne(n* and *renne(n* are mainly, if not entirely, due to the influence of ON. *rinna* and *renna*. To a great extent they first appear in texts where Scand. influence is prominent.

The different OE. and ME. types, partly by natural development of the vowels and partly by interaction of the various tenses of the strong verb, gave rise to a large number of variations, for which see the forms below. The weak conjugation, properly belonging to the causative but soon extended to the intransitive verb, remained fairly common until *c* 1400, and still survives to some extent in dialects.

In the sense 'to curdle' the causative form exists in mod. dialects as EARN *v.*[2] For the ME. forms representing the OE. compound *ʒe-yrnan*, see YERN *v.*]

A. Inflexional forms.

I. Forms with metathesis.

1. *Infinitive.* *α.* **1 irnan, iernan, 1–2 yrnan, 2 yrnen, 3 irne(n), 9 *dial.* hirn.**

c **888** K. ÆLFRED *Boeth.* xxxv. §7 Wildu dior ðær woldon to irnan. *c* **897** —— *Gregory's Past. C.* xvi. 103 Ðæt hi mægen iernan & fleon. *c* **900** WÆRFERTH tr. *Gregory's Dial.* 118 Se hræfn..ongan yrnan ymb þone ylcan hlaf. *c* **1205** LAY. 19750 He..hahte hine..irne to þere welle. *Ibid.* 21229 His hors he lette irnen. **1825** JENNINGS *Obs. Dial. W. Eng.* 180 I'll hirn auver an zee where I can't help 'em.

β. **1 iornan, [eornan], 3 eornen(n), 3–4 eorne (3 heorne).**

a **900** in *O.E. Texts* 178 Ðæt ða wildan hors scealden iornan. *c* **1200** ORMIN 1336 He..let itt eornenn forþwiþþ. *c* **1275** LAY. 19750 [He] hehte him..heorne to þare wille. *c* **1400** *Trevisa's Higden* (Rolls) VIII. 61 Swyn were i-seie..renne [*v.r.* eorne] up and doun.

γ. **3 urnen, 3–4 urne, vrne, 9 *dial.* (h)urn.**

c **1205** LAY. 24696 Summe heo gunnen urnen. *a* **1250** *Owl & Night.* 638 þat node makeþ old wif urne. *a* **1300** *K. Horn* 936 Hi gunne awei vrne. **1886** ELWORTHY *W. Somerset Wd.-bk.* 635, I zeed the stoat urn 'long the wheel-ruck. **1894** BLACKMORE *Perlycross* 257 Zippy..hath orders to hurn for her life.

δ. **1 ærnan** (*dat.* **ærnenne, earnenne**), **3 ærne(n), eærne, earn(n)e, earnee, hearn, 4 (9 *dial.*) arn; 3–4 ernen, ernyn, erne, 3 ernne, 5 eerne.**

These are properly forms of the causative verb.

c **825** *Vesp. Ps.* xviii. 6 He..ʒefaeh swe swe ʒiʒent to earnenne on weʒ. *c* **900** tr. *Baeda's Hist.* v. vi. 400 þæt hio ærnan moste. *Ibid.*, To ærnenne & to flitenne. *c* **1205** LAY. 1638 Þeond þat lond he gon ernen. *Ibid.* 8542 þa com an gume ærnen. *c* **1275** *Ibid.* 21229 His hors he makede earnee. *a* **1300** in *E.E.P.* (1862) 9 As bestis þat wer wode a-ȝe oþir to erne her and þare. *c* **1330** *Arth. & Merl.* 1228 (Kölbing), He oȝaines hem fast gan erne. *c* **1440** *Promp. Parv.* 142/2 Ernyn, as horse (*P.* eerne), *cursito.* **1876** *Mid. Yorks. Gloss.* 163 *Arn*, to run, or walk hastily.

2. *Present Participle.* *α.* **1 irn-, 1–2 yrnende.**

c **893** K. ÆLFRED *Oros.* I. i. 8 Seo is irnende of norþdæle. *c* **1000** *Sax. Leechd.* III. 234 Æfre heo byð yrnende ymbe ðas eorðan. *a* **1100** in Napier *O.E. Glosses* 5/2 *Uagans*, i. *circumiens*, yrnende.

β. **1 eorn-, iornende, 4 eornynge.**

c **825** *Vesp. Ps.* lvii. 8 Swe swe weter eornende. *c* **950** *Lindisf. Gosp.* Matt. xxvii. 48 Hræðe iornende an of hiora ʒenom spyngc. *c* **1320** *Cast. Love* 728 A welle þat euere is eornynge.

γ. **2 ernende, 4 erninde, ernyng(e.**

a **1100** in Napier *O.E. Glosses* 12/2 *Labentibus*,.. ernendum. **13..** *Guy Warw.* 719 Riche stedes..erninde. **1377** LANGL. *P. Pl.* B. xix. 376 Water..ernynge out of mennes eyen.

δ. **4 arnand, arnyng, 5 arnende.**

13.. *K. Alis.* 2098 (Laud MS.), Ac a kniȝth þer comeþ arnyng. *c* **1330** *Arth. & Merl.* 8494 (Kölbing), Arnand wiþ al his miȝt. **14..** *Sir Beues* (E) 1679 He prekyd hys hors al arnende.

3. *Present Indicative*: *3rd pers. sing. and pl.* *α.* **1 irn(e)ð, yrn(e)ð, *pl.* irnað, yrnað, 3 irneð.**

c **888** K. ÆLFRED *Boeth.* xxxvi. §6 Ða dysegan..irnað hidres ðidres. *c* **893** —— *Oros.* I. i. 8 Seo ea..irnð þonan suðryhte. *c* **1000** *Ags. Gosp.* Luke xxii. 10 Eow aʒen yrnð an man. *c* **1000** *Ags. Ps.* (Thorpe) cxlvii. 4 His word yrneð wundrum sniome. *c* **1205** LAY. 29664 þe ueȝereste welles stæm þe irneð on uolden.

β. **1 iorn(e)ð, 2 eornð, 1, 3 eorneð, 3 *Orm.* eorneþþ, 4 eorneþ, -eth.**

c **825** *Vesp. Ps.* cxlvii. 13 Hreðlice eorneð word his. *c* **950** *Lindisf. Gosp.* Luke xxii. 10 To-gægne iorneð iuh monn. *c* **1050** *Voc.* in Wr.-Wülcker 378 *Cursat*, iornð. *c* **1160** *Hatton Gosp.* Luke xxii. 10 Eow an-ȝen eornð an man. *c* **1200** ORMIN 8832 All þiss weorrldess ald Bi seoffne daȝhess eorneþþ. *a* **1225** *Juliana* 74 As weter þat eorneð. *c* **1400** *Trevisa's Higden* (Rolls) I. 115 þe brook..eorneth in to þe valey of Iosephat.

pl. *a* **1225** *Ancr. R.* 80 Heo eorneð boðe togederes. *a* **1250** *Owl & Night.* (J.) 375 If hundes eorneþ to him ward. *a* **1400** *Trevisa's Higden* (Rolls) I. 59 þe strong stremes þat renneþ [*v.r.* eorneþ] þat course.

γ. **3 *pl.* urneþ, 4 urn-, vrneþ, 9 *dial.* urnth, *pl.* hurneth.**

a **1250** *Owl & Night.* (C.) 375 ȝif hundes urneþ to him ward. *a* **1300** *Floris & Bl.* 225 He vrneþ in o pipe of bras. *c* **1400** *Trevisa's Higden* (Rolls) V. 329 þat ryver renneþ [*v.r.* urneþ] under..Wygan. **1881** BLACKMORE *Christowell* ii, They little holes hurneth all round 'em. **1886** ELWORTHY *W. Somerset Word-bk.* 50 The water..urnth down his ditch.

δ. *pl.* **1 ærnað, 3 ærneð, erneþ, 4 erniþ; *sing.* 3 erneþ (*Orm.* -eþþ), 4 ernnes.** Also *2nd sing.* **3 ernst.**

c **893** K. ÆLFRED *Oros.* I. i. 20 þonne ærnað hy ealle toweard þæm feo. *c* **1200** ORMIN 13183 Ure wukedaȝȝ Bi twellfe timess erneþþ. *c* **1205** LAY. 13999 þurh þi lond heo ærneð [*c* **1275** erneþ]. **1297** R. GLOUC. (Rolls) 6570 þat lond vp wan þou ernst. *a* **1300** in *E.E.P.* (1862) 20 Be-hold..how þe stremis erniþ of is swet blode. **13..** *Guy Warw.* (A) 6730 He ouer-ernnes dounes & cuntre. *c* **1400** *Trevisa's Higden* (Rolls) V. 329 þat ryver renneþ [*v.r.* erneþ] under þe citee of Wygan.

4. *Present Subjunctive.* **1 irne (*pl.* irnen), yrne, ierne, 3 vrne.**

c **888** K. ÆLFRED *Boeth.* xi. §1 þæt he irne [*v.r.* ierne] on his willan. *Ibid.* xxxiv. §1 Swa swa..irnen mæneʒe brocas & riða of. *a* **1000** in Grein *Bibl. Ags. P.* I. 352 Nefne he under seʒle yrne. *a* **1225** *Ancr. R.* 164 ȝif a wode liun vrne ȝeont þe strete.

5. *Imperative.* *sing.* **1 yrn, irnn, eorn, 9 *dial.* (h)urn; *pl.* 3 ierneð, ærneð, herneþ, eærne.**

c **850** *Kentish Gloss.* in Wr.-Wülcker 59 *Discurre*, irnn. *c* **900** WÆRFERTH tr. *Gregory's Dial.* 115 Broðor Maurus! yrn

B. Signification.

I. Intransitive senses.

The conjugation of the perfect and pluperfect tenses with *be* instead of *have* (as *is run*, *was run*, etc.) is occasionally found in literary use down to the end of the 18th century.

* *Of persons and animals, in literal or fig. senses.*

1. a. To move the legs quickly (the one foot being lifted before the other is set down) so as to go at a faster pace than walking; to cover the ground, make one's way, rapidly in this manner.

Run may be construed with a large number of preps. and advs., as *about*, *after*, *against*, *at*, etc. Some idiomatic uses arising from such phrases are treated under III and IV, and others will be found under some other distinctive word in the phrase (as RANDOM *sb.* 3).

c **888** K. ÆLFRED *Boeth.* xxxvii. §2 Færð ðonne micel folc to, & yrnað ealle endemes. *c* **950** *Lindisf. Gosp.* Matt. xxviii. 8 [Hia] eodun hreconlice from byrʒenne..iornende. *c* **1000**

**** *Of time, money, practices, or other things having course, continuance, or extension.*

26. a. Of a period of time: To come to an end, be complete, expire. Only in pa. pple.

a **1000** *Phœnix* 364 Oþ þæt wintra bið þusend urnen. *a* **1300** *Cursor M.* 10927 Fiue thusand yeir was runnun Efter þis werld it was bigunnen. *c* **1375** *Sc. Leg. Saints* x. (*Matthew*) 497 Of his elde quhene rownyn war be reknyne fyfe & thretty ȝere. *c* **1400** *Sc. Trojan War* I. 150 Sene he has this debate bygonnyne, Per awenture, or it all be ronnyne, Als gret defoule may fall hyme till. **1486** *Rec. St. Mary at Hill* (1905) 7 After that the said xv daies be past & ronne. **1530** in *Vicary's Anat.* (1888) App. II. 105 The somme of vli, for ij quarters fully ronne at the natiuitie of saint Iohn Baptiste. **1610** WILLET *Daniel* 283 From Daniels time vntill now there are not aboue 2200 yeares runne. **1722** DE FOE *Col. Jack* (1840) 320 The night was almost run. **1884** *Law Rep. 27 Chanc. Div.* 530 Delay is no bar to our enforcing it, as the Statute of Limitations has not run.

transf. **1546** J. HEYWOOD *Prov. & Epigr.* (1867) 37 A bed were we er the clocke had nine runne.

†**b.** Of persons: To become advanced *in* years.

c **1400** *Rom. Rose* 4495 A rympled vekke, fer ronne in age, Frownyng and yelowe in hir visage. **1430–40** LYDG. *Bochas* I. i, The progenitours, Of all mankynd farre I-ranne in age. **1533** BELLENDEN *Livy* II. ix. (S.T.S.) I. 161 Howbeit he was walk, and fer rvn in ȝeris. *c* **1550** H. LLOYD *Treas. Health* G ij. Youre grace beyng nowe sumwhat runne in yeares.

27. a. Of time: To pass or go by; to elapse; also, to be passing or current.

c **1200** ORMIN 11251 All þiss middell ærdess ald Eorneþþ aȝȝ forþ wiþþ ȝeress. *a* **1300** *Cursor M.* 11178 þe tide þat bringes al to fine, Ran wit þis to monet nine. **1423** JAS. I *Kingis Q.* clxxi, Thy tyme, Ane houre and more It rynnis ouer prime. **1447** BOKENHAM *Seyntys* viii. 1318 Long tyme aftyr, whan þe yere of grace On seuen hundryd ran & fourty & nyne. **1559** W. CUNNINGHAM *Cosmogr. Glasse* 40 Because the tyme doth so faste ronne, and I have also other matters to intreate on. **1581** MULCASTER *Positions* xxxvii. (1887) 148 The time to preuent it, is almost runne to farre. **1604** E. G[RIMSTONE] *D'Acosta's Hist. Indies* VI. ii. 435 Noting by those figures the yeare that did runne. **1634** FORD *Perk. Warbeck* III. i, How runs the time of day? Past ten, my lord. **1726** AYLIFFE *Parergon* 154 The Time of Instance shall not commence or run until after Contestation of Suit.

b. To continue, go on, last; to remain existent or operative.

a **1300** *Cursor M.* 24897 For to halu þis ilk fest dai,..In hali kirc rinnand bi yer. **1384** CHAUCER *L.G.W.* 1943 *Ariadne*, This wekede custome is so longe I-ronne. *c* **1460** FORTESCUE *Of Abs. & Lim. Mon.* xiv. (1885) 143 In the arrerages off such livelod..wich shall renne aftir þat resumpcion. **1558** WARDE tr. *Alexis' Secr.* 24b, If..the disease bee olde or hath runne longe, giue the pacient..this glister. **1573** *Reg. Privy Council Scot.* II. 226 And swa hes ordanit the said Parliament to ryn and be continewit quhill the last day of August. **1677** YARRANTON *Eng. Improv.* 20 Their way of Dealing I knew, and what Security they took, which was impossible should run long. **1843** *Jrnl. R. Agric. Soc.* IV. II. 299 Leases run in general for nineteen years. **1850** *Tait's Mag.* XVII. 4/1 Must his exclusion run only during the currency of other parts of his sentence? **1893** *Strand Mag.* VI. 217/1 Her contract..had two years more to run.

c. Of a play: To keep the stage or be played continuously (for a specified time). Also of a cinematographic film: (to continue) to be shown to the public.

1808 MRS. INCHBALD *Brit. Theatre* 4 Having, on its first appearance, run, in the theatrical term, near thirty nights. **1828** *Examiner* 85/2 The piece..will run the season. **1890** *Sat. Rev.* 22 Nov. 574/2 The play now running at the Lyceum. **1923** H. CRANE *Let.* 5 Oct. (1965) 149 Charlie [Chaplin]..is here in New York at present to see that the first film he has produced in it gets over profitably... It's running now for just a week or so more at the 'Lyric' theatre. **1940** G. MARX *Let.* 5 Sept. (1967) 25 He also hates Noel Coward and even refuses to see his playlets, which are now running at El Capitan. **1976** *Oxf. Compan. Film* 646/1 Rodgers and Hammerstein's stage musical, which opened in New York in 1959 and ran for four years.

28. a. Of money: To have currency; to be in circulation; to go, pass current.

a **1300** *Cursor M.* 14038 þis riche man lent to þat tan An hundreth penis, suilk als ran. *c* **1400** MAUNDEV. (1839) xxii. 239 Whan that Money hathe ronne so longe, that it begynnethe to waste. **1444** *Rolls of Parlt.* V. 109 That Half penyes and Ferthinges renne..in paiement in grete sommes amonge the peple. **1626** SIR R. COTTON in *Posthuma* (1651) 297 The said Royall of Eight runnes in account of Trade at 5.s. of..English money. **1662** in J. Simon *Ess. Irish Coins* (1749) 130 All sorts of small silver moneys of the denominations of or running for groates..or under. **1888** *N. & Q.* 7th Ser. VI. 338 Are not these the Spanish 'pillar dollars'; and did they not run current in England as crown pieces?

b. Of a writ, proclamation, etc.: To issue; to have legal course or effect; to operate.

c **1400** *Apol. Loll.* 7 þat..silk indulgencis rennun not forþ aȝen þe ordinaunce of God. **1436** *Rolls of Parlt.* IV. 497/2 Countrees where the Kynges Writt renneth night. **1610** HOLLAND *Camden's Brit.* (1637) 589 That Writs out of the Kings Courts, should in certain cases have no place nor runne among them. **1689** T. R. *View Govt. Europe* 51 The Process and Decrees of the Court ran in the Emperor's name. **1768** BLACKSTONE *Comm.* III. 78 In all these..the king's ordinary writs..do not run; that is, they are of no force. **1852** LEVER *Daltons* xiii, Not knowing that they were in another land where the King's writ never ran. **1890** LANE-POOLE *Barbary Corsairs* I. viii. 86 It may be doubted whether the Sultan's writ would have run in either of his new provinces.

c. Of payments, practices, etc.: To be current or generally prevalent.

1429 *Rolls of Parlt.* IV. 252/1 At alle tymes when poundage hath ronne. *c* **1460** *Reg. Oseney Abbey* 126 Whenne scutage renneth generally thorowgh all Inglonde.

Fig. 21

II. Transitive senses.

* *To traverse, accomplish, aim at or avoid, etc., by running.*

34. a. (*a*) To pursue or follow (a certain way or course) in running, sailing, etc. † ***to run one's way***, to run away, make off hurriedly.

c **888** K. ÆLFRED *Boeth.* xxi, þæt hie ne moton toslupan, ac bioð ȝehwerfde eft to þam ilcan ryne þe hie ær urnon. *a* **1300** *E.E. Psalter* xviii. 6 He gladed als yhoten to renne his wai. **1375** BARBOUR *Bruce* xx. 558 At mydday to turne agane The sone, that rynnis his cours all playn. **1480** *Robt. Devyll* 488 in Hazl. *E.P.P.* I. 238 Yt was no hede to bydde hym begone. He ranne hys waye. **1535** COVERDALE *Job* i. 14, I only ranne my waye, to tell the. **1562** *Child-Marriages* 72 Wher-of Richard Pierson was so ashamid, that he wold have runne his way. **1600** SHAKS. *A.Y.L.* III. ii. 138 How briefe the Life of man runs his erring pilgrimage. **1669** STURMY *Mariner's Mag.* IV. iii. 148 You are more Easterly or Westerly, by running or sailing that Course and Distance. **1775** BURKE *On Conciliation with America* Sel. Wks. 1897 I. 176 Others run the longitude, and pursue their gigantic game along the coast of Brazil. **1814** *Sporting Mag.* XLIV. 87 Being headed on the Ipswich road, he again ran the same cover, on his way to Somes-Wood. **1892** *Field* 20 Feb. 245/3 Our fox . . did not run the chain of woodlands, but held on southwards.

(*b*) In figurative contexts.

c **1000** *Lambeth Ps.* cxviii. 32 Weȝ beboda þinra ic arn. *a* **1300** *E.E. Psalter* cxviii. 32 Wai ofe þi bodes ran i. **1572** in *Buccleuch MSS.* (Hist. MSS. Comm.) 23 Erle of Lenox . . wes persuaditt . . to rin a cours with England, attempting mony things innaturallie agains his native realme. **1622** MABBE tr. *Aleman's Guzman d'Alf.* II. 330 Wee were fellowes and Companions in one Prison, and . . had runne both of vs one and the same Carreere. **1881** GARDINER & MULLINGER *Study Eng. Hist.* I. vii. 148 The members encouraged one another in running the Christian course.

b. *Hunting.* To pursue, follow up (a scent). Also † ***to run one's country*** (see quots. 1611).

1607 MARKHAM *Caval.* III. (1617) 10 Then laying on fresh dogges, . . make your Horse run the traine with good courage and liuelinesse. **1611** COTGR., *Fendre le vent*, to runne his countrey. *Ibid.*, *Tirer pais*, (in hunting) to runne his countrey; or, to flye directly forward. **1826** SCOTT *Woodst.* iv, Hunting counter, or running a false scent. **1890** *Blackw. Mag.* CXLVIII. 548/1 Hounds are running a high scent through a stiff country.

fig. **1857** WHEWELL in Todhunter *Acc. W.'s Wks.* (1876) II. 411 The dynamical-heat men are running their scent very eagerly.

c. *transf.* Of immaterial things.

1864 W. T. FOX *Skin Dis.* 11 It is not associated with any special form of ill health, is non-contagious, . . runs a definite course [etc.]. **1881** GARDINER & MULLINGER *Study Eng. Hist.* I. v. 97 Lollardism, too, ran much the same course. **1889** TRAILL *Strafford* xiii. 169 Affairs ran their fated course.

35. To traverse or cover by running, sailing, etc.: **a.** a specified distance. Also *fig.* in colloq. phr. ***to run a mile***, to seek safety in flight; to evade through fear, reluctance, etc.

c **1200** ORMIN 6969 þatt follc rideþþ onn a der . . þatt onn a daȝȝ . . Erneþþ an hunndredd mile. *c* **1300** *Havelok* 1831 He was ded on lesse hwile, þan men mouthe renne a mile. *c* **1380** WYCLIF *Wks.* (1880) 30 Prelatis schulden not . . make a pore man to renne two or þre þousand myles [etc.]. **1555** EDEN *Decades* (Arb.) 379 Runnynge southwest in the sea, [we] dydde runne .xii. leagues. **1669** STURMY *Mariner's Mag.* IV. ii. 146 So many Knots as the Ship runs in half a Minute, so many Miles she saileth in an Hour. **1728** CHAMBERS *Cycl.* s.v. *Courier*, Pliny, . . and Cæsar, mention some of these, who would run 20, 30, 36 . . Leagues per Day. **1748** *Anson's Voy.* III. vi. 345 We had a . . gale blowing right upon our stern: So that we generally run from forty to fifty leagues a day. **1812** *Sporting Mag.* XXXIX. 53 Flying Childers . . once run four miles in six minutes and forty seconds. **1846** A. YOUNG *Naut. Dict.*, With reference to the ship's progress . . we say she has run so many knots in an hour and so forth. **1861** *Temple Bar* I. 345 The engine had run more than 10,000 miles. **1949** D. SMITH *I capture Castle* v. 64 Men . . run a mile from obvious fascination. **1952** 'R. GORDON' *Doctor in House* xvii. 188 The ones that run a mile if they see a nurse and talk big about staying single. **1963** A. HERON *Towards Quaker View of Sex* 67 Were a woman to whom he exposed himself to respond sexually, the average exhibitionist would run a mile. **1969** H. E. BATES *Vanished World* x. 98, I run a mile from intellectual swank words such as 'esoteric' and 'proliferate'. **1973** J. WILSON *Truth or Dare*

III. With prepositions, in specialized uses.

In all of these the verb is intransitive; for prepositions following the transitive verb, see senses 43 to 56.

59. run across ——, to meet or fall in with.

1880 'MARK TWAIN' *Tramp Abroad* xxi. 202 If I don't run across you in Italy, you hunt me up in London before you sail. **1887** J. HAWTHORNE *Tragic Myst.* viii, The young man who happens to run across one of them and to make a good

IV. With adverbs, in specialized uses.

In most of these both intransitive and transitive uses are very fully represented.

72. run away.

a. To make off, retreat hurriedly, flee, in the face of danger or opposition.

c **1380** *Sir Ferumb.* 2438 þan runne þai away & saide alas. **1530** PALSGR. 695/2, I runne awaye from myne enemye, or any daunger. **1542** UDALL *Erasm. Apoph.* 335 b, That same manne, that renneth awaye, May again fight, an other day. **1642–4** VICARS *God in Mount* 164 The present was the season, else the enemy would bee run away. **1724** DE FOE *Mem. Cavalier* I. 94 The King . . rated them for running away, as he called it, though they really retreated in good Order. **1804–5** NELSON in *Sotheby's Catal.* 15 June (1897) 17 That gentleman has thought proper to write a letter stating that the fleet under my command ran away. **1848** THACKERAY *Van. Fair* xxxii, This . . Belgian hussar . . was too good a soldier to disobey his Colonel's orders to run away.

b. To abscond; to depart surreptitiously *from* or *to* a person; to elope *with* some one. Also *transf.* Freq. used jocularly in the negative (as, ***it won't run away***) to give assurance of the permanence or fixity of something or someone.

c **1460** *Towneley Myst.* iv. 227 'Where is he,' . . will she spyr; If I tell her, 'ron away', hir answere bese . . 'nay, sir!' **1530** PALSGR. 695/2 He was aboute to ronne awaye, and he had done it in dede if I had nat taken the better hede. *a* **1568** ASCHAM *Scholem.* Pref. (Arb.) 18 Scholers . . be runne awaie from the Schole. **1614** J. COOKE *Greene's Tu Quoque* C ij b, Doe not I know that thou wilt run away with the Gentleman? **1632** LITHGOW *Trav.* III. 127 There were foure-score Christian slaues, who hauing cut their Captaines throat . . , runne away from Constantinople. **1754** RICHARDSON *Grandison* IV. xiv. 105 The next girl that run away to a dancing master, or an ensign. **1793** 'A. PASQUIN' *Life Earl of Barrymore* (ed. 3) 13 Mr. Stone had a tenant run away. **1892** *Daily News* 8 Jan. 3/6 It was true that the land could not run away, but they knew that rent could run away. **1882** C. M. GASKELL in *Nineteenth Cent.* Sept. 460 The landowner has been credited with the . . most valuable form of security; . . it could not 'run away'. **1888** C. M. YONGE *Beechcroft at Rockstone* II. xxi. 191 The charms of 'the halls of Ivor' . . which, after all, would not run away. **1908** A. BENNETT *Old Wives' Tale* IV. iii. 515 There's no earthly reason why you should go back. . . The house won't run away. **1928** A. M. M. DOUTON *Bk. with Seven Seals* 21 Sunday will be round again in a week, and Park Chapel won't run away. **1942** A. E. W. MASON *Musk & Amber* i. 15 'What of Grest [*sc.* an estate] meanwhile?' 'Grest won't run away, Sir.' **1973** J. PORTER *It's Murder with Dover* vii. 65 What's your sweat? This Tiffin bird's not going to run away.

transf. **1920** E. O'NEILL *Beyond Horizon* III. i. 152 You've spent eight years running away from yourself. **1934** —— *Days without End* I. 36 It's a rocky road . . this running away from truth in order to find it? **1944** B. HUTCHISON *Hollow Men* vi. 79 It's his mask. It fools nearly everybody. He's always running away from himself. **1966** *Listener* 17 Nov. 718/2 The whole of the world ran away from the pound, and if this doesn't reveal an inflationary situation, what does?

c. ***run away with***: (*a*) To depart surreptitiously with, to carry off (something).

1624 *Capt. Smith's Virginia* Wks. II. 401 The strongest preparing once more to run away with the Pinnace. **1660** F. BROOKE tr. *Le Blanc's Trav.* 12 The rest of the Jewes gave

V. 82. In various collocations used attributively or as sbs., as **run and fell** *Needlework* (see quot. 1968); also *attrib.*; **run-and-read**, given to hasty reading (see 1 e); **run-flat** *a.*, applied to a kind of tyre on which a vehicle may run after a puncture has occurred; **run-over**, due to being run over by a vehicle; **run-sheep(y)-run** *N. Amer.* and *Sc.*, a children's hiding game (see quot. 1909); **run-the-hedge**, a vagabond; **runther(e)out** (only in Sc. form *rin-*), a vagabond, roving person; also *attrib.*; **run-through**, applied to a particular stroke in billiards.

1882 CAUFEILD & SAWARD *Dict. Needlework* 428/1 **Run and fell* . . is a method sometimes adopted in lieu of Oversewing, and employed in making seams, either in underlinen, or in the skirts and sleeves of dresses. **1961** M. SPARK *Prime of Miss Jean Brodie* iii. 69 In the worst cases

Fig. 22

ran). Section **B.** covers 'Signification', the eighty-two main senses of the word, and employs five roman numeral subdivisions (**I.** to **V.**) to group intransitive senses; transitive senses; the verb with prepositions, in specialized uses; with adverbs, in specialized uses; and collocations used attributively.

The arabic numeral (**1.**, **2.**, **3.** . . .) level is employed in Section **A.** to itemize the various grammatical forms. As can be seen in Fig. 21, Greek letters (*α*, *β*, *γ* . . .) are then used, in accordance with the convention followed in other variant forms lists, to group similar sets of variants. Each set is followed by a quotation paragraph. In Section **B.**, arabic numerals and lower case letters (**a.**, **b.**, **c.** . . .) are used to list senses and sub-senses in the normal linear fashion. Where further subdividing is necessary, bracketed and italicized lower case letters are employed ((*a*), (*b*), (*c*)). Over and above this grammatical organization, the senses are also assembled semantically. Italicized descriptive headings, prefaced by an increasing number of asterisks, alert the reader to the contents of each broad subject area. For example, intransitive senses (**I.**) are grouped under the following headings, two of which can be seen in Fig. 21:

* *Of persons and animals, in literal or fig. senses* (Senses 1–8)

** *Of inanimate things in rapid motion* (Senses 9–18)

*** *Of liquids, sand, etc. (or vessels containing these)* (Senses 19–25)

**** *Of time, money, practices, or other things having course, continuance, or extension* (Senses 26–30)

***** *Of things passing into, assuming, or maintaining a certain condition or quality* (Senses 31–33)

The senses within these categories are further classified, as can be seen in the portion of the entry relating to the fourth item (time, money, practices, etc.) in Fig. 21. Sense 26, for example, defines **run** as it applies to time expiring or coming to an end, first (**a.**) in a general sense and then (**b.**) specifically relating to persons. Sense 27 and its subdivisions cover the passing or continuance of time, while Sense 28 subdivisions pertain to the currency of money, writs, payments, and so forth.

As illustrated in Fig. 22, a similar system of asterisked headings is used in part **II.**, transitive senses (Senses 34 to 58), which, according to the note at the beginning of part **III.**, also includes prepositions used with this form of the verb. Specialized uses of prepositions when the verb is intransitive are dealt with in part **III.** (Senses 59 to 71), and each occupies a separate main sense with relevant sub-senses. Thus, Sense 59 refers to **run across**, Sense 60 to **run after**, Sense 61 to **run against**, Sense 62 to **run before**, etc. Part **IV.** (Senses 72 to 81), on the other hand, itemizes, also in alphabetical order, specialized uses with adverbs, such as **run away, run down, run in**, etc., for both the intransitive and transitive verb. Where one such collocation is used both ways, the intransitive sub-senses are listed first (designated * *intr.*), followed by transitive sub-senses (** *trans.*). In all cases, quotation paragraphs support each individual sub-sense.

Finally, part **V.**, the initial half of which is shown in Fig. 22, lists alphabetically in one paragraph (Sense 82) a few collocations used attributively or as nouns, including **run and fell, run-and-read, run-flat**, etc., followed by a quotation paragraph arranged in the same order.

Although lengthy entries for nouns or other parts of speech may vary in their components, all such entries can be analysed in a similar fashion if one has some understanding of the *OED*'s organizational philosophy and the flexible structural scheme established by Sir James Murray.

CROSS-REFERENCE ENTRIES

WHAT IS A CROSS-REFERENCE ENTRY?

A cross-reference entry is primarily a user aid that leads the reader from an obsolete or variant spelling, or from an irregular inflection, to the main form headword(s) where complete information is given. Such entries are useful to readers who encounter, in early texts, unusual words or usages that may not be obvious variants of the headword. There are over 60,000 such entries in the second edition, the majority of which consist of a single line. Note that 'cross-reference entries' should not be confused with the 580,000 'cross-references' *within* entries.

For example, in the variant forms list of the main entry for **marmalade** (Fig. 2), there are a number of variant spellings listed; nine cross-reference entries cover most of these variations. In Fig. 23, the headword section of the main entry is duplicated, together with the nine cross-reference entries. Some of these, such as **marmaled**, appear in close proximity to the main entry; others, such as **marmulade, -ate, -et**, are found at some distance. In some instances, variants may well have an initial letter which is different from the main form as in the case of a number of Middle English or archaic forms with a 'y' prefix.

Readers who have used the first edition or who have read the introductory material in the second edition may have also encountered the expression 'subordinate entry'. This term was originally used to refer primarily to cross-reference entries. The first edition attempted to distinguish such entries by using lighter bold type for their headwords. The convention was dropped in the *Supplement* and the second edition because the definition of the category was somewhat ambiguous and the typographical distinction appeared to serve no useful purpose.

STRUCTURE AND CONTENT OF CROSS-REFERENCE ENTRIES

Usually the format of cross-reference entries is quite simple, as illustrated in those referring to **marmalade**. The headword appears in the same large bold type as used in main entries, in keeping with a policy established by the *Supplement*. As can be seen, entries sometimes cover more than one variant. No further information is given about the headword, except that it is an obsolete form of a main word (printed in small roman capitals, the usual convention for cross-referencing headwords).

Irregular or obsolete inflections of verbs are handled in a similar fashion, as in the entry for **ypleynted** (Fig. 23), identified as the Middle English past participle of the verb **plaint**. Sometimes, cross-reference entries refer to combinations within other entries, as is the case with the entries for **ypodeakon** and **ypointing** (note that the combinations are referenced in bold italic type). In the latter case, the reader is directed to the combination *star-ypointing* within two entries—first, in Sense **20.** of the entry for **star** *sb.*[1] and secondly, in the entry for the prefix **y- 3.c**. The initial item to look for in such entries is the referenced main headword(s) in small roman capitals.

While one-line entries with minimal information are the norm, about five per cent of the cross-reference entries give additional information, usually in the form of quotations illustrating the uses of the variant form. The entries for **vermion** and **wrappe** exemplify this type of entry. Note that the entry for **vermion** also includes a note suggesting the reader should compare the form with the mediaeval Latin *vermeum*.

marmalade ('mɑːməleɪd), *sb.* Forms: 6 marmylate, -elad, -ilat, -ilade, mormelade, marmlet, mermelado, 6–7 marmelet(t, -alad, -alate, 6–8 marmalet, -elade, 7 marmilad, -ilitt, -alit, -alett, -ulade, -ulate, -ulet, -aled, -eleta, -elate, mermalade, 8 marmolet, mermelade, 6– marmalade. [a. F. *marmelade*, in Cotgr. *mermelade*, a. Pg. *marmelada*, f. *marmelo* quince, repr. (with dissimilation of consonants) L. *melimēlum*, a. Gr. μελίμηλον ('honey-apple', f. μέλι honey + μῆλον apple) the name of some kind of apple which was grafted on a quince. From the Pg. word are also Sp. *marmelada*, It. *marmellata*, and (through Fr.) G., Du., Da. *marmelade*, Sw. *marmelad.*]

marmaled, -et(t, obs. forms of MARMALADE *sb*.

marmelade, -ate, -et(t, obs. ff. MARMALADE *sb.*

marmilad(e, -at, -itt, obs. ff. MARMALADE *sb.*

marmlet, obs. form of MARMALADE *sb.*

marmolet, obs. form of MARMALADE *sb.*

marmulade, -ate, -et, obs. ff. MARMALADE *sb.*

mermalade, obs. form of MARMALADE *sb.*

mermelade, obs. form of MARMALADE *sb.*

mormelade, obs. form of MARMALADE *sb.*

vermion, -eon, obs. varr. VERMILION *sb.*

Cf. med.L. *vermeum*, var. of *vermellum*, etc.

1399 *Mem. Ripon* (Surtees) III. 129 In j lib. de vermion emp. pro prædicto vale [= veil], 22*d.* *a* **1400–50** *Alexander* 3945 Þan come a fliȝtir in of fowls as fast as it dawid, To vise on as vowtres, as vermeon hewid. **14..** *MS. Harl.* 2257, *Miniographus* a writer with vermion. *Minium est genus coloris rubei,.. anglice* vermion.

wrappe, obs. var. (and pa. t.) of WARP *v.* 1.

1303 R. BRUNNE *Handl. Synne* 7517 Alle naked hym-self he wrappe Among þe þornes þat were sharpe. **1426** LYDG. *De Guil. Pilgr.* 21932 Yiff I hadde wrappyd the, Nakyd, cast the vp and doun In thornys for thy savacioun. **15..** *Henryson's Paddock & Mouse* 171 (Harl. MS.), Now hie, now law,.. Now on the quheill, now wrappit [*Bann. MS.* wappit] to the ground.

ypleynted, ME. pa. pple. of PLAINT *v.*

ypodeakon, var. *hypodeacon* (see HYPO- II).

ypointing, in *star-ypointing*: see STAR *sb.*[1] 20 and Y- 3 c.

Fig. 23

PART II

A COMPANION TO THE *OED*

NOTE TO THE READER

Articles in this section appear in letter-by-letter alphabetical order, ignoring spaces and punctuation, according to their heading. Cross-references are indicated by an asterisk (*) in front of the word to be looked up, or by the use of 'See' or 'See also' to refer the reader from a topic to another entry where further information will be found. Cross-references are also included to page numbers in Part I where explanations and/or examples are given of Dictionary conventions and elements within entries. For example, the reference 'pp. 19–20' tells the reader to refer to pages 19 and 20 of Part I for additional information. Headings for grammatical, etymological, and linguistic technical terms are, where applicable, followed by the abbreviation generally used in the Dictionary for that term.

Because the subject matter of the entries is interrelated, an effort has been made to asterisk cross-references only when it is judged that they will contribute to the reader's understanding of the topic about which he or she is currently reading. In the case of the major structural elements found in almost all Dictionary entries and familiar to most readers, it was considered that repeated cross-referencing asterisks might be more annoying than helpful. Thus, the many references to the following Dictionary elements are not, in most instances, preceded by an asterisk, even though an entry will be found under each term: **entry, cross-reference, headword, part of speech, pronunciation, etymology, sense, definition, quotation**, and, within quotations, **date, author**, and **title**.

There are also frequent references within articles to specific typefaces, such as bold, italic, small roman capitals, etc. Readers who would like clarification and examples of these conventions should refer to the article on TYPOGRAPHY. In addition, it should be noted that the term 'word form', as it is employed throughout this text, means the word, phrase, combination, affix, etc. that is the subject of a Dictionary entry or sense, and technical terms such as 'lemma', 'lexeme', or 'lexical item', which are subject to varying interpretations, are avoided.

A few references are made within articles to relevant books or journal articles. Full bibliographical details for these citations are given in the selective bibliography on pages 205–206.

A

abbreviation (abbrev.) Abbreviations in the *OED* consist of shortened forms of a word or words (Feb., etc., mod., f.) initialisms (B.B.C., P.S.), and acronyms (Unesco, AIDS). Initialisms and acronyms are both formed from the initial letters of the words they stand for, but differ in their style of pronunciation; the letters of an initialism are pronounced separately, whereas the acronym is pronounced as a word. Abbreviations are encountered in the Dictionary as *main and *subordinate headwords, or as shortened forms and initialisms used within entries to conserve space:

1. *abbreviations as main and subordinate headwords*: the Dictionary includes main entries for a number of frequently used abbreviations which are treated in the same fashion as other headwords (see p. 59 for examples). Many other abbreviations are listed alphabetically (letter-by-letter) as subordinate headwords in bold type within the entry for their initial letter (pp. 55–57). As subordinate headwords, the information immediately following each abbreviation is minimally its expanded form, but further defining or explanatory text is sometimes included, such as the date of establishment of an organization or award; a subject *label; or the English translation of a term (e.g., '**D.V.** = L. *Deo volente*, God willing'). Each abbreviation is supported by one or more quotations grouped in the same alphabetical order as the listed forms. To assist the reader, the first citation for each abbreviation is normally preceded by an asterisk (*), and where more than one quotation is given for an abbreviation, the listing is chronological, with the earliest quotation first. Following the list of abbreviations, it is usual to include a cross-reference to the other abbreviations beginning with the same initial letter for which there are main entries. 'See also (as main entries) D-DAY, D.D.T., DORA, D.T.' is a typical example from the entry for the letter 'D'. Abbreviations are usually listed with full stops (periods), or occasionally with other punctuation such as an apostrophe or hyphen (see p. 59 for examples such as *'flu* or *flu* for 'influenza' and *sci-fi* for 'science fiction'). However, some abbreviations may appear without punctuation as an alternative form, or as the main form where no recorded instance of punctuation is found in the accompanying quotations. These include, in addition to initialisms and acronyms, entries for a number of commonly used shortened forms, such as 'demo', 'gym', and 'pop'.
2. *editorial abbreviations*: numerous abbreviations are used throughout the text of the Dictionary and their correct interpretation is an important aid to understanding entries. The full form of most abbreviations can be found in the *List of Abbreviations, Signs, etc.* included at the front of

each volume. While it is recognized that textual abbreviations may create some initial obstacles for the occasional reader of the Dictionary, their use is dictated by the need to save space. Many abbreviations such as those for parts of speech and other labels will be obvious to the user; names of languages in etymologies may cause more difficulty. Since there are approximately 250,000 references to foreign word forms, the use of abbreviated language names, such as 'G.' for German and 'Gr.' for Greek, is essential. Abbreviations for older languages and dialects are often more obscure ('OS.' for Old Saxon, 'cl.L.' for Classical Latin, etc.), so that it is advisable to refer to the explanatory *List* until one becomes accustomed to the forms. (See also TITLES for an explanation of abbreviations used in titles of cited works.)

absolute, -ly (*absol.*). Employed as a *label to indicate that the word form under discussion may be used without its usual syntactic or grammatical complement. For example, an adjective may stand alone with its noun understood, as in 'the poor' or 'the wealthy' ('people' understood). In the quotation 'What say to La Coupole? It's one of the few places . . . where we don't have to reserve', the normally *transitive verb 'reserve' ('a table' understood) is used absolutely. Proper nouns also frequently appear absolutely. For instance, one may refer to 'an Amati' ('violin' understood) or 'a Bokhara' ('rug' or 'carpet' understood). (Compare with ELLIPTICAL which describes a more *colloquial form of omission.)

acronym. An abbreviated form which is pronounced as a word, usually made up of the initial letters, or occasionally several letters, of the words it stands for. See ABBREVIATION.

adaptation of (ad.). A term used in etymologies to refer to the process by which a foreign word enters a language with some alteration to its original form, in order to conform to the receiving language's word structure. The English word 'indicative' is an adapted form of the French *indicatif*. Similarly, the French word *panache* is an adaptation of the Latin *phalangium*. Note, however, that the English usage of the word 'panache' is *adopted (that is, brought into the language *without change*) from the French form. (See pp. 24–25 for further examples.)

adopted from, adoption of (a.). A term used in etymologies to describe the process by which a foreign word enters another language without significant change. The English word 'restaurant', for example, is a *naturalized form of the identical French word. The present definition represents a formalization of *Murray's original, somewhat inexact, distinction between adoption as a 'popular process and '*adaptation of' as a 'learned or literary process'. (See pp. 24–25 for further examples and compare with NATURALIZED WORD.)

affix. An element added to a word which qualifies or modifies its meaning, or which changes its grammatical function. There are three types of affix:

1. a prefix (*pref.*), which is added to the beginning of a word. For instance, the prefixes *un-* and *dis-* negate or reverse the meaning of the base form in words such as 'unusual' and 'disembark'.
2. a suffix (*suff.*), which is added to the end of a word. Suffixes are often used to change grammatical function. For example, the suffix *-ly* in words such as 'quickly', 'rapidly', and 'slowly' converts adjectives to adverbs, while the suffix *-ness* in 'kindness', 'blindness', and 'slowness' is used to form nouns from adjectives.
3. an infix, which is inserted within a word and is found in languages such as Tai.

Since the use of prefixes and suffixes is very common in English word formation, there are many entries for words formed in this manner. In addition, all major prefixes and suffixes (as well as *combining forms) are given entries of their own which document their history and explain their usage (pp. 58–64).

Aldenham, Lord. See GIBBS, HENRY HUCKS.

alien. See NATURALIZED WORD.

allusive, -ly. Used to describe the application of a word or proper name to a different but analogous thing, situation, or act. Many proper names of people and places, both fictional and real, are used allusively. For example, 'Svengali', the name of a character in the novel *Trilby* by George du Maurier, is often used allusively to typify a person who exercises a controlling or mesmeric influence on another. (Also compare with FIGURATIVE and TRANSFERRED.)

alphabetical order. The letter-by-letter order in which entries are arranged by headword in the Dictionary. 'Letter-by-letter' means a system of alphabetizing that ignores punctuation, capitalization, accentuation, or spacing between compound words or phrases in headwords (compare with the **Bibliography* at the end of Volume XX in which the alphabetical ordering of entries is word-by-word). 'Alphabetical' also means that the order is based strictly on the standard, modern English alphabet. *Diacritics are ignored, *ligatures are treated as sequential vowels, and early English characters are allocated their modern equivalents. Thus, 'cañon' is treated as 'canon', and the ligatures *æ* and *œ* are alphabetized as *ae* and *oe*. The *special English characters *thorn* (þ) and *edh* (ð) are regarded as equivalent to *th*, and *yogh* (ȝ) is equated with *gh*.

Following the convention of ignoring punctuation, headwords that show optimal endings enclosed within parentheses (brackets) are treated letter-by-letter as if no parentheses existed. The exception to the rule is that when a single left-hand parenthesis is used to mark off a letter such as the final silent 'e' in the headword 'anachoret(e', the final letter itself is ignored and the word is alphabetized as 'anachoret'.

The general rule for headwords with the same spelling (or those treated as having the same spelling) is to order them by their grammatical category. This is usually considered to be noun (*substantive), adjective, verb, and adverb, followed by the minor categories, although deviations will be found from this order. Each group of *homonyms is arranged by the following superior number or superscript which usually indicates the order of historical development. Note that *affixes, *combining forms, and some *acronyms and *abbreviations are treated as separate grammatical categories, and are distinguished by superior numbering from other identical forms in the same category. *Variant and *obsolete forms are usually listed after all other entries with the same spelling. (See p. 5 for an example of the alphabetical ordering of entries.)

American contributors. See CONTRIBUTORS.

Anglo-French (AF., AFr.). The language of the ruling class and of the law in England for approximately two centuries following the Norman Conquest in the eleventh century; now usually referred to as Anglo-Norman, although this term is rarely found in *OED* etymologies. Originally a mix of northern French dialects, Anglo-French was later modified by other regional dialects and by literary French. It influenced the spelling of many words, such as 'colour', 'gracious', 'award', and 'benefit', and the terminology of particular subject areas, such as law (assize, crime, juror, justice), and ecclesiastics (chaplain, doctrine, faith, surplice, vice, and virtue).

Anglo-Norman. See ANGLO-FRENCH.

Anglo-Saxon. In its rare appearance in *OED* etymologies, Anglo-Saxon normally refers to the Saxon, as opposed to the more commonly surviving Anglian, dialect of *Old English, the language of England prior to the twelfth century. (Note that the Dictionary distinguishes between Old English and Anglo-Saxon although, in common usage, the terms are often used interchangeably.)

anonymous works. Books, pamphlets, and other works written by an unidentified author. Where an author's name is not known, quotations from the text are cited by the title, rather than by the abbreviation 'anon.' as is the practice in some library catalogues and bibliographies (although the Dictionary does contain a few instances of this designation). Anonymous works should not be confused with articles from journals, magazines, and newspapers where authors' names are deliberately omitted as a matter of Dictionary policy, except in some cases where the quotation represents the first located use of a word or sense or the author is very well known. It should be remembered, however, that the use of authors' names in periodicals only became widespread in the twentieth century.

An author's anonymity is frequently a matter of choice. For example, some pamphlets or books contain radical political or religious statements, pornographic material, or other content which the author, for one reason or another, prefers not to acknowledge. However, where the author is later discovered and is generally recognized as having written a work, quotations appear under his or her name. In other instances, especially with very early works, the author's name may have been lost, or it may never have been recorded, as is the case with many early manuscripts written by anonymous clerics. The authors of some of the most widely used sources for early English word forms are therefore unknown, including *Beowulf*, one of the earliest extant *Old English epic poems, and the great *Middle English epic **Cursor Mundi*. (See also PSEUDONYMOUS WORKS.)

ante (*a*). Latin word meaning 'before'. The abbreviation '*a*' preceding a quotation date indicates that the precise date of writing or publication is not known, but it is assumed to be before, or not later than, the date given (See also DATES, pp. 41–43, and compare with CIRCA).

antedating. Ever since the *OED* began publication, readers have enjoyed the scholarly exercise of antedating, that is, finding quotations for words and senses earlier than those given in the Dictionary. Over the years, journals such as *Notes and Queries* have documented many of these findings, which were often the accidental by-product of research in other areas.

The *OED* editors, however, have never claimed that the earliest quotations cited are the first to have appeared in print, and they were fully aware of the hazards of doing so. In fact, James *Murray once observed that probably three-quarters of the headwords could be antedated. However, his estimate that any potential gaps should not exceed more than several decades has been challenged by some scholars' findings. The current *Reading Programme emphasizes not only quotations for new words and uses, but provides both older and more recent quotations for existing words and senses, since the need to postdate Dictionary quotations is as great as the antedating requirement. It is also interesting to note that the Dictionary, not unexpectedly, contains material which sometimes antedates or postdates itself; that is, a quotation used to illustrate one word may include an earlier or later quotation for a second word. The capability for searching the *OED* electronically greatly increases the potential of the Dictionary itself as a source for generating needed examples. (See Jürgen Schäfer, *Documentation in the OED* (1980), for a scholarly critique of antedating questions with particular reference to Shakespeare and Nashe.)

aphetic, aphetized (aphet.). A term suggested by James *Murray and used in the Dictionary to describe a word form which has undergone the loss of an unstressed initial vowel or syllable, as in the case of the word 'squire', derived from the earlier 'esquire'.

appositive, -ly (appos.). Used to describe the combining of one noun with another noun in expressions such as *amateur painter*, *woman doctor*, or *dilettante musician* in which the first word is grammatically parallel to the second word, i.e., a doctor who is a woman. Less frequently employed to describe the relationship of a noun to a noun clause as in the *phrase, *the fact that* ... where the noun *fact* is in apposition with the explanatory clause that follows it. (Compare with ATTRIBUTIVE in which a noun preceding a noun functions as an adjective.)

archaic (*arch.*). A *label attached to a word, sense, or phrase that is no longer in common use, but is still employed for special purposes (poetical, liturgical, in dialogue in a period novel, etc.), or sometimes as an affectation. Such usages include *afore* for 'before', *methinks* for 'I think', and *chimney-side* for 'fire-side'. Readers should be aware that a word or sense labelled archaic at the time when the entry was first written may now be regarded as *obsolete (*Obs.*). In some instances, the lexicographer may have considered the usage as borderline so that occasionally one finds the designation '*obs.* or *arch.*'. Equally, a few words that were labelled *arch.* when an entry was compiled may have experienced a revival. Revision of such entries for future editions has to be a continuing process.

Aryan. See INDO-EUROPEAN.

ash. See SPECIAL ENGLISH CHARACTERS.

assimilate, assimilation. Literally, the process by which a thing is made, or becomes, similar to another thing. In the Dictionary 'assimilate', 'assimilated' (form), and 'assimilation' are used to describe two distinct categories of the process, both of which result in changes to a word's form:

1. 'Assimilated to' is often used in etymologies to mean 'altered in form to be similar to' another word (e.g. the spelling of a similar word in English or another language). For example, 'abbacy' (meaning the dignity, estate, or jurisdiction of an abbot) is 'a modification of the earlier *abbatie*, assimilated to forms like *prelacy*', and in the case of the alternative spellings *ardour* or *ardor*, the first reflects the word's adoption from French, while the second is a spelling 'assimilated to' Latin in the sixteenth century.
2. Assimilation is also employed in accordance with the terminology of modern phonetics to describe a specific process by which a speech sound gradually becomes similar or identical to a neighbouring sound. Conse-

quently, the spelling of a word may be affected as is the case with many words formed with Latin prefixes. For example, the prefixes *ac*-, *af*-, *ag*-, *al*-, *ap*-, *ar*-, and *at*- are all assimilated forms of the Latin prefix *ad*- when used before the relevant consonant sound. This alteration is the result of a sound being produced or articulated by the same action of the lips, tongue, throat, etc. as an adjacent sound. For instance, the articulation of the letters *m* and *p* is *bilabial*, that is, it requires the compression of the upper and lower lips, while the sound *n* is referred to as *alveolar* because the tongue touches the *alveolar ridge* behind the upper teeth. Thus, for ease of pronunciation, the prefix *in*- became *im*- in the words 'impossible' and 'immemorial'. A similar process takes place in the formation of the proper name 'Harry' from 'Henry' by assimilation of *nr* to *rr*, or in the word 'best', a reduction of the earlier forms *betst* and *betest*. (Compare with ELISION and METATHESIS.)

attributive, -ly (*attrib.*). A term applied to the use of a word, usually a noun, which performs a defining or adjectival function before another noun, as the noun *library* in the phrase 'library book'. Proper nouns are also frequently used attributively; for example, in '*Wankel* engine' or '*Rorschach* test', both named after their inventors. When such a grouping occurs with some degree of regularity, the Dictionary often refers to it as a *combination; thus the usage of a word may be described as '*attrib.* and *Comb.*'.

Attrib. is also frequently employed to distinguish the use of an adjective before a noun from a *predicative (*pred.*) adjective (one that follows a verb). For instance, 'big' is attributive in 'the big Dictionary' and predicative in 'the Dictionary is big'.

authors. The second element in a quotation following the date is normally the author's name, printed in large and small roman capitals. A general exception is that quotations from journals, magazines, and newspapers omit authors' names, except when the citation illustrates the first located use of the word or sense. However, it should be noted that periodical articles before the twentieth century were often *anonymous, and that the Dictionary frequently includes the name of a celebrated author even if the quotation is not the earliest. Other special instances include *translations and *pseudonymous works (see also pp. 43–45 for examples of these and other conventions).

The majority of well-known authors of standard English literary and popular works are represented in the Dictionary's quotations. When the initial inventory of words was undertaken by the *Philological Society, and later by James *Murray, comprehensive lists of the significant literature of earlier periods were compiled. Volunteer readers were then invited to select particular authors or titles. Many of these early works were made available by the editions of the *Early English Text Society. In effect, a policy of 'literary inclusiveness' was adopted for authors such as Chaucer, Milton and *Shakespeare, which included *hapax legomena* (words with only one known occurrence). This policy, together with the extensive writings and vocabulary of these authors, contributed to the fact that Shakespeare is the most widely quoted author in the *OED*, with Milton and Chaucer in third and fourth places, respectively. The popular and prolific nineteenth-century author, Sir Walter Scott, who was responsible for the revival of much older Scottish vocabulary, is the second most frequently quoted author. The policy instituted by the **Supplement* (1972–86) called for a liberal, but not necessarily all-inclusive, representation of the vocabulary of important contemporary authors, as well as of a broad selection of lesser-known writers. It was also recognized that the first edition was Britocentric. To redress this bias, the *Supplement* included in its *Reading Programme many authors from other English-speaking countries, such as Australia, Canada, the United States, and the West Indies. This policy is continued through the present North American Reading Programme, and by deliberate efforts to ensure that writers from other English-speaking areas are read.

B

back-formation. The process of creating a word, usually a verb, from an existing word by the subtraction or replacement of a real or supposed *suffix (or rarely, a *prefix). This type of word formation is the basis for many modern verbs, such as *cybernate* from 'cybernation', *televise* from 'television', *wire-tap* from 'wire-tapping', and *fluoresce* from 'fluorescent', as well as older words such as *burgle* from 'burglar' and *greed* from 'greedy'.

Bible. The *OED* contains an estimated 25,000 quotations extracted from the various English versions of the Bible, including Wyclif (1382, 1388); Tindale (1526, 1534); Coverdale (1535); Matthews (1537); Cranmer, also known as 'the Great' (1539); Becke's edition of Matthews (1551); the Geneva (1560); the Bishops' (1568); the Rheims-Douay (1582); the Douay (1609–10); the Authorized or King James (1611); the Revised New Testament (1881), Old Testament (1884), and Apocrypha (1894); and the New English (1961, 1970). Most of these versions are listed in the *Bibliography* at the end of Volume XX under their individual translators or titles, as well as under an entry headed 'Bible, versions of'. In addition, there are also quotations from partial versions of the Bible, such as the portions of the first seven books of the Old Testament, known collectively as the *Heptateuch*, translated into *Old English by the late tenth-century scholar Ælfric. Numerous quotations from the same period were also taken from the *Anglo-Saxon Gospels*, cited as *Ags. Gosp.*, edited by *Skeat for the *Early English Text Society. The exact number of quotations is difficult to assess, because of the many versions cited, the differences in citation style, and the fact that, for the purpose of comparison, references to several versions may be given for a single quotation.

In general, there are two basic ways in which citations from a version of the Bible are given. First, the name BIBLE is included in the citation, followed by a reference to the specific book, chapter, and verse in which the quotation may be found. Secondly, and in an even greater number of cases, only the translator's name is given, followed by the book, chapter, and verse information. Thus, a quotation might begin '**1535** COVERDALE *1 Kings* xxii.13'. Most commonly, the King James version is cited simply as '**1611** BIBLE'. Other versions which do not bear the name of an individual translator are also cited as BIBLE followed by the identifying familiar name in parentheses, such as 'BIBLE (Geneva)', 'BIBLE (Great)', BIBLE (Bishops)', BIBLE (Douay)', or in the case of the 1881–94 revision 'BIBLE (R.V)', '(Revised)', or '(Rev. Vers.)'. A variation of this form is found in the case of the 1961, 1970 version which is usually cited as NEW ENG. BIBLE, or sometimes NEW ENGLISH BIBLE. One of the exceptions to the generalization on versions by individual translators is that when the quotation is taken from the dedication, introduction, preface, prologue, etc. (that is, where no specific book, chapter, and verse are involved), the title *Bible* is normally used. For example, if the quotation was found in Coverdale's Dedication, the citation reads '**1535** COVERDALE *Bible* Ded.' Finally, one will also find examples where the citation is to the New Testament or the Old Testament (usually abbreviated as N.T. or O.T.), as for example, '**1582** N.T. (Rhem.)', '**1557** N.T. (Genev.)', or '**1881** N.T. (Revised)'. In those instances where no translator's name follows the date, the text name is cited in large and small roman capitals as if it were the author, and the name of the book appears in italics, the usual style for the title of a work.

Other exceptions can undoubtedly be found, but, in most cases, the reader of the printed Dictionary should not have any problem in identifying the source. Where some doubt exists, the date is often an important identifier, as well as the reference to a Biblical chapter and verse. The major difficulty resulting from these variations will be experienced by the user (or lexicographer) attempting to search an electronic version of the Dictionary text for all Bible quotations or for all quotations from a certain version.

Note that the names 'Wyclif' and 'Tindale' are normally cited in this form, although modern usage sometimes gives preference to the spellings 'Wycliffe' and 'Tyndale'.

Bibliography. An alphabetical list giving bibliographical details of the principal sources commonly quoted in the Dictionary. The original bibliography was compiled for the 1933 **Supplement* and entitled 'A List of Books Quoted in the Oxford English Dictionary'. The later **Supplement* (1972–86) included, under the title 'Bibliography', a similar listing of the works most frequently cited within its four volumes. The second edition's *Bibliography* consolidates the two lists. The reader should be aware that, in all instances, no claim is made that the bibliographies are complete; nevertheless, the consolidated listing is a considerable aid to users who wish to obtain fuller information about particular titles or authors since both normally appear in abbreviated form within quotation texts.

The *Bibliography*'s alphabetical arrangement follows the normal word-by-word listing (in contrast to the letter-by-letter arrangement of Dictionary entries) found in most bibliographies, library catalogues, and telephone directories. As is also often the practice, names beginning with 'Mac' and 'Mc' are interfiled (as if they were all spelled 'Mac'), and initialisms precede words beginning with the same letter:

R., B. 1584 *See* RICH, B.
R., H. *News from the Levane seas* 1594
R., T. *A view of government in Europe* 1689
R.A.F. news See *Royal Air Force news*
RCA review, 1936–
RADDALL, Thomas Head *Hangman's Beach* 1966
RADIN, Paul tr. *J. Vendryes's Language* 1925
Radio Times, The 1923–

Authors' names are printed in large and small capitals, and titles in italics, in the same way as they appear in quotation paragraphs. Entries are listed under authors' surnames, when appropriate or known; otherwise, the listing is by title. Journals are normally entered by title, together with their inclusive dates if they have ceased publication, or, if they are still published (as in the case of *RCA review* above) the starting date followed by a dash is given. Frequently, the place of publication of a journal or newspaper is included in parentheses, especially when the source is somewhat obscure, or where there are several publications with the same name. Numerous cross-references are included. For example, the reader is directed from the initials 'B.R.' to the author's surname, where an entry is found under 'RICH, Barnaby'. The *main entry for joint authors is normally under the first author's name with references from the name(s) of the other author(s). Author and title information is followed by the date of the first edition (or the date of the principal edition or the edition 'read') and, in some instances such as journals and diaries, the date of composition.

Works by *pseudonymous authors are usually listed under the pseudonym enclosed in single quotation marks in the same way as they appear within quotation paragraphs. Thus, the works of Lewis Carroll are listed under 'Carroll, Lewis' followed by his real name in parentheses—'(C. L. Dodgson)'. In general, the practice is to list works by the name under which they were published. When an author has written under his or her own name as well as under one or more pseudonyms, works are usually listed by the name under which they appeared in print with a 'See also' cross-reference from the listing under the actual name to the pseudonymous listing. In the case of *translations, as in the above entry for 'RADIN', the translator is considered to be the author of the English-language text, as it is in quotations, with the original foreign author's name in italics as part of the title. The *Bibliography* is first and foremost a list of works written in English, or translated into English, so that foreign titles cited in the Dictionary, particularly in etymologies, are only occasionally given (Littré's *Dictionnaire de la langue française*, for example, is listed, but *Grimm's *Deutsches Wörterbuch* is not).

*Abbreviations will frequently be encountered for organizations which undertook the editing and printing of earlier works. These include the *English Dialect Society (E.D.S.), the *Early English Text Society (E.E.T.S.), the Scottish History Society (S.H.S.), and the Scottish Text Society (S.T.S.). Normally the date, if known, of the original manuscript or publication is given with the relevant society's initials and the date of its edition in parentheses.

blend. A descriptive term sometimes applied to a fusion of two or more words into one. Also referred to as a 'portmanteau' word from Lewis Carroll's explanation of 'slithy' (combining 'lithe' and 'slimy') in *Through the Looking Glass* as 'like a portmanteau—there are two meanings packed into one word'. Blends include words such as 'anecdotard' (a blend of 'anecdote' and 'dotard'), obviously referring to a dotard given to the tedious recounting of anecdotes; 'cyborg' [a blend of *cyb(ernetic* and *org(anism*] to describe an integrated man-machine system; and 'franglais' [a blend of *fran(çais* and *an)glais*], a form of French corrupted by the addition of English words.

A modification of this practice, however, will be observed in more recent entries where the term 'blend' is only applied if the original words share a common letter or letters so that brackets cannot be placed exactly, as, for example, with the *proprietary name 'Selectric', a blend of 'select' and 'electric'. Otherwise, the etymology notes that the word is *formed on (f.) the two original words in a similar fashion to other *combinations, except that the appropriate parts of the original words are bracketed. An example is found in the etymology for 'Valspeak' which reads 'f. VAL(LEY *sb.* + -SPEAK'.

BRADLEY, Henry (1845–1923). Philologist, lexicographer, and second editor of the first edition of the *OED* from 1888 until his death. Bradley was born in Manchester, and largely self-educated, having attended grammar school only until the age of fourteen. He was employed as a corresponding clerk for a Sheffield cutlery firm from 1863 to 1883. During these years, he pursued his philological interests, mastering modern European and classical languages, and acquiring a knowledge of Hebrew.

In 1884, for economic reasons and out of concern for his wife's health, he moved to London where he undertook miscellaneous literary work, mainly writing book reviews. In the same year, his review of the first part of the recently published **New English Dictionary* (*NED*, later the *OED*) demonstrated such an unusual knowledge of *philology that *Murray began consulting him on etymological problems. In 1886, Bradley was employed by the *Delegates of Oxford University Press to assist with the letter *B*, and in January of 1888 he was appointed as the Dictionary's second editor. He continued to work in London, using a room provided by the British Museum, with his own staff. Finally, in 1896, he moved to Oxford, although he, and the two subsequent editors, worked separately from Murray in quarters allocated to them in the *Old Ashmolean Museum.

Bradley's forty years' work on the Dictionary encompassed the letters *E–G*, *L–M*, *S–Sh* (a section which included the longest entry '*set'), *St*, and part of *W*. Bradley was a modest, unassuming scholar; although their backgrounds were similar, his quiet manner was a contrast to Murray's occasionally volatile temperament, and their methods were quite different. *Onions, who worked under both men before becoming the fourth editor contrasted Murray's formal, schoolmasterly instruction with Bradley, the 'philosophical exponent', who taught 'by hint, by interjectional phrase, or even a burst of laughter'.

In 1891, Bradley's work on the Dictionary was recognized with an honorary MA from Oxford, and in 1914, both he and Murray received honorary D.Litts. Bradley became senior editor after Murray died in 1915 and continued to work on the Dictionary until his own sudden death in 1923.

BURCHFIELD, Robert William (b. 1923). Scholar and editor of the four-volume *Supplement*. Born in Wanganui, New Zealand, Burchfield came to Oxford as a Rhodes scholar in 1950, following service in the Second World War. On graduation he became a college lecturer in English Language and Literature, first at Magdalen and then at Christ Church, Oxford. While at Magdalen, he met C. T. *Onions and was encouraged by the former *OED* editor to take an interest in lexicography. Burchfield subsequently, together with G. W. S. Friedrichsen, assisted in editing the *Oxford Dictionary of English Etymology* (1966) which was Onions's chief occupation in his later years. In 1957, Burchfield was appointed editor of the *Supplement*. He immediately embarked upon re-establishing the Dictionary's editorial offices, and developing a *Reading Programme to collect material for the new volumes. Burchfield was responsible for directing the updating of the Dictionary's coverage of standard language, as well as for broadening its scope to include, in particular, other varieties of written English such as that of North America, Australia, New Zealand, South

Africa, India, Pakistan, and the West Indies. He also instituted increased coverage of *scientific and technical terms, as well as *slang and *colloquialisms. His policies continue to serve as guidelines for the Dictionary. (See also VOCABULARY and SUPPLEMENT (1972–86).)

C

cant. A status *label used in some older entries compiled for the first edition. While 'cant' in general use is often applied to the jargon or secret language of any particular group, the *OED* uses it with specific reference to the early slang of 'thieves, rogues, and beggars'. Many of these words were taken from specialized sources, such as the *Dict. Cant. Crew* (*A New Dictionary of the Terms Ancient and Modern of the Canting Crew*, a. 1700), and include such oddities as 'nub' (to execute by hanging), 'smash' (to pass counterfeit money), 'tallman' (dice loaded to turn up high numbers), and 'lag' (a convict transported for penal servitude). Words and senses in this category will also be found with the labels *thieves' cant, thieves' slang, criminals' slang*, or simply *slang*.

casual. See NATURALIZED WORD.

catachrestically (*catachr.*). A *label applied to the use of a word judged to be improper (e.g., ungrammatical or based upon a misconception), and employed primarily in entries written for the first edition. More commonly the catachrestic *status symbol (¶) is used for this purpose. (Also compare with SPURIOUS WORD.)

chronological order. The ordering of items according to date. The *OED* normally employs chronological order, with the earliest date first, for numbering senses within entries and for listing the illustrative quotations that support each sense. (See also SENSE DEVELOPMENT and DATES.)

circa (*c*). A Latin word meaning 'approximately' or 'around' which is used in its abbreviated form preceding dates that cannot be definitely established. It is most often employed to indicate the approximate date of publication or writing of a source work cited in a quotation. (See also DATES, p. 43 and compare with ANTE.)

Clarendon Press. See OXFORD UNIVERSITY PRESS.

coarse slang. See TABOO AND OFFENSIVE LANGUAGE.

cognate with (cogn. w.). Used principally in etymologies to introduce a word which belongs to the same linguistic family as another word, although there is no direct lineal connection between the two. Many *Old English words, are cognate with older forms in other related languages. For example, the word 'after' is descended from the Old English *æfter* which is cognate with the Old Saxon and Old High German *aftar*, *er*, Old Frisian *efter*, Old Norse *aptr* or *eptir*, Gothic *aftra*, etc. (p. 26).

coinage. A term employed in the Dictionary to refer to the deliberate formation of a word, usually attributable to an individual; also applied to the word so formed. Information regarding coinage is normally included in the etymology, although it may sometimes appear in a definition or *definition note. Numerous word forms in general use may be attributed to an individual, such as 'doublethink' (George Orwell) and 'serendipity' (Horace Walpole). The origin of such words is also frequently confirmed by the initial supporting quotation, although coined words are sometimes known to have been in use before they were recorded in print. (Compare with INVENTED WORD.)

Coined *scientific words which are adopted into several modern languages, but whose origins can be traced to a specific foreign source, are treated somewhat differently. It was customary in etymologies in the first edition to attribute a coined scientific term to its author, when known, with or without a date. However, the **Supplement* (1972–86) extended this practice by providing more explicit bibliographical information such as the journal or book title, volume, and page number in which the term first appeared in the foreign language. The references were in all instances verified, since specialized dictionaries and bibliographies sometimes cited sources incorrectly. However, given the international nature of science, it is not always possible to identify the language in which a scientific term first appeared and in these cases the word is usually designated as a *modern formation (*mod. f.*) (see p. 25). Note also that foreign quotations which contribute to the history of a word are sometimes included in square brackets within the quotation paragraph (see p. 40–41).

COLERIDGE, Herbert (1830–61). Philologist, active member of the *Philological Society, first editor of the Society's proposed complete New English Dictionary, and a great-nephew of the poet Samuel Taylor Coleridge. Educated at Eton and Balliol College, Oxford, and a barrister by profession, Coleridge became one of the three members (together with *Trench and *Furnivall) in 1857 of a committee to collect older words not registered in existing dictionaries. When the Society decided to pursue its larger dictionary project, Coleridge was appointed editor in 1859, the year in which his *Glossarial Index to the Printed English Literature of the Thirteenth Century* was published. He immediately drafted a set of

'Canones Lexicographici', rules for the compilation of the dictionary, which were largely consistent with the principles suggested by Dean Trench in his influential papers *On Some Deficiencies in Our English Dictionaries*. Coleridge confidently had fifty-four pigeon-holes built to hold the 100,000 *dictionary slips which he anticipated would be generated by the volunteers who were assigned to read English literature within three time periods (1250–1526, 1527–1674, and 1675 onwards). Coleridge's plans were cut short by his untimely death in 1861 of consumption, aggravated, so it is said, by a chill caught while sitting in damp clothes at a Philological Society meeting. He was succeeded as editor by Frederick Furnivall.

collective, -ly (*collect.*). A label used to indicate that a word, normally a noun, refers in some fashion to a number, or collection, of beings, objects, or things as an entity. Collectives may be singular (*collect. sing.*) or plural (*collect. pl.*), with 'singular' and 'plural' in each instance referring to the grammatical form of the word, e.g., stair, stairs. Their use is perhaps most readily understood by citing examples. The simplest collective singulars are what are sometimes referred to as 'nouns of multitude', such as 'crowd', 'herd', or 'flock'. The noun 'management', however, although not a noun of multitude, can be used in the singular in a collective sense to refer to the members of a governing body. The plural of the noun 'stair' in the sentence 'he climbed the stairs' is an example of a collective plural since it refers, in this instance, to a single flight of stairs, or a staircase. On the other hand, the noun 'clothes' is a collective plural without a singular, while 'sheep', 'deer', and 'salmon' are singular nouns without plurals that can be used either to refer to one animal or fish, or, collectively, to a number of them.

collocation. In modern linguistic terminology, a collocation is sometimes defined as the context, or the habitual way, in which a particular word is used together with another word or a group of words. The term is interpreted in the *OED* in its more conventional sense of placing something adjacent to, or side-by-side with, something else, or the grouping formed by this action (specifically, one word in juxtaposition with another). Collocations or 'special collocations' may often appear to the reader to be similar to *combinations. For example, 'environmental engineering' is a 'special collocation' of 'environmental'. It should be noted that 'environmental' is an adjective joined to a noun, but when a noun, functioning *attributively is joined to another noun, it is usually referred to as a combination. Normally, the Dictionary makes this distinction, although there are instances, especially in the case of proper names, where the two terms appear to overlap. For example, the name of the city 'Paris' is defined as being 'used in various collocations' (Paris cut, Paris dress, Paris gown, Paris hat). (See also pp. 46–50 for specific examples of collocations and the manner in which they are listed in entries.)

colloquial (*colloq.*). A *label indicating that a particular usage is found in the informal, standard language of the native speaker, rather than in formal, literary contexts. Obviously, the judgement of what constitutes colloquial language is somewhat subjective. James *Murray addressed the problem graphically in a chart originally drafted for the first edition which still appears at the beginning of the 'General Explanations' in Vol. I. In the centre is 'common' vocabulary, which Murray explained is the area in which 'literary and colloquial usage meet', but he noted that for everyone 'the domain of "common words" widens out in the direction of his own reading, research, business, provincial or foreign residence, and contracts in the direction in which he has no practical connexion: no one man's English is *all* English'.

The borderline between colloquial usage and *slang is also not always clear-cut, as is also indicated by Murray's chart and his comment that '"slang" words ascend through colloquial use'. This distinction is perhaps even more difficult today because media such as television, films and popular music often rapidly promote 'slang' words to the 'colloquial' category. In general, however, the label *slang* is applied to language that is less widely accepted by or acceptable to all native speakers; that is likely to be ephemeral; or that is employed by a particular social or interest group rather than speakers at large.

combination(s) (*Comb.*). A term used in the Dictionary to identify word forms resulting from the joining of two or more existing words, whether separated, hyphenated, or combined as a single word, which function as one grammatical unit (for example, 'school phobia', 'school-learning', and 'schoolboy'). In keeping with the *OED*'s policy of inclusiveness, the Dictionary attempts to record all major established combinations, as well as numerous examples of minor or less established forms. Minor combinations are usually instances in which a noun is attached *attributively to another noun with both words retaining their own meaning; in other words, the first noun performs a descriptive or adjectival function. Major combinations often require further definition, while the meanings of most simple, attributive combinations are obvious. The Dictionary therefore includes definitions only for major forms, but illustrates the use of both types of combinations with quotations.

Many combinations are included in the entry for their main (usually the first) word. Major, defined combinations, often referred to as 'Special Combinations', are printed in bold type and function as *subordinate headwords, while minor combinations, usually preceded by the wording '***attrib***. (attributive) and (***Comb.***)', are listed in heavy italics. Numerous combinations, however, have acquired independent status and have developed their own history and senses. For example, words such as 'postman' and 'newspaper' are obviously combinations, but it is also apparent that they function, and indeed are largely thought of by the user, as independent words which merit main entries in their own right. Note also the distinction between the terms 'combination' and '*collocation'. In most instances, the Dictionary refers to a noun joined to a noun as a 'combination', while the form resulting from the habitual joining of an adjective to a noun is called a 'collocation', or 'special collocation', although examples may be found where the two terms appear to overlap. (See also COMPOUND for the way in which this term is applied to certain established combinations.)

The form in which combinations are recorded in the Dictionary is frequently problematic for lexicographers. In theory, a hyphen implies that the relationship between two words is closer than if they were written separately, but not as close as if they were joined. In practice, there are no hard-and-fast rules as to whether combinations should be written as two words, hyphenated, or one word. As in other instances, the *OED*'s decision is primarily based on usage since its aim is to record language as it exists, not as it 'should be'. (See pp. 46–50 for specific examples of types of combinations and a description of the way in which they are structurally integrated into entries.)

combining form (comb. form). The form taken by a word when it is combined with another *word form to produce a new *compound word. Most combining forms in English are based on Greek or Latin roots. For example, 'bio-' is a combining form of the Greek word meaning 'a life, course, or way of living' as used in 'biography', and is also extended to mean 'organic life' in words such as 'biocentric' or 'biochemistry'. Similarly, 'matri-' is a combining form based on the Latin word 'mater' for mother, and is used in words such as 'matriarch'. It is the Dictionary's policy to treat combining forms in the same way as words; that is, they are accorded main entries which document their history, define the senses in which they are used, and illustrate their use. There are more than 600 entries for such forms in the Dictionary. Combining forms differ from *affixes in that they generally represent a word (although frequently they undergo some change in the process as can be seen in the above examples), whereas affixes represent a grammatical element (*un-* negates in the same way as 'not') or function (*-ist* indicates an agent). (See also pp. 58–64 for examples of entries for combining forms and affixes.)

comparative philology. See PHILOLOGY.

compound (comp., cpd.). The terms 'compound' or 'compound word' in the *OED* are most often found in entries for *combining forms, such as 'geo-, 'bio-', or 'matri-', where reference is made to words resulting from this type of formation ('geography', 'biology', 'matriarchy', etc.). In most other instances, words formed by combining two, or more, existing English word forms are called *combinations or *collocations.

computerization. See DATABASE, INTEGRATION, NEW OED PROJECT.

concrete, -ly (*concr.*). A *label used to identify a noun which refers to an object or a thing, and which is derived from an abstract noun or *verbal substantive describing an action, state, or quality. For example, an *organization* as an entity is the product of 'organization' (the noun describing the act of organizing), and a *painting* (a representation or picture) is the result of the act of 'painting' (verbal noun formed from the verb 'paint').

construction, construed with (const.). Terms widely employed in definitions and etymologies to describe the grammatical construction in which a word or sense is used. Note that the somewhat ambiguous word 'construed', in this case, is used in its grammatical sense and is perhaps more easily understood as 'constructed'. Specifically, what is being described is the way in which a verb, noun, adjective, or some other part of speech is combined grammatically with a relational form such as a preposition, infinitive, adverb, singular or plural verb, case, etc. For example, a word sense may be 'construed with' certain prepositions such as *of*, *to*, *with*, *for*, *out*. The verb 'recoil' (meaning to rebound, or spring back) is 'const. *against*, *to*, *on*, *upon*', as in the sentence 'their treason recoiled *on* their own hands', or the noun 'substitution' can be 'const. *for*, *to*', as exemplified in 'the substitution of words *for* reason'. A word form may also be used 'without construction'; the *verbal substantive (noun) 'smattering' (meaning a slight or superficial knowledge) is usually followed by the prepositions *in* or *of*, but Ruskin's statement that 'there is a wide difference between elementary knowledge and superficial knowledge—between a firm beginning and a feeble smattering', illustrates the use of the word without construction. Alternatively, a word may be 'const. as' singular or plural, as in the case of the noun 'physics' which is plural in origin (literally, 'natural things'), but 'now construed as a singular' (physics *is* . . .). Other examples are the construction of the *obsolete verb 'behappen' with a dative object ('many remarkable occurrences behappened *this Martyr*'), and the verb 'contrive' with an infinitive ('an editor should always look at the MSS for himself, if he can possibly contrive *to do* so').

While the introductory terms 'const.' or 'construed with' are frequently used, other means of indicating similar constructions are often encountered. For example, a definition may include a comment such as 'Also with *in*' to point to an alternative construction, or a preposition may be incorporated as part of the definition. For instance, sense **2** of the verb 'saturate' reads 'to impregnate, soak thoroughly, imbue *with*'. Note that in all cases, the relational word is indicated by italics.

contributors. The *OED* could not have been produced without the help of the hundreds of men and women—scholars, scientists, and dedicated amateurs—who contributed their services as consultants, readers, sub-editors, and proof-readers. Their work is acknowledged in the introduction to each of the original *fascicles, and the names of the major contributors are listed, together with the regular editorial staff, in the initial volume of the first edition and the **Supplement* (1972–86). Although volunteers still play an important role in the continuous updating of the quotation files, the majority of regular readers receive some payment under the current directed *Reading Programmes, but it may still be said that their dedication is primarily 'a labour of love'.

The first public appeal for readers to collect words and quotations was issued by the *Philological Society in their 'Proposal for the Publication of A New English Dictionary' in January 1859, although some sixty volunteers, many of them members of the Society, had already begun the task almost two years earlier. When *Furnivall assumed the editorship in 1861, he also recruited volunteer sub-editors to begin the preliminary editing of individual letters. While the initial response to the programme was enthusiastic, the work of the volunteers was not consistently of high quality—or even legible, as James *Murray discovered when he became editor of the future *OED* in 1879. Under Murray's firm guidance, the readers (over 1,000 strong) in Britain and the US who responded to 'An Appeal to the English-speaking and English-reading Public' issued in April 1879, were somewhat more zealous in their adherence to rules.

The contribution of some individuals was remarkable. The first edition notes numerous volunteers whose contributions numbered in the thousands, with Thomas Austin (who extracted 165,000 quotations) leading the list, closely followed by William Douglas of London, who is credited with 136,000. One can only imagine the labour involved in copying by hand thousands of quotations from a work such as **Cursor Mundi*, a task apparently undertaken by Dr H. R. Helwich of Vienna. Citations from this great Middle English work must have made up a good percentage of his 50,000 submissions. It is apparent that the spouses of some of the more diligent workers did not share their enthusiasm; 'that wretched dictionary' is a phrase reported to have been used by the wife of one Mr A. Caland of Wageningen, Holland who for some years read all the Dictionary proofs. Prominent names also figure among the early principal contributors including Flinders Petrie, the Egyptologist, William Rossetti, a well-known literary critic and brother of Dante Gabriel and Christina, and Leslie Stephen, the first editor of the *Dictionary of National Biography* and father of Virginia Woolf.

From the first call for volunteers by the Philological Society, the American contribution has been significant. Although the initial plan for readers in the United States to be responsible for 'the whole of eighteenth-century literature' was never seriously pursued, Murray's later appeal for readers elicited an enthusiastic response from Americans, a number of whom appear as principal contributors in the list of names included in Volume I of the first edition. In his presidential address to the Philological

Society in 1880, Murray especially referred to the cooperation of American academics and their students, under the direction of Prof. Francis A. March of Lafayette College, noting somewhat testily that 'we have had no such help from any college or university in Great Britain'. Professor Fitzedward Hall, an American who had taught in India and later moved to England, routinely devoted about four hours a day to collecting quotations and reading proofs. His death in 1901 was noted by Murray in the preface to Volume V as 'an incalculable loss'. The importance of American and Canadian readers, particularly for coverage of North American vocabulary and idiom, is recognized in the current North American Reading Programme, based in the United States, which was established in 1989.

The contribution of women to the Dictionary is by no means insignificant. Of the principal readers for the first edition, nearly twenty per cent of those enlisted before 1884 were women, and about one-quarter of the post-1884 readers. Notable is the contribution of 18,700 quotations by Miss E. F. Burton of Carlisle, while the Misses Edith and E. Perronet Thompson of Bath jointly contributed over 15,000 quotations, and are frequently acknowledged for their proof-reading efforts as well. The number of unmarried women or pairs of unmarried sisters is particularly interesting, as is the number of clergymen from both sides of the Atlantic. In fact, twenty-seven per cent of the listed sub-editors have the title Reverend, although it was not unusual for men initially educated for the church, such as Walter *Skeat, to pursue an academic career later.

The record of the greatest number of quotations submitted by any one individual, however, must be held by Marghanita Laski (1915–88) who first participated in the Reading Programme established in 1957 for the *Supplement*. Miss Laski, a British broadcaster, journalist, and author, who sometimes wrote under the name 'Sarah Russell', is credited with extracting at least a quarter of a million quotations for the Reading Programmes of the *Supplement* and the second edition. The *Supplement* also benefited from major collections of quotations contributed by scholars in America, South Africa, Australia, and other locations, and from the work of numerous librarians in cities throughout the world who researched and verified information.

The roster of international scholars, scientists, and specialists who acted, and continue to act, as voluntary consultants on the history and definition of specialized terms or words of foreign origin is also an indication of the high regard in which the Dictionary is held.

Finally, one cannot overlook family involvement with the *OED*. The contribution of Murray's extensive family to the first edition is apparent since the names of his two eldest sons Harold and Ethelbert, the former with 27,000 quotations to his credit, as well as Lady Murray and her brother and sister-in-law, the Ruthvens, appear in the list of principal contributors to the first edition. Among the 'assistants', two Murray daughters, Rosfrith and Elsie, as well as a daughter of editor Henry *Bradley, are also prominent. (See also READING PROGRAMME.)

CRAIGIE, William Alexander (1867–1957). Philologist, lexicographer, third editor of the first edition, and co-editor (with *Onions) of the 1933 **Supplement*. Like James *Murray, Craigie, who was born in Dundee, was a Lowland Scot. He graduated from St. Andrews University in 1888 and later attended Balliol College, Oxford. In common with his two colleagues, he had a remarkable knowledge of languages, specializing in Celtic, Older Scots, and Scandinavian, particularly Icelandic.

Craigie was appointed by the *Delegates of the Press to *Bradley's staff in 1897 and worked on the letter *G*. In 1901, he became the third editor and was responsible for editing *N, Q, R, Si-Sq, U, V*, and *Wo–Wy*, as well as approximately one-third of the *Supplement* (1933). He was knighted in 1928 upon the completion of the first edition. While working on the Dictionary, Craigie was also a lecturer in Scandinavian languages at Oxford, and in 1916 became a professor of Anglo-Saxon. He has been called 'the most productive lexicographer of his time', and in his later years worked simultaneously on three major dictionaries, the *OED*, his own *Dictionary of the Older Scottish Tongue (DOST)*, and the historical *Dictionary of American English* (1936–44). In order to edit the latter, he took a post as professor of English at the University of Chicago in 1925. In 1936, he resigned from that position to devote his full attention to the *DOST* and finished the letter *I* before handing over the editorship to his successor at the age of 88.

cross-reference. A direction to the reader to refer to another section of the entry being consulted, or to an entry for another headword. Cross-references in the *OED* are found in many forms *within* entries. There are also some 60,000 entries which are in themselves cross-references, the purpose of which is to direct the reader from a variant spelling or obsolete or erroneous form of a word to the comprehensive *main entry for its most recent or common form. (See also pp. 79–81 for examples of cross-reference entries, and 14, 25–27, 38–39, and 41 for cross-references within entry components.)

Cursor Mundi. One of the major extant works of the *Middle English period, this northern poem was based on the work of earlier Latin writers and compiled around 1300. It survived in seven manuscripts which were edited by Richard Morris and published by the *Early English Text Society between 1874 and 1893. As a primary source of early English for the *OED*, *Cursor Mundi* is, next to the multiple versions of the text and partial text of the **Bible*, the most frequently quoted single work in the Dictionary. The exacting task of extracting quotations from the work appears to have been undertaken largely by Dr H. R. Helwich of Vienna. The poem was written by an unknown cleric and purports to be a spiritual history of mankind's seven stages from the Creation to the Last Judgement.

D

database. A collection of data organized by a conceptual framework (a 'schema') that provides the basis for storing and accessing its contents on one or more storage devices, such as tape or disk, and by any number of software programs. The *OED* database consists of text and is defined in terms of the functional elements found within a Dictionary entry, such as the headword, part of speech, pronunciation, definition, etc., forming a hierarchically nested structure in which each element fits within another. For example, an individual quotation is part of a quotation paragraph, which is part of a sense, which is part of an entry, and the sub-elements of a quotation are the date, the author, the title of the work, and the text of the quotation. In current practice, the beginning and ending of each of these elements and sub-elements as they occur in an entry are identified by a designator called a tag enclosed in angle brackets. Each entry, for example, is preceded by a 'start' tag ⟨e⟩ and the last character of each entry is followed by an 'end' tag ⟨/e⟩ (note that the end tag is differentiated from the start tag by an oblique slash). Thus, when seen on a computer screen in its unformatted form (that is, without structure) the entire content of the Dictionary appears as one long string of characters composed of text interspersed with tags (see fig. 24 opposite for a sample of a string of text from the beginning of the entry for **trade-in**).

The original editors of the Dictionary established a consistent, although complex, model for entries and *typography had always been used to indicate certain functional elements, e.g., bold type for headwords and small italic type for titles of works. Based on these conventions and other criteria, much of the labour of inserting structural tags was done automatically by sophisticated computer transduction tools, following the manual insertion of minimal structural and typographical indicators when the text was first recorded in *machine-readable form (see NEW OED PROJECT). Once the text was fully tagged, a variety of software programs could be developed to access it for editing, searching, augmenting, deleting, and printing, and for viewing the text in the format most appropriate for the user. For example, an editor may wish to examine the text in its fully tagged form, while the average reader is probably more comfortable working with untagged text, formatted so that it closely replicates the structure and typography of the printed Dictionary.

Organized in this form, the Dictionary database becomes a whole that is much more than the sum of its parts. Not only does it record the text of the *OED* as it appears in print, but it offers the potential for reformatting the information, or combining parts of the contents with other data, to create, if wished, an entirely different print form. It also serves as a central

<e><hg><hw>trade-in</hw> <pr><ph>
"treIdIn</ph></pr>.</hg> <etym>f.
vbl. phr. <cf>to trade in</cf> s.v.
<xr><x>trade</x> <ps>v.</ps> <xs>10
</xs>.</xr></etym> <s4 num=1><s6
num=a>A transaction in which
something is traded in; a part
exchange.</s6> <s6 num=b>An item
traded in, esp. a used car; also <la>
fig.</la></s6> <s6 num=c>A sum
allowed in return for a trade-in.
</s6></s4> <qp><q><qd>1917</qd> <w>
Horseless Carriage</w> <lc>1 Aug. 28
</lc> <qt>A used car in a trade-in.
</qt></q> <q><qd>1934</qd> <a>J.
O'Hara</a> <w>Appointment in Samarra
</w> <lc>ii. 39</lc> <qt>That
Studebaker sedan, the black one.&es.
The one we took on a trade-in from
Doc Lurie.</qt></q> <q><qd>1945</qd>
<w>Word Study</w> <lc>Dec. 3/1</lc>
<qt>So useful and practical is
English becoming that the time may
not be far off when many small
nations&dd.may consider some sort of
&oq.trade-in&cq. with their national
language for the English language.
</qt></q> <q><qd>1954</qd> <a>P.
Highsmith</a> <w>Blunderer</w> <lc>
(1956) xxii. 140</lc> <qt>Since he
hadn't the money for a brand-new car,
Kimmel preferred to keep his ancient
one rather than acquire something
slightly newer on a trade-in.</qt>
</q> <q><qd>1960</qd> <a>V. Packard
</a> <w>Waste Makers</w> <lc>xiii.
137</lc> <qt>The high trade-in proved
to be enormously effective in luring
prospects.</qt></q> <q><qd>1969</qd>
<a>F. Sargeson</a> <w>Joy of Worm</w>

Fig. 24

resource for other reference works published by Oxford University Press, and, of course, with appropriate software, it provides both editors and users with the opportunity of searching not only within one entry but across all the elements within all entries in the Dictionary.

dates. The first element in virtually all illustrative quotations in the Dictionary is a year-date in bold type, although it may be modified in some way when the precise date cannot be established (by preceding the date with **ante (a)* or **circa (c)*, or by replacing the last one or two digits with dots, e.g., 18. .). In general, the date is that of the year in which the cited work was first published. However, certain modifications are made when the original text is unavailable, when a later revised edition is used, or when the quotation is extracted from a letter, journal, diary, or manuscript published after the date of composition (for details and examples of these and other conventions, see pp. 41–43).

In the first edition, some quotations appeared without dates. The computer system for automatically processing the text of the second edition expected each quotation to begin with a date. Since this was a desirable stipulation, dates, or approximate dates, were researched and supplied for most quotations where they were lacking. A few regular exceptions were made, the most notable being most of the numerous quotations from the *Old English epic poem *Beowulf*.

In addition, some discrepancies may exist, especially in the dating of quotations in entries prepared for the first edition. Given the long period over which the Dictionary was compiled and the number of sometimes widely scattered sub-editors that were used, bibliographical consistency was understandably somewhat less rigorous than at present.

definition. A brief statement that explains the meaning of a headword, or of a particular sense, *sub-sense, *derivative, *combination, *phrase, *abbreviation, or other word form. The definition text may also take the form of a direction to the reader to refer elsewhere for this information (for example, to a quotation, to another sense within the same entry, or to another entry), or it may simply describe the way the word form functions within some grammatical or syntactical structure.

It is important to remember that the purpose of a historical dictionary, such as the *OED*, is not simply to define words and their senses, but to explain and document their form, function, and development over time. A definition is therefore only one explanatory element in an entry and, in writing it, the lexicographer takes into account the supporting information surrounding it, such as a *label which tells the reader the context in which the definition is to be considered, or the degree to which the accompanying quotations explain the meaning of the sense or sub-sense under consideration. In addition, a definition, especially in a long entry, must be presented so that the reader is able to comprehend its semantic and/or syntactic relationship to the headword and to the preceding or following senses and sub-senses. Thus, the definition may contain one or more elements, such as expositions, synonyms, antonyms, grammatical constructions, cross-references, direct quotations or paraphrasing from other acknowledged sources, phrases, and minor derivatives and combinations. (For a further explanation of examples of *explanatory, structural*, and *cross-reference* definitions, see pp. 37–39.)

definition note. A statement or paragraph, in small print, appended to a definition, which provides supplementary or explanatory information about the usage of a word or sense. (See p. 39 for an example.)

Delegates. A committee of senior members of the University of Oxford who direct the affairs of *Oxford University Press and approve the publication of its books, including the *OED*. The chief executive officer of the Press is called 'the Secretary to the Delegates'. The Delegates played a critical role in the initial negotiations between the Press and the *Philological Society for the printing and publication of a historical dictionary based on the Society's collected material. They were also responsible for initially contracting with James *Murray to serve as editor and for subsequent decisions to appoint additional editors in order to hasten the completion of the Dictionary.

In the difficult early years when it became increasingly apparent that the Press had committed itself to a project far exceeding the original estimates of time, size, and money, conflicts often arose between the senior editor and the Secretary to the Delegates, particularly after the resignation of the supportive Dr Bartholomew Price, who held the position until 1884. Anxious to expedite the Dictionary's completion, the new Secretary, Philip Lyttelton Gell, appointed *Bradley as second editor in 1888. The committee was still disappointed with the output and did not hesitate to express its displeasure to the two editors, who were constantly urged to reduce the size of the Dictionary, using *Webster's Unabridged Dictionary* (1864) as their benchmark. Originally conceived as four times the size of *Webster's*, entries had increased to almost eight times the size. Fortunately, by 1896 when the Press resigned itself to accepting the increase in size and to publishing 64-page quarterly sections, relations between the Delegates and the editors had eased, although the need to conserve time and space was a constant concern for Murray.

denizen. See NATURALIZED WORD.

derivative. Used in the *OED* to describe a word derived from another word. Typically, a derivative is formed by the addition of a *suffix to an existing word also treated in the Dictionary. The purpose of the word ending is normally to change the grammatical function of the main word.

For example, the suffix *-ly* is often employed to convert an adjective to an adverb, as in the case of the foregoing adverb 'normally' (derived from the adjective 'normal'). The suffixes *-er* and *-ness* are typical examples of endings used to create nouns. 'Commoner' (referring to an ordinary citizen) is derived, partly from the verb and partly from the noun 'common', and the noun 'commonness' from the adjective 'common'. Note, however, that 'commoner', the comparative (meaning 'more common'), is an *inflected form.

The *OED* distinguishes derivatives from other similar word forms, noting that they stand midway between *combinations (formed by combining two meaningful existing words) and inflected forms that result from the addition of a grammatical ending, such as that required to indicate the tense or person of a verb form, or the plural of a noun. Thus, 'common sense' is a combination, while 'commons' as in the 'House of Commons' (the common people) is an inflected form.

The Dictionary attempts to include all major derivatives and treats them according to their importance. Derivatives straightforwardly related to their main word are included within the entry for that word, frequently as the last unnumbered item in the entry (for examples, see p. 51). It will also be found that a few words treated within entries as minor derivatives are identical in form to the *main word, and are deemed derivatives because of a change in grammatical category (see p. 52 for an example). Many derivatives, however, have developed their own complex histories, apart from their parent word, and are treated as main words (pp. 68–72).

diachronic. An adjective applied to dictionaries, such as the *OED* and the *Deutsches Wörterbuch*, which are principally historical; that is, they present the history of a language, tracing the changes in form and meaning of words over a specified period of time (see also HISTORICAL PRINCIPLES). Most dictionaries, by contrast, are 'synchronic', meaning that they primarily document language that is contemporary with a particular point in time.

diacritic. A mark placed over, under, or through a letter or character to distinguish a sound or value assigned to it. For example, the French acute (*é*) and grave (*è*) accents, the cedilla (*ç*), the German umlaut (*ü*) and the Spanish tilde (*ñ*) are diacritics. Diacritics are also employed in *phonetic transcription to represent a particular sound, although the *IPA (International Phonetic Alphabet) used in the *OED* to transcribe *pronunciation is distinguished from other systems by its avoidance of diacritics. The only diacritic used in the Dictionary for transcription is the *tilde*, indicating nazalization (e.g. ɔ̃, as in the French word *bon*).

dialect, -al (*dial.*). A status *label applied to a word form or usage arising from local or regional peculiarities of vocabulary, pronunciation, and idiom. While dialect in the modern sense is often perceived as referring to the spoken language of uneducated, rural, or geographically isolated people, it is frequently recorded in printed form in dictionaries and word books compiled for that purpose, and in literary works containing dialogue that attempts to incorporate its use. The *OED* must, of necessity, place restrictions on its coverage of dialect in this sense, but as a historical dictionary, it takes into account the fact that the English language, until the end of the fifteenth century (in Scotland until the nineteenth century), existed only in dialects, all of which had a literary standing. Therefore, for this early period, 'words and forms of all dialects are admitted on an equal footing into the Dictionary'. With regard to dialectal forms after that period, the policy, as originally stated, was to exclude such forms 'except when they continue the history of a word or sense once in general use, illustrate the history of a literary word, or have themselves a certain currency'. In general, this policy is still followed.

The label *dial.* for post-fifteenth-century forms is therefore usually attached to an individual *variant form, to a sense, or an idiomatic expression, rather than to an entire entry, although it may appear comprehensively in a phrase such as 'now *dial.*', indicating the current status of a headword that was once used more generally. The designation is also frequently defined or modified by other descriptors, such as the regional labels '*north. dial.*' (northern dialect), '*mod. Sc.*' (modern Scottish), or '*U.S. dial.*'. For example, the lengthy entry for 'they' notes a '*U.S. dial.*' adverbial use of 'they' in place of 'there' in the quotation 'They's music in the twitter of the bluebird and the jay'. Similarly, the dialect designation is often combined with other status labels, such as '*dial. rare*', '*dial.* and *arch.*', or '*dial.* and *colloq.*'. (See also ENGLISH DIALECT SOCIETY.)

dictionaries, earlier. When the editors of the Dictionary compiled their original inventory of the English language, earlier dictionaries, glossaries, lexicons, and other word books were quite naturally used as sources, not only for what they contained, but also for what they left out, since it was one of the Dictionary's objectives to compensate for previous omissions. They were scanned as well for erroneous entries which sometimes perpetuated non-existent words resulting from misreadings, typographical mistakes, and so forth (see SPURIOUS WORD). The exact number of such works is difficult to assess, but the **Bibliography* in Volume XX lists nearly eight hundred titles in the first three categories. In addition to earlier general dictionaries, they cover an astonishing array of specialized subjects and topics, as well as various *dialects, *slang, *cant, and regional speech.

References to such sources within definitions appear for a variety of reasons. They may be used to provide additional information about the meaning of a word or sometimes, for example, with *scientific and technical terms, the entire definition may be a quotation from another source. On the other hand, the reference may correct an error in interpretation contained in another dictionary. Older dictionaries compiled by one individual are usually cited by the author's surname, sometimes abbreviated. The older dictionaries that are most commonly referred to, such as Cawdrey, Florio, Cockeram, Blount, Bailey, *Johnson, and *Webster, have full citations in the *Bibliography* and, where abbreviated, are often included in the *List of Abbreviations, Signs, etc.* at the front of each volume (this information was expanded in the **Supplement*). Some of the later and more comprehensive dictionaries, which are usually the work of a number of lexicographers and one or more editors, are often referred to by title. Examples of both types of citations include *D.A. (Dictionary of Americanisms), D.A.E. (Dictionary of American English), D.O.S.T. (Dictionary of the Older Scottish Tongue), E.D.D. (English Dialect Dictionary)*, J. (Johnson's *Dictionary*), and Jam. (Jamieson, *Scottish Dictionary*). (See also pp. 37–38 for examples of Dictionary citations within definitions.)

Within quotation paragraphs, references to earlier dictionaries serve different purposes. A notation may be made in square brackets that the word is to be found in Blount or Johnson, or, alternatively, that it was not found, suggesting that the word was possibly not in use at that time. Sometimes, the phrase 'in mod. Dicts.' or 'in Johnson' (or some other source) is used to indicate the word's apparent existence when no other contextual quotations were found. (For examples of this usage, refer to p. 41 and see also RARE.)

Finally, etymologies contain numerous references to information found in other dictionaries and word books, usually cited by the author's or compiler's surname. The majority refer to sources containing etymologies of foreign words from which the headword under discussion is in some way derived. While a full citation for the work referred to can often be found in the *Bibliography*, there are also a number of references that are not documented, since the *Bibliography* is primarily a list of works in English used as sources for quotations. For example, a citation such as 'Diez 351, and Grimm Dict. I. 22' assumes that the reader is familiar with the etymological dictionary (*Etymologisches Wörterbuch der romanischen Sprachen*) compiled in 1853 by Friedrich Christian Diez, and Jakob and Wilhelm Grimms' historical dictionary, the *Deutsches Wörterbuch*. Similarly, there are numerous references in botanical entries to 'de Tournefort' which again assumes a familiarity with the works of the French botanist, Joseph Pitton de Tournefort. (See also pp. 26–27 for specific examples of dictionary references within etymologies.)

dictionary slip. The traditional Dictionary slip is a 6 × 4 in. sheet of paper (originally specified as a slightly larger 'half-sheet of notepaper') used by a reader to record a word, phrase, etc. of potential use to the Dictionary. The *reading programme established by James *Murray was explicit in defining the format. The word selected was to appear in the upper left-hand corner, with the date, author, title, page, etc. of the work from which it was taken written below, followed by the quotation with its original capitalization, punctuation, and spelling retained. Despite Murray's best efforts, some readers ignored the instructions and jotted quotations on fragments of paper such as the backs of envelopes, grocery bags, and book jackets. Historically, Dictionary slips have been vulnerable to time, weather, rodents, and the vagaries of handwriting, none more notably than the two and a half million slips (and sundry items such as clippings, unread books, and letters) that Murray inherited from the *Philological Society in 1878.

Dictionary slips are sorted in letter-by-letter alphabetical order (a task formerly assigned the younger Murray children) and filed for later use by lexicographers. In Murray's original *Scriptorium, slips were first filed in the 1,016 wooden pigeon-holes created for the purpose, which eventually had to be converted to shelves to accommodate the constant shifting of quotation bundles. It has been estimated that eventually some five million slips were accumulated for the first edition. Remarkably, losses in the mail do not seem to have been a factor, despite the fact that thousands of parcels of slips were sent, and continue to be sent, by post.

In current practice, a similar meticulous routine is followed, although the bibliographical facilities are more sophisticated. An editor selects entries to be drafted or revised and assigns them to a lexicographer who is given a bundle of relevant quotation slips. Lexicographers are responsible for the accuracy of the quotations they decide to use and for assuring that the source is, where possible (and appropriate), the first edition of the cited work. The Dictionary Department's reference library may be consulted or the lexicographer may decide to use the *OED*'s *library research network which has researchers located in a number of key centres, principally in England and the US. Thus a typical Dictionary slip often passes through a number of hands and accumulates a variety of handwritten notes specifying what has been checked, what was found, or not found, and so forth. Not only are dictionary slips used to record quotations, they are also traditionally used by lexicographers to record their handwritten draft entries. While Dictionary slips continue to be used by readers and lexicographers to the present day, computerized storage is gradually replacing the pigeon-holes and filing cabinets that have often housed them. The Reading Programme established in the US in 1989, for example, converts quotations to machine-readable form. A similar practice is also being incorporated in the British programme. However, provision is made for individual quotations to be printed on demand in the format of the traditional slip since portability is still a desirable feature for editors and library researchers.

diphthong. Strictly speaking, 'a union of two vowels pronounced as one syllable' used only in reference to the spoken word, while the more general term 'digraph' is applied to any two letters representing a single sound in written form, such as the *ea* in 'head' or the *gh* in 'rough'. The diphthongs *ae* and *oe* in Latin loanwords are generally printed in the Dictionary as *ligatures (æ and œ), e.g. *archæology*.

E

Early English Text Society (E.E.T.S.). Founded in 1864 by Frederick *Furnivall 'for the purpose of bringing the mass of Old English Literature within the reach of the ordinary student, and of wiping away the reproach under which England had long rested, of having felt little interest in the monuments of her early language and life'. In general, the Society concentrated on the printing of manuscripts and texts compiled before 1558. The Original Series of works selected for editing was supplemented by an Extra Series, begun in 1867, and devoted to 'fresh editions' of early works that had previously been printed. These two series provided ready access to many documents which had been difficult to obtain or interpret, and supplied much of the early material that was perused by readers, initially for the *Philological Society's New English Dictionary and later for the *OED*.

The scheme devised by Furnivall was ambitious, and remarkably successful. By 1928 when the first edition of the Dictionary was completed, the Society had published approximately 175 texts in the Original Series, and roughly 125 in the Extra Series. The fact that about the same number of texts edited by the E.E.T.S. are listed in the *OED*'s **Bibliography* in Volume XX indicates the close relationship between the Society and the Dictionary. The Society continues to publish today, with around 300 texts in the Original Series to its credit. Its accomplishments are all the more astonishing because it laboured in its early years under severe financial difficulties as frequently pointed out to the membership by the Society's founder. Furnivall bemoaned as 'a scandal' the fact that the Society numbered only 300 subscribers compared to the Hellenic Society's 1,000 members. He was particularly incensed by the death of one G. N. Currie who was editing a text for the Society and who, on his deathbed, instructed a friend to burn a pile of his manuscripts. Furnivall notes indignantly that this collection included several texts belonging to the E.E.T.S., and the Society 'will be put to the cost of fresh copies, Mr. Currie having died in debt'.

The relationship of the *OED* to the Society has always been a close one. James *Murray edited several of the Society's editions between 1868 and 1878, the first of which was *The Complaynt of Scotlande*, published in 1872. More recently, Robert *Burchfield, the editor of the **Supplement*, was the Society's Honorary Secretary from 1955 to 1968, and served as a member of its council from 1968 to 1980.

Although the *OED*'s use of E.E.T.S. texts was widespread, it is not always clear, from an individual quotation, that the source is the Society's edition. The Society's initials are sometimes incorporated in a quotation reference. For example, '*c* **1450** METHAM *Wks.* (E.E.T.S.)' is an obvious reference to the Society's edition of John Metham's *Works, including the romance of Amoryus and Cleopes* (the full title being given in the **Bibliography*). However, the 1,400 references of this type represent only a small percentage of quotations taken from E.E.T.S. editions. Another form of citation is '**1561** AWDELAY *Frat. Vacab.* (1869)'. If one refers to the entry in the *Bibliography*, one finds 'Awdelay, John. *The fraternitye of vacabondes* 1561 (E.E.T.S. 1869)' which explains the 1869 reference. On the other hand, the same work by Awdelay is often cited with only the 1561 date, although, in checking the *Bibliography*, it may be assumed that the Society's edition was the source. The same unevenness in citations is found with editions of works reprinted or edited by other organizations or publishers, such as the *English Dialect Society (E.D.S.). Therefore, the *Bibliography* is often the best source of information for the reader who is anxious to identify the exact edition from which a quotation is taken.

echoic. A term coined by James *Murray and used in the Dictionary to describe a word form which imitates or echoes the sound associated with the thing or action it represents, for example, *blip*, *ding-dong*, *purr*, or *zoom*. To a lesser extent, the word 'imitative' is also employed to describe similar formations. Both terms are alternatives to the familiar word 'onomatopoeic'.

edh. See SPECIAL ENGLISH CHARACTERS.

editions. There have been only two complete editions of the *OED* in print. The Dictionary was initially published in a series of 125 paper-bound *fascicles or sections over a period of forty-four years between 1884 and 1928. The entire text was then printed in ten volumes in 1928 under the title *A New English Dictionary on Historical Principles*. It was made available in various formats, the least expensive form being twenty half volumes 'in quarter-persian' (morocco leather), or the ten volumes bound as twelve in 'half-morocco' binding at 50 guineas per set. A more expensive set of twenty half-volumes in 'half-morocco' was also sold at 55 guineas (*The Periodical*, 15 Feb. 1928). In 1933, this edition was reprinted with minor corrections in twelve volumes under the title *The Oxford English Dictionary*, together with a one-volume **Supplement*. Subsequent reprints of the first edition were issued in 1961, 1970, 1975, and 1978 without change, except that the three 'lists' (additions and emendations, *spurious words, and the *bibliography), at first included in the supplemental volume, appear instead at the end of Volume XII. Between 1972 and 1986, a new four-volume *Supplement*, which subsumed almost all of the entries in the old 1933 *Supplement*, was issued. The second edition of the *OED*, amalgamating the first edition and the four-volume **Supplement* in one alphabetical sequence, and adding some 5,000 new words and senses, was published in 1989. The first edition was also released in compact one-volume form in 1971, and again in 1987 in combination with the four-volume *Supplement*. The second edition appeared in a compact single volume in 1991.

Since the conversion of the *OED* text to *machine-readable form for the production of the second edition, the Dictionary has increasingly been made available to users for searching electronically. A CD-ROM of the first edition was released in 1987, and the second edition has been marketed in a magnetic tape version and, more recently, on a CD-ROM in 1992.

editors. From the time the decision was made by the *Philological Society in 1858 to undertake the publication of a New English Dictionary, the Dictionary has had nine editors. The names of the editors of the Society's proposed dictionary and the editors of the *OED* itself, together with the dates during which they held the position or, in the case of the current editors, were appointed, are listed below:

Herbert *Coleridge 1858–61 (Phil. Soc.)
Frederick James *Furnivall 1861–78 (Phil. Soc.)
James Augustus Henry *Murray, 1879–1915 (*OED*, ed. 1)
Henry *Bradley, 1888–1923 (*OED*, ed. 1)
William Alexander *Craigie, 1901–33 (*OED*, ed. 1 and 1933 *Supplement*)
Charles Talbut *Onions, 1914–33 (*OED*, ed. 1 and 1933 *Supplement*)
Robert William *Burchfield, 1957–86 (1972–86 *Supplement*)
Edmund Simon Christopher Weiner, 1984– (*OED*, ed. 2)
John Andrew Simpson, 1986– (*OED*, ed. 2)

It is interesting to note that this editorial chain, and thus the *OED* tradition, has been unbroken in the Dictionary's long history. Murray was closely connected with his Philological Society predecessors, and Bradley, Craigie, and Onions all worked under the direction of Murray. Burchfield was guided into lexicography by Onions, while Weiner and Simpson worked on the *Supplement* under Burchfield's direction.

elision. The process by which the sound of a letter or syllable in a word is suppressed or lost in speech, leading to an alteration of the word's spelling. For example, the letter 'v' has been dropped in some dialects of Scotland and northern England, producing vernacular spellings such as *deil* for 'devil', and the modern word 'hamper' is 'a phonetic reduction by elision' of the middle vowel of the obsolete form *hanaper*, a type of plate-basket. (Compare with ASSIMILATION.)

elliptical, -ly (*ellipt.*). Characterized by the process of ellipsis or 'leaving out' which, in general use, refers to the omission of a word or clause that is, grammatically speaking, necessary. For example, in the sentence 'she opened the Dictionary and read the definition', the subject 'she' is omitted, but understood, in the second clause. The *label *ellipt.* in the *OED*, however, is normally used to indicate that a familiar *combination is *colloquially referred to by its initial word as, for example, *symphony* for 'symphony orchestra', *shag* for 'shag carpet', or *Bermudas* for 'Bermuda shorts'. (Also compare with ABSOLUTE.)

English Dialect Society (E.D.S). Founded in Cambridge by Walter *Skeat in 1873 with the objective of promoting the study of English *dialects and of publishing editions of dialect word books and similar sources. The Society moved its headquarters to Manchester in 1876, and in 1893 to Oxford, where Joseph Wright served as secretary. Wright later became the editor of the *English Dialect Dictionary* (1896–1905), based on the Society's work. As founder and president of the Society, Skeat strongly supported Wright's lexicographical endeavours and was active in raising funds and even contributed his own money to support the dictionary. The *E.D.D.* remains the most comprehensive single source of information on regional use within the British Isles. It is frequently cited in the *OED* by title as a direct source (that is, a dictionary definition is quoted), or as the source of a secondary quotation (that is, a quotation taken from another source, used as an illustration in the *E.D.D.*, is quoted). Typically, a citation to a direct quotation from a dictionary entry reads in a similar fashion to the following example from the entry for 'boss-shot'—'**1898** *Eng. Dial. Dict.* s.v. A bad shot with a stone is called a boss-shot' (indicating that the quotation appears 'under the word', i.e., in the entry for, 'boss-shot' in the *E.D.D.*). Alternatively, a secondary quotation is often encountered in the form in which it appears in the entry for 'ringled' (marked by circular bands)—'**1899** *Shetl. News* 14 Oct. (E.D.D.) My blue an' rid ringl'd socks.'

The Society's editions of glossaries, dictionaries, etc. are also used as sources for *OED* quotations, many of which are followed by the organization's initials. The citation in the last quotation paragraph of the entry for 'vervain', beginning '**1548** TURNER *Names Herbes* (E.D.S.)', is typical of this type of reference. However, as with editions published by other similar organizations, some irregularities will be found in the way the editions are cited. Readers who are interested in establishing whether an E.D.S. edition was used are advised to consult the **Bibliography* in Volume XX (see also EARLY ENGLISH TEXT SOCIETY for comments on similar types of citations).

entry. The basic unit of a dictionary consisting of a headword in bold type, indicating the subject of the entry, followed by relevant information pertaining to it; also referred to as an 'article'. There are two types of entries in the *OED*: 1) the *main entry which documents, normally in *chronological order, the headword's origin and subsequent history both as to form and meaning, together with illustrative quotations; and, 2) the *cross-reference entry, the purpose of which is to direct the reader from an *obsolete form or *variant spelling of a headword to the appropriate main entry. There are over 290,500 entries defining over 500,000 words in the second edition, including some 60,000 cross-reference entries. The longest entry is for the verb '*set' which has more than 430 senses and sub-senses. (For a full explanation and examples of the structure and individual components of main and cross-reference entries, see Part I, as well as the entries in this section for each component, such as HEADWORD, PRONUNCIATION, ETYMOLOGY, etc.)

especially (*esp.*). A *label often found preceding a statement within a sense or *sub-sense which notes the context or circumstances in which the word form is most often applied. For example, the definition of 'afterthought' used colloquially is given as 'the youngest child in a family, *esp.* one born considerably later than the other children'. Less frequently, *esp.* is used as a label for a separate sub-sense when a word is used concurrently in both a broad and special sense or context, such as the word 'contract', referring to a mutual agreement or *esp.* to a business agreement, and the word 'torrid' applied *esp.* in the context of the phrase 'torrid zone'.

etymological note. A statement or paragraph in small print added to an etymology to provide supplementary information, usually of an unsubstantiated or speculative nature. For example, widely held 'folk' or popular theories of the origin of the word form under discussion may be cited and discounted, or possible explanations or associations, which cannot be clearly confirmed but which appear to be potentially valid may be offered (see p. 27 for examples.)

etymology. The process of tracing the origin or derivation of words or elements of words. The term is applied to both the discipline and its results. Thus, one may speak of the study of etymology in general, or the etymology of an individual word. In the *OED*, the etymology is that portion of an entry's *headword section enclosed in square brackets (p. 22).

Etymologies compiled for the first edition of the *OED* represented a significant step forward in the history of English *lexicography, which had remained attached to conjectural etymologies well into the nineteenth century, largely owing to the popularity of Horne *Tooke's philosophical *philology. Implicit in the new comparative philology was the recognition of a common ancestral *Indo-European language, of which the Germanic languages (including English) represent one branch. Although, in the late eighteenth century, the British orientalist William Jones had postulated the kinship of Sanskrit to Greek and Latin, it was only through the investigations of Danish and German scholars, such as Friedrich Schlegel, Rasmus Rask, Franz Bopp, and Jakob *Grimm that the comparative study of related languages was formalized.

Many members of the English *Philological Society, including *Skeat, who compiled *The Etymological Dictionary of the English Language* (1879–84), *Sweet, who had studied at Heidelberg, and the future *OED* editor James *Murray, strongly supported the new systematic and genealogical approach to the study of word origins. Skeat condemned methods which based etymologies on the resemblance of a form to that of a language with different phonetic laws as 'commonly a delusion', while Murray in his Romanes Lecture of 1900 referred contemptuously to 'the notion that derivations can be elaborated from one's own consciousness'. 'Etymology', he said, 'is simply Word-history, and Word-history, like all other history, is a record of the *facts*, not a fabric of conjectures as to what may have happened.' When the Society in 1858 drew up its original 'Lexicographic Creed' for a New English Dictionary, it noted a 'most pressing need' for the improvement of etymologies. However, in the negotiations with *Oxford University Press, the inclusion of etymologies became a contentious issue, partially because the Press had just agreed to publish Skeat's *Etymological Dictionary* and there was concern that the two publications might duplicate their coverage. The *Delegates of the Press suggested that etymologies should either be abbreviated or eliminated entirely from the Society's dictionary. From the point of view of Murray, who was negotiating for the editorship, the elimination of etymologies was unthinkable. Finally, a compromise proposed by *Müller was accepted. It was agreed that etymologies of non-native words should be traced to the foreign words or elements from which they were immediately adopted or formed, and native words to their earliest English form and, where possible, to their earliest Germanic form. Anything beyond that, it was argued, belonged to an etymological dictionary, not a historical dictionary of the English language. In practice, however, *OED* etymologies sometimes exceed these limitations, and, to the credit of the standards set by the Philological Society and by Murray in particular, most have stood the test of time.

euphemistically (*euphem.*). A *label applied to a word, phrase, or sense intended as an inoffensive or evasive substitute for an action, thing, or truth considered to be too blunt, unpleasant, or impolite to call by its common name. Since euphemisms abound and many are accepted as part of everyday language, the judgement as to what constitutes this form is somewhat subjective. The *OED* confines its occasional use of the term to obviously oblique references to such things as sexual intercourse ('a fate worse than death'), or criminal behaviour ('to find' or 'to help onself' for theft), or unpleasant truths such as death and dying ('to cross over') or, the dismissal or 'firing' of an employee ('to dehire'). As well as occurring as an italicized label, words 'used euphemistically' sometimes preface a definition involving an ironic reversal of meaning, for example, 'blessed' to mean 'cursed', 'holiday' for 'imprisonment'.

F

factitious word. See INVENTED WORD.

fascicles. The instalments of a book published in parts. The *OED* was originally issued in 125 paperbound fascicles (often spelled 'fascicules' in earlier references) over a period of forty-four years between 1884 and 1928. The first instalment of Volume I (A and B) covered the entries A–Ant. A list of fascicles according to the sections they covered and the dates at which they were ready for publication is given in Fig. 25. Each section was numbered as a 'part' of a volume, for example, 'VOL. III, PART I. E–EVERY', with the complete Volume III consisting of the letters D and E. All fascicles bear the title *A New English Dictionary on Historical Principles; Founded Mainly on the Materials Collected by The Philological Society*, although on the covers of fascicles issued from 1 Jan. 1895 onwards, the designation *The Oxford English Dictionary* appears above the title.

As a rule, fascicles were initially published in parts of 352 pages at a price of twelve shillings and sixpence each. Because of the length of time between publication of new sections, it was decided towards the end of 1894 to shorten the intervals by issuing sections containing sixty-four pages on the first day of each quarter. This policy was followed for the next twenty years (though occasionally a double section of 128 pages was issued on the quarter) until the First World War forced a reduction in staff. However, the larger twelve-and-sixpenny parts were still sometimes made available for the convenience of those who preferred them. For this reason, original sets of *OED* fascicles may vary in the number of volumes, depending on the individual subscriber's preference. The fascicles are of particular interest to anyone studying the history of the Dictionary because they contain editors' prefaces which are not available elsewhere. (The prefaces are reprinted in D. R. Raymond, *Dispatches from the Front* (1987).)

figurative, -ly (*fig.*). A *label applied to the use of a word or phrase in other than its literal or concrete sense in order to suggest a comparison, i.e., metaphorically. For example, the literal sense of the verb 'unspool' is to unwind (thread or tape), but it is used in a figurative sense in the quotation 'A new play . . . unspools inside Christopher's head'. Similarly, the use of 'cobweb' to refer to anything that is flimsy, frail, or insubstantial as in Tennyson's lines—'The questions men may try, The petty cobwebs we have spun'—is figurative. Many phrases are also figurative, such as the following employing the noun 'rope'—'to know the ropes', 'to give someone plenty of rope', or 'to come to the end of one's rope'.

It will be noted that a word or even a single sense is often employed both

Fascicles

The following list shows the parts or sections in which the Dictionary was originally published, the dates at which they were ready for publication, and how they were combined in the ten volumes of the finished work:

VOLUME I

A–Ant	January	1884
Anta–Battening	November	1885
Battenlie–Bozzom	March	1887
Bra–Byzen	June	1888

VOLUME II

C–Cassweed	June	1888
Cast–Clivy	November	1889
Cloaca–Consigner	October	1891
Consignificant–Crouching	May	1893
Crouchmas–Czech	November	1893

VOLUME III

D–Deceit	November	1894
Deceit–Deject	December	1894
Deject–Depravation	July	1895
Depravative–Development	September	1895
Development–Diffluency	December	1895
Diffluent–Disburden	June	1896
Disburdened–Disobservant	September	1896
Disobstetricate–Distrustful	December	1896
Distrustfully–Doom	March	1897
Doom–Dziggetai	July	1897
E–Every	July	1891
Everybody–Ezod	March	1894

VOLUME IV

F–Fang	November	1894
Fanged–Fee	April	1895
Fee–Field	September	1895
Field–Fish	March	1896
Fish–Flexuose	September	1896
Flexuosity–Foister	March	1897
Foisty–Frankish	October	1897
Franklaw–Gaincoming	January	1898
Gaincope–Germanizer	October	1898
German–Glass-cloth	March	1899
Glass-coach–Graded	January	1900
Gradely–Greement	July	1900
Green–Gyzzarn	December	1900

VOLUME V

H–Haversian	March	1898
Haversine–Heel	June	1898
Heel–Hod	December	1898
Hod–Horizontal	March	1899
Horizontally–Hywe	June	1899
I–In	October	1899
In–Inferred	March	1900
Inferrible–Inpushing	July	1900
Input–Invalid	October	1900
Invalid–Jew	December	1900
Jew–Kairine	June	1901
Kaiser–Kyx	October	1901

VOLUME VI

L–Lap	March	1901
Lap–Leisurely	January	1902
Leisureness–Lief	March	1902
Lief–Lock	January	1903
Lock–Lyyn	October	1903
M–Mandragon	October	1904
Mandragora–Matter	July	1905
Matter–Mesnalty	March	1906
Mesne–Misbirth	December	1906
Misbode–Monopoly	June	1907
Monopoly–Movement	March	1908
Movement–Myz	September	1908
N–Niche	September	1906
Niche–Nywe	September	1907

VOLUME VII

O–Onomastic	July	1902
Onomastical–Outing	March	1903
Outjet–Ozyat	January	1904
P–Pargeted	March	1904
Pargeter–Pennached	December	1904
Pennage–Pfennig	September	1905
Ph–Piper	June	1906
Piper–Polygenistic	March	1907
Polygenous–Premious	December	1907
Premisal–Prophesier	December	1908
Prophesy–Pyxis	September	1909

VOLUME VIII

Q	October	1902
R–Reactive	July	1903
Reactively–Ree	July	1904

Ree–Reign	March	1905
Reign–Reserve	January	1906
Reserve–Ribaldously	June	1908
Ribaldric–Romanite	March	1909
Romanity–Roundness	December	1909
Round-nosed–Ryze	March	1910
S–Sauce	June	1909
Sauce-alone–Scouring	June	1910
Scouring–Sedum	March	1911
See–Senatory	December	1911
Senatory–Several	September	1912
Several–Shaster	June	1913
Shastri–Shyster	March	1914
VOLUME IX		
Si–Simple	December	1910
Simple–Sleep	September	1911
Sleep–Sniggle	June	1912
Sniggle–Sorrow	March	1913
Sorrow–Speech	December	1913
Speech–Spring	September	1914
Spring–Standard	March	1915
Standard–Stead	September	1915
Stead–Stillatim	June	1916
Stillation–Stratum	December	1917
Stratus–Styx	September	1919
Su–Subterraneous	December	1914
Subterraneously–Sullen	December	1915
Sullen–Supple	January	1917
Supple–Sweep	March	1918
Sweep–Szmikite	September	1919
T–Tealt	September	1910
Team–Tezkere	June	1911
Th–Thyzle	March	1912
VOLUME X		
Ti–Tombac	December	1912
Tombal–Trahysh	September	1913
Traik–Trinity	June	1914
Trink–Turn-down	June	1915
Turndun–Tzirid	March	1916
U–Unforeseeable	October	1921
Unforeseeing–Unright	July	1924
Unright–Uzzle	July	1926
V–Verificative	October	1916
Verificatory–Visor	August	1917
Visor–Vywer	April	1920
W–Wash	October	1921
Wash–Wavy	May	1923
Wavy–Wezzon	August	1926
Wh–Whisking	May	1923
Whisking–Wilfulness	November	1924
Wilga–Wise	August	1926
Wise–Wyzen	April	1928
X Y Z	October	1921

Fig. 25

figuratively and in '*transferred' use (*transf.*). Sometimes a single quotation paragraph illustrates both usages and the distinction is normally apparent. For example, the quotation from Ogden Nash—'they will give you a look that implies that your spine is spaghetti and your soul is lard'—is clearly an example of the figurative use of the noun 'spaghetti'. In contrast, a quotation referring to the same word as a name for 'insulating tubing used over bare wire' illustrates the way in which the characteristic tubular form of spaghetti is applied in a 'transferred' or extended sense to wiring that resembles it.

floruit (fl.). In its abbreviated form, occasionally found preceding a date or a date range to indicate a period during which a person 'flourished', or is known to have been active (especially when precise dates of birth and death could not be established). For example, in the entry for the proper name 'Schrader', used in connection with air valves, the definition begins 'The name of George H. F. Schrader (fl. 1895) . . .'.

foreign script. In the first edition, foreign words cited in etymologies were printed, where appropriate, in non-roman script (for example, Arabic script, the Cyrillic alphabet, or the Hebrew alphabet), usually with transcriptions. In the **Supplement* (1972–86) and throughout the second edition, transliterations alone are used, except when Greek forms are cited. In quotations, however, a small number of characters from non-Roman alphabets, and a very few words made up of them (chiefly in Hebrew), are retained in keeping with the policy of reproducing the original source as precisely as possible.

foreign words. See ADAPTATION OF, ADOPTED FROM, NATURALIZED WORD.

formed on (f.). The abbreviation 'f.' occurs frequently in etymologies, since together with *adoption (a.) and *adaptation (ad.), new formation is one of the three primary ways in which words enter the English language. In this instance, words are formed by combining native or foreign elements, or a combination of both, consisting of existing words, *affixes, or other syllables which may not exist as separate words, but which carry meaning. Examples include the word 'roundish' in which the adjective 'round' is combined with the *suffix '-ish' (f. ROUND *a.* + -ISH), or 'television' in which the *combining form 'tele-' is attached to the noun 'vision' (f. TELE- + VISION *sb.*). Similarly, a foreign word may be combined with an affix, as in the case of 'rotate' which is formed on the Latin word *rota* meaning wheel, and the suffix '-ate' (f. L. *rota* wheel + -ATE). Alternatively, the formed word may be a *combination of two or more words, native or foreign, such as 'postman' (post + man), 'afternoon' (after + noon), or the *proprietary name 'Ouija', formed on two foreign words meaning 'yes' (the French *oui* and the German *ja*). Readers may also trace the origin of any English language components which are printed in small roman capitals, since the typography signifies a cross-reference, indicating that there is an entry for that element elsewhere in the Dictionary.

form-history. That part of an etymology, following information on the origin or derivation of a headword, which offers an explanation of special factors contributing to subsequent changes in the English word form. These may include contractions or corruptions derived from the word's usage in the spoken language, *metathesis, erroneous associations with other words (pseudo-etymological spellings), scribal errors, etc. All or part of the explanation may also be incorporated as supplementary information in an *etymological note (in smaller print). Examples of form-histories can be found in the etymologies of words such as 'purlieu', 'acton', 'equerry', 'cranny', 'periwinkle', and 'turmeric'. For instance, the form-history for 'equerry' notes that the surviving English form is due to an erroneous connection with the Latin word for horse (*equus*).

frequentative. A term used in etymologies to denote a verb or verbal form expressing a frequent or repeated action of a *root (or base) form. Typically, the literal sense of repetition is lost over time, and the new word comes to denote an independent mode of action in its own right. Such formations are commonly made by adding a frequentative *suffix, principally *-le* or *-er*, to an earlier simple word form or root. Examples of frequentative formations include words such as trample (from 'tramp'), jiggle (from 'jig'), curdle (from 'curd'), stutter (from 'stut', an obsolete verb with a similar meaning), linger (from 'leng', an obsolete verb meaning 'lengthen'), and crankle (from 'crank').

FURNIVALL, Frederick James (1825–1910). Scholar, editor, educator, and inveterate organizer. Furnivall became one of the two honorary secretaries of the *Philological Society in 1853 and sole secretary from 1862 until his death.

Although Furnivall was famous for his lack of tact and his impulsive and sometimes ill-advised actions, the *OED* owes a good share of its existence and survival to his persistence and energy. It is probable that Furnivall, in the spring of 1857, suggested to Richard Chenevix *Trench that the Society collect early words not recorded in contemporary dictionaries. As a result, an 'Unregistered Words Committee' was formed, consisting of Trench, Furnivall, and Herbert *Coleridge, with the objective of producing a supplement to existing dictionaries. Later in the same year, the Society decided to produce a complete New English Dictionary with Coleridge as editor, and to recruit volunteer readers to collect words and quotations. Following Coleridge's untimely death in 1861, Furnivall assumed the editorship. He immediately organized a group of sub-editors to handle *dictionary slips sent in by readers. Recognizing the shortage of readily available English literature, particularly from the *Old and *Middle English period, Furnivall created the *Early English Text Society in 1864, to publish modern editions of manuscripts and texts, in part to support the *reading programme. Motivated by his commitment to popular education, he later founded Chaucer, Shakespeare, Wyclif, Browning, and Shelley societies. Furnivall's ideas, however, sometimes exceeded his capacity to carry them through. The reading programme initially thrived, then lagged, and twenty years later, by the time it was agreed that *Oxford University Press would undertake the publication of a dictionary based on the Society's collection, the material was in a somewhat chaotic state.

Furnivall actively supported *Murray as editor, and over the years the two men shared their enthusiasm for, and dedication to, the Dictionary, although their personalities sometimes conflicted. Despite his eccentricities Furnivall's establishment of the Early English Text Society contributed immeasurably to the Dictionary. He also made a personal contribution of quotations from his morning and evening newspapers. As the 'Historical Introduction' to the Dictionary observes—'if the Dictionary at one period quotes the *Daily News* and at another the *Daily Chronicle*, it is because Furnivall had changed his paper in the meanwhile'.

Furnivall was still rowing on the Thames and sending his daily offering of quotations to the *OED* in his eighties. However, when it was found he had an incurable tumour, he wrote to Murray expressing regret that he would not live to see the Dictionary completed. Murray was shocked that their forty-year, somewhat tumultuous friendship was about to end, and typically responded—'Would it give you any satisfaction to see the gigantic *TAKE* in final? before it is too late?' The completed entry was the most appropriate gift he could think of for a man who had helped conceive the idea of the Dictionary and has supported it for over fifty years.

G

general, -ly (*gen.*). A *label normally found preceding the definition of a sense or *sub-sense to indicate a broadening of meaning. For example, the verb 'deforest' was used in an early legal sense to refer to the reduction of an area from the status of forest to ordinary land. Its second sense covers the later general use of the word to mean 'to clear or strip of forests or trees'. The label is also sometimes used to differentiate a meaning or sense from a more specific (*spec.*) use of a word. Both labels may appear within a single definition, or they may appear as separate sub-senses. For example, the term 'tariff-reform' is first defined in a *gen.* sense as 'reform of a tariff, or existing tariff conditions', and then in the *spec.* sense in which it is used in US politics.

In addition, *spec.* is sometimes used *within* a sense or sub-sense if the specific use is not established enough to merit separate treatment, or if the word is mainly applied in its specific sense as in the case of the noun 'meseta' which has a single sense defined as 'a plateau; *spec.* the high plateau of central Spain'.

Germanic. See TEUTONIC.

GIBBS, Henry Hucks, Lord Aldenham (1819–1907). Scholar, bibliophile, head of his family's banking firm, and a Director of the Bank of England. Gibbs was also an active member of the *Philological Society and one of the most competent sub-editors for its projected dictionary, as well as an editor of manuscripts for the *Early English Text Society. He continued his support of the Dictionary after James *Murray became editor, reading and annotating every proof until his death.

Murray not only sought Gibbs's advice on criteria for the Dictionary, but often turned to him when he was discouraged or angered by what he considered the unreasonable expectations of the *Delegates of the Oxford University Press. In fact, in the critical 1883–4 period, it is likely that Murray would have resigned without the support and sensible advice of Gibbs, who also used his influence and diplomacy to convince the Press to reconsider its demands and to resolve some of the editor's financial problems.

Murray acknowledged the contribution of Gibbs, whom he once called 'my best of friends', in the section *Plat-Premious* published in 1907, noting that 'the Dictionary was only one of many interests to which his sagacity and beneficence extended themselves; but he watched over its progress as assiduously as if it had been his only interest'.

grammatical label. See LABEL.

Greek-English Lexicon (1834). See LIDDELL & SCOTT.

Greek letters. See FOREIGN SCRIPT.

GRIMM, Jakob Ludwig Karl (1785–1863). German lexicographer, folklorist, and one of the founders of comparative *philology. This new scientific approach to language was later adopted by the *Philological Society and was a major impetus for their dictionary project.

Based partially on the work of the Danish philologist Rasmus Kristian Rask, and concurrent with the comparative studies of Franz Bopp, Grimm's four-volume *Deutsches Grammatik* (1819–37) identified regular shifts, later known as Grimm's Law, by which certain Germanic consonants developed from their *Indo-European forerunners. (See also ETYMOLOGY.) Grimm, together with his brother Wilhelm (1786–1859), was also responsible for initiating in 1851 the great historical dictionary of the German language from the fifteenth century onward, the *Deutsches Wörterbuch* (the first edition of which was completed in 1960). The dictionary was based on the *historical principles first stated by *Passow and later adopted by the *OED*. The Grimms' method of recruiting numerous volunteer readers to collect words and quotations was also a model for the *OED*.

Despite their major philological and lexicographical achievements, the brothers Grimm are perhaps best known to English readers for their ethnographic contribution, a collection of Germanic folktales, the *Kinder- und Hausmärchen* (1812–15), popularly translated as *Grimm's Fairy Tales*.

H

headword. The subject of a dictionary entry. In the *OED*, the headword may be a word, *phrase, *prefix, *suffix, *abbreviation, *variant form, or other lexical entity. All headwords in the second edition are printed in bold type and capitalized when it is normal practice to do so. This follows the convention established by the **Supplement* (1972–86), and differs from the first edition which made a distinction between main headwords, capitalized in heavy bold, and 'subordinate entry' headwords, consisting primarily of variant or obsolete forms, in lighter bold capitals. The headword is usually the most common form of a word in current use or the most typical of the later forms of an *obsolete word. (See also p. 16 and the section on 'Special Types of Main Entries', pp. 52–77, for examples of entries for headwords such as letters of the alphabet, acronyms, abbreviations, affixes, and combining forms.)

headword section. The term currently used to refer to that section of a Dictionary entry containing the headword, and, where applicable, information concerning the status of its usage in the language (*status symbol), pronunciation, parts of speech, *homonym number, special applications or status (*label), earlier or alternative *spellings (*variant forms), and origin, history, or *form-history (etymology). In other words, it is the part of an entry preceding the senses and quotations which describes the subject of an entry as a linguistic unit. (For an explanation of headword section elements and examples of how they are shown in the Dictionary, see pp. 13–27, as well as the separate entries in this part for each of the elements mentioned. Also compare with SIGNIFICATION and SENSE SECTION.)

HED. Abbreviation for *Historical English Dictionary*, an early form used for a number of years by the journal *Notes and Queries* to refer to the *OED*. The abbreviation never gained general currency. (See also *NEW ENGLISH DICTIONARY* (*NED*).)

historical principles. The *OED* is a *diachronic, or historical, dictionary since it is concerned not only with the current status of words, but with documenting their changes in form and meaning over time. The Dictionary's rationale and presentation is therefore consistent with the historical perspective of comparative *philology. The method used to illustrate these changes is the chronological and hierarchical documentation of *sense development, supported by illustrative quotations. Although compilers of earlier English language dictionaries such as *Johnson and *Richardson had employed quotations to illustrate the use of words, their work was based on somewhat primitive concepts of language development and even more questionable ideas of word derivation.

With the introduction of comparative philology in Europe, a 'scientific' approach to language was emphasized and in the early years of the nineteenth century was slowly adopted by English philologists. Probably the first comprehensive and most articulate statement on historical principles was made by the German scholar Franz *Passow in his essay *Über Zweck, Anlage, und Ergänzung griechischer Wörterbücher* in 1812. Passow stated that the history of each word should be set down in an orderly fashion, noting its origin and its changes in meaning and form, and when and how old meanings had been replaced by new. In contrast to the conventional approach to *lexicography, Passow urged that a historical dictionary should report accurately what was found; that is to say, it should be 'descriptive' in its coverage, rather than 'prescriptive'. Implicit in Pasow's principles was that usage, as illustrated by quotations from the literature, should dictate the chronological sequencing of a word's history. Passow incorporated his criteria in his *Handwörterbuch der griechischen Sprache* (Greek-German Lexicon), which was the basis of *Liddell & Scott's highly acclaimed *Greek-English Lexicon* (1843). Their work, as well as that of Jakob and Wilhelm *Grimm who had just begun to publish their great historical dictionary, the *Deutsches Wörterbuch*, was noted by Dean *Trench in his influential addresses to the *Philological Society in 1857. Trench emphasized the importance of descriptive historical principles and the use of volunteer readers (a method which was being employed by the Grimms) since the task of documenting the history of the English language was well beyond the scope of the lone lexicographer. As a result, the *OED* from its earliest beginnings was committed to these principles, as implied in the original title of the first edition, **A New English Dictionary on Historical Principles*, and in James *Murray's 'Introduction' which emphasized that each word should be 'made to exhibit its own history and meaning'. Thus quotations normally provide the basis for the *chronological arrangement of senses, except in a few instances, where *logical order (based on an assumption that the principles of language development suggest an order for which quotation evidence has not been discovered) is used (see SENSE DEVELOPMENT for a further explanation of chronological versus logical order).

homonym. A term used in *OED* entries in the special sense of a word which is spelled in exactly the same way as another word and is the same part of speech, but whose etymological history is different. For example, the noun 'mint' in the sense of an aromatic plant and the noun 'mint' meaning a place where money is coined have quite different origins, and are thus given separate entries in the Dictionary. The word 'homonym' is most often employed in the context of 'homonym number' which is the superior number, or superscript, attached to the part-of-speech designator (*sb.*[1], *v.*[3], etc.) or, in the case of some nouns, to the headword itself. Its purpose is to differentiate homonyms and to ensure that each has a unique 'address' which can be used as a reference to the particular entry which covers it. (For examples of usage of the homonym number, see p. 19.)

hyperbole. See INTENSIVE, JOCULAR.

hyphenation. The second edition of the *OED*, in contrast to the first edition and the **Supplement* (1972–86), is printed without line-end hyphenation, meaning that, in most cases, so-called 'soft' hyphens are not introduced to split a word at the end of a line of print in order to justify the right-hand margin. Only true or 'hard' hyphens (that is, hyphens which form part of the normal punctuation of the word form) are used, in order to avoid extraneous and potentially confusing hyphenation, particularly in the citing of various linguistic forms. In a few cases, it was unclear from the first edition and Supplements whether hyphens in quotations were hard or soft. Where a usage was doubtful, a special symbol (~) was employed to replace the hyphen in the parent text. In addition, the symbol is occasionally used to split a *combination or *derivative at a line break to indicate that the word is not normally written with a hyphen. (See also COMBINATION(S) for the use of hyphenation in words formed by the joining of two existing words.)

I

identification. The term used in the first edition to describe the elements of the *headword section, excluding the etymology. (Compare with SIGNIFICATION.)

idiom. See PHRASE.

imitative. See ECHOIC.

Indo-European. The family of languages of which most European and the majority of languages of northern India and Iran are members. The identification of linkages came through the recognition of systematic resemblances among the various members, and, specifically, similarities between Sanskrit and European languages. This eventually led to a hypothesis of the existence of a parent language, or common ancestor, referred to as '*Proto-Indo-European', of which no written record exists, but which has been painstakingly reconstructed by philologists and linguists on the evidence of descendant languages. Indo-European includes among its extant members Germanic (the branch to which English belongs and which is referred to in the *OED* as *Teutonic), Celtic, Italic (Romance languages), Hellenic (Greek), Balto-Slavic, and Indo-Iranian. The most frequently used term for this family, and its common ancestor language, in the *OED* is 'Aryan', which is limited in its application in modern scholarship to that branch of the family containing the Indian and Iranian languages (in accordance with the derivation of the word from Sanskrit *arya* and Old Persian *ariya*). The Dictionary often refers to this sub-group as 'Indo-Aryan'. The term 'Indo-Germanic' (also no longer used by scholars) to mean 'Indo-European' will also be encountered in some entries. (See also PHILOLOGY.)

inflection (generally *inflexion* in the *OED*—an older spelling). The modification of a word's form, usually by the addition of a *suffix, in order to express a grammatical relationship, such as number, tense, person, case, or gender. The most common English inflections are *-s* (or *-es*) added to a noun to create a plural and *-ed* added to a verb *stem to form the past tense and past participle. The word form that results from this process, such as 'cats' or 'dogs', and 'rained' or 'snowed', is referred to as an 'inflected form', although this term is also sometimes applied to the inflectional element or suffix itself. Inflection, however, may involve other kinds of changes to the stem, for example, 'he' to 'him' 'man' to 'men', or, in the case of an irregular verb, 'go' to 'went' and 'gone'. Unusual or irregular inflections for nouns (*substantives), verbs, and other grammatical categories are given in the *headword section, usually immediately following the part of speech. However, some word forms, such as verbs which have been in the language for a long time, may, historically, have had many inflectional forms, and the *OED* documents and illustrates the primary variants. For example, the first (**A**) grouping of the entry for the irregular verb 'say' is devoted to 'Inflexional Forms', divided into seven categories (*Infinitive, Indicative present, Indicative past, Subjunctive present, Imperative, Present participle, Past participle*), some of which, in turn, are subdivided into further headings, such as **a.** *1st person sing.*, **b.** *2nd person sing.*, etc. (See also REGULAR.)

Inflected forms should not be confused with *participial adjectives, *verbal substantives, or *derivatives which they often resemble in form, but not in function. The purpose of adding suffixes or making other form changes in these instances is typically to create an adjective from a verb, a noun from a verb, an adjective from a noun, and so forth. Note, therefore, that the entry for 'said' in the Dictionary is for the participial adjective (defining something named or mentioned previously), *not* for its use as the past tense of 'say'. While inflected forms do not normally warrant main entries, irregular or variant forms sometimes appear as *cross-reference entries, directing the reader to the entry for the relevant main word.

initialism. See ABBREVIATION.

integration. The process of combining the entries in the **Supplement* (1972–86) with those in the first edition of the *OED* in order to produce an amalgamated, alphabetically-arranged sequence of entries for the second edition. Much of this complex task, involving additions, deletions, substitutions, and transference of information, was, in the first instance, performed automatically by computer. Subsequent verification and emendation was done on paper by lexicographers, and the changes were then entered interactively on to the computer.

The editorial process involved a number of steps. Proofs of entries which had been modified in any way by the automatic integration were checked and marked up by lexicographers, and passed to keyboard operators who incorporated the necessary corrections. At this stage, numerous changes and additions, over and above those related to the integration process, were also made. Galley proofs were then generated, distributed to more than sixty proof-readers, and corrections were again made and checked by the editorial group. Once again, these were incorporated on magnetic tape and fully formatted page proofs were produced for checking, correcting, and production of the final proofs for printing and publication.

The meticulous checking and double-checking was necessary in order to cope with the various levels of integration and change. For example, there were two major categories of entries in the *Supplement*—entries that were completely new and independent without counterparts in the original edition, and entries which related in some fashion to existing entries in the *OED* proper. Midway between these two categories were a number of separate entries in the *Supplement* for *combinations and *derivatives which had originally been treated under their *root or main words. In the context of the *Supplement*, many of these words had reached independent status through increased usage or extended senses. It was therefore necessary to produce new entries for the second edition which transferred the older subordinated information and combined it with the more recent information. In other cases, some separate entries in the *Supplement* represented current spellings or more recent variants of a form which was the subject of an older entry, necessitating a change in the headword itself, or in its *form-history.

Entries that related to existing entries with directions to add, delete, or substitute new senses, more recent quotations, corrections, and a myriad of other instructions, all needed to be inserted in the proper place within the original entries, and any necessary adjustments made. For example, senses occasionally had to be renumbered, and new combinations and derivatives that were added to old entries had to be fitted into the correct alphabetical sequence in lists, with their supporting quotations integrated in proper chronological order. There were numerous deletions of items such as obsolete status *labels, or transference of labels to individual senses.

Finally, one of the most difficult tasks was to assure that the approximately 600,000 cross-references in the Dictionary were adjusted where necessary. This required changes to approximately 20,000 of the cross-references, including a few corrections to make references more precise.

intensive. A term applied to the use of word forms, senses, or phrases to intensify or exaggerate a statement. The adjective 'very' is a common example of an intensive. Adverbs such as 'devilishly', 'diabolically', 'terribly', 'awfully', 'terrifically', and 'dreadfully' are frequently used in an exaggerated way. The phrase 'armed to the teeth' is also intensive, and the compound word 'lifelong' is described as an 'emotional intensive' of 'long'. Some prefixes may function as intensives when attached to verbs. The prefix *be-*, for instance, is used as an intensive in words such as 'bedazzle' for 'dazzle' and 'bedrench' for 'drench'. (See also JOCULAR.)

intransitive (*intr.*). See TRANSITIVE.

invented word. A term sometimes applied, particularly in recent entries, to describe a word which is 'made up' or contrived. These include a few current *proprietary names such as 'Pyrex' and 'Xerox', as well as fanciful words such as 'schmoo' and 'Shazam'. A small number of words in the latter category are designated 'factitious' in older entries, especially some of Lewis Carroll's inventions, including 'chortle', 'frumious', 'tove', and 'wabe'. Occasional use of the term 'nonsense word' to describe forms such as 'eeny' (found in the first line of children's counting rhymes) and Edward Lear's 'runcible' will also be encountered. (Compare with NONCE-WORD and COINAGE.)

IPA (International Phonetic Alphabet/International Phonetic Association). The system used to transcribe pronunciation in the second edition of the Dictionary is the International Phonetic Alphabet devised by the International Phonetic Association. The organization was established in 1886. Although from its beginning the objective had been to devise an international alphabet to represent sounds in all languages, its earliest interests tended to be pedagogical, since a number of its original members were French nationals who were teaching English in their own country. Included in their number was Paul Passy whose leadership was instrumental in the group's founding. However, the Association also attracted many prominent international scholars, including a number of men, such as *Sweet and *Müller, who later played key roles in decisions relating to the *OED*. Melville Bell, whose system of 'Visible Speech' helped foster James *Murray's interest in phonetics, and Otto Jespersen were also among the leading members. By 1891, the Association's interests were almost wholly directed to phonetics rather than teaching.

By the time the Association was founded, individual sounds had already been quite effectively represented in phonetic alphabets devised by Isaac Pitman (best known, perhaps, for his shorthand system based on the phonetic analysis of speech sounds), Ellis, and Sweet. As early as 1888 the Association formulated six basic principles, most of which have been adhered to over the years. These included the use of a separate sign for each distinctive sound and the same sign for the same sound across all languages, the employment of ordinary letters of the Roman alphabet to the greatest extent possible, the criterion that any necessary new letters should suggest their sound by their resemblance to existing letters, and the avoidance of *diacritics. An early form of IPA was based on Sweet's 'Broad Romic', although it also drew on Ellis's 1870 'Glossic' and Pitman's 1876 alphabet. Since that time, the IPA has undergone a number of changes and gained increasing acceptance for use in teaching, in research, and in dictionaries.

One of its earliest uses in dictionaries was in the *Phonetic Dictionary of the English Language* (1913), compiled by H. Michaelis and Daniel Jones, and in the latter's well-known *English Pronouncing Dictionary* (1917). Since the publication of the second edition of the *OED* in which Murray's system of pronunciation was converted to IPA, the latter is now used in almost all English language dictionaries published by the Oxford University Press, where pronunciation is given. (See also PRONUNCIATION and, for a history of the IPA and its predecessors, refer to R. W. Albright, *The International Phonetic Alphabet; its backgrounds and development* (1958).)

irregular (irreg.). See REGULAR.

J

jocular, -ly (*joc.*). A number of descriptors or *labels are used to describe words or senses which are either deliberately humorous in themselves, such as 'made-up' words like 'artsy-craftsy', 'splendiferous', or 'telephonitis', or which are used out of their normal context, such as 'press-gang' to refer to a group of journalists. The term most frequently applied to this kind of usage is 'jocular, -ly', or the label *joc.* The label *facetious, -ly* is similarly attached to senses of words such as the adjective 'blushing' used 'often somewhat facetiously with "bride"'. 'Jocular' may also appear in the phrase 'in jocular hyperbole', indicating an exaggerated use of language, such as 'fiend' to describe a person causing mischief or annoyance, or the verb 'melt' to describe suffering from extreme heat (see also INTENSIVE). There are also a number of other terms specifying the type of humour intended, including 'ironic, -al' and 'sarcastic, -ally' which normally refer to the use of a word to imply its opposite, e.g., the application of adjectives such as 'charming' or 'eminent' to ridicule rather than compliment. Since humour frequently mocks, or scoffs at, its target, phrases such as 'humorous or derisive', 'derisive or playful', 'ironical or derisive' will be encountered. More deliberately offensive or biased attempts to express humour will be found with designators such as 'derisive or hostile use' and 'opprobrious, -ly' (see also TABOO AND OFFENSIVE LANGUAGE).

JOHNSON, Samuel (1709–84). Lexicographer and prominent eighteenth-century man of letters, whose life, achievements, eccentricities, and wit were minutely chronicled by his biographer, James Boswell. Although he was responsible for a variety of works including biographies, journal articles, essays, political pamphlets, and an edition of Shakespeare's works, he is perhaps best remembered today for his *Dictionary of the English Language*.

There was a strong movement in the eighteenth century to produce a 'standard' dictionary of English to register proper usage, as it was generally thought that the language had come to its full flowering. To this end, a syndicate of five booksellers contracted with Johnson in 1746 to produce a dictionary. Johnson drew up a highly prescriptive and ambitious *Plan of a Dictionary of the English Language*, which was published in 1747. While the document showed a far greater grasp of lexicographical problems than might be expected of a writer without experience in dictionary-making, a number of Johnson's goals proved unworkable in practice. Notable among these was his proposal that language should be 'fixed' or standardized to preserve its 'purity', a view not unlike that espoused by the French Academy and, incidentally, by Lord Chesterfield, the potential patron to whom the *Plan* was addressed. Johnson later reversed this view, albeit somewhat ambiguously. In the preface to his *Dictionary*, he expresses the hope that 'the spirit of English liberty' will 'hinder or destroy' an academy on the French model. At the same time, he urges that, if such a body were to be created, it should endeavour to stop translators who inevitably, he maintains, introduce foreign terms that corrupt the native language.

Johnson's contract called for the production of the dictionary in three years, but, with the aid of several assistants, the work, which defined 40,000 words, eventually took nine years to complete and was published in two folio volumes in 1755. Its numerous quotations were mainly drawn from books in Johnson's own library which he underlined and gave to his assistants to copy. No writers prior to the sixteenth century were quoted, and dates and titles of works were usually omitted. The dictionary, which was extremely popular on both sides of the Atlantic well into the nineteenth century, went through a number of editions and printings. After Johnson's death, it was revised by Henry John Todd in 1818 and again in 1827. The work was authoritative and unabashedly 'literary' and its shortcomings, as well as its merits, served as a benchmark for subsequent lexicographers. It provided *Webster with the incentive to produce a similarly authoritative American dictionary, but one which would have a much wider coverage of the popular language of commerce and business (which Johnson referred to as 'fugitive cant'), science, and other areas that Johnson omitted. *Richardson, on the other hand, considerably expanded Johnson's use of quotations to include those from earlier writers. The initiators of the *OED*, while appreciating the usefulness of Johnson's division of word senses and his employment of 'Examples from the Best Writers' to illustrate them, saw the need to reject his notion of a dictionary as a means of teaching 'correct' usage in favour of a historical and non-judgemental approach, as well as to employ numerous volunteers to undertake reading on a much wider and more systematic scale. Nevertheless, Johnson's *Dictionary* remains a remarkable work that can still be enjoyed for its definitions as well as for the obvious biases and humour of its compiler.

L

label. An italicized designation, often abbreviated, that informs the reader of the boundaries within which a word or sense is used. In *OED* terminology, the five primary categories of labels are *status*, *regional*, *grammatical*, *semantic*, and *subject*. A *status* label identifies a word or sense that either deviates in some way from, or is not a part of, current standard usage, or is no longer used at all. Terms such as *obsolete (*Obs.*) and *colloquial (*colloq.*) are examples of status labels. A *regional* label such as *Austral.*, *U.S.*, indicates that use is confined to a particular geographical area. A grammatical label describes the syntactical role of a word or sense, such as plural (*pl.*), *collective (*collect.*), or *attributive (*attrib.*). The fourth category, *semantic*, specifies how the meaning of a word or sense is to be interpreted within a particular context, that is, whether its use is *figurative (*fig.*), *specific (*spec.*), *transferred (*transf.*), etc. Finally, subject labels such as Music (*Mus.*) or Chemistry (*Chem.*), describe the form's use within the context of a particular profession, trade, or interest (see also p. 19 for further examples).

Readers should realize that subject labels will be found to have varying degrees of specificity, largely due to historical changes in terminology and increased specialization within disciplines. For example, Natural History (*Nat. Hist.*) is a label that is used quite extensively in the Dictionary, but as a single discipline it has been largely superseded and subdivided. Such labels, however, should be considered within the context of the chronological period illustrated by the quotations.

Latin (L.). References found, principally in etymologies, to Latin as a language have a number of variations. In general, Latin (L.) alone, and Classical Latin (cl.L. or classical L.) refer to the language down to approximately A.D. 200; Late Latin (late L.) extends from around 200 to 600; Mediaeval Latin (med.L. or med.Latin) from 600 to 1500; and Modern Latin (mod.L. or mod.Latin) from roughly 1500 onwards. In addition to identification by time periods, the language is frequently classed by type, such as Popular Latin (pop.L. or popular L.), vulgar Latin (vulg.L. or vulgar L.), ecclesiastical Latin (eccl.L.), and Christian Latin (Chr.L. or Christian L.). The terms 'popular' and 'vulgar' refer to the language as spoken by the common or ordinary people as opposed to the formal, written language. Christian Latin usually refers to early forms adopted from the Greek, while ecclesiastical Latin encompasses terms developed at a later period in Church history. Note also that the above examples of abbreviations are those most frequently used, but other variations may be encountered.

lexicography. The art, craft, and science of compiling dictionaries. The two editions of the *OED* represent significant milestones in English lexicography—the first because of its comprehensive documentation of the history of the English language, and the second because it combines traditional lexicographical skills with the potential of a constantly updated electronic database.

English lexicography had its foundations in glosses, the notations that scholars added to manuscripts to explain difficult terms. These notes were often collected in 'glossaries' which, in turn, led to the bilingual Latin-English and French-English dictionaries of the fifteenth century. It was not until the sixteenth century that a need was recognized for dictionaries to explain English words in English, although initially they often contained only 'hard words' and were intended for users such as 'the more-knowing Women, and less-knowing Men', as Blount said in the introduction to his 1656 dictionary.

The eighteenth century marks the beginning of modern lexicography and the publication of increasingly comprehensive dictionaries defining both common and difficult words. The best known of the eighteenth-century lexicographers is undoubtedly Dr Samuel *Johnson, whose idiosyncratic *Dictionary* (1755), with 40,000 headwords, was compiled in just nine years. It was notable for its inclusion of many illustrative literary quotations, although Johnson often depended on his memory, which was occasionally faulty. As with other English dictionaries of the period preceding the *OED*, including *Webster's major 70,000-word *An American Dictionary of the English Language* (1828) and *Richardson's *A New Dictionary of the English Language* (1837), etymologies were often conjectural. Webster, however, was notable for his comprehensiveness and the quality of his definitions, and Richardson for his attempt to compile a dictionary containing a vast number of historical quotations dating back to the fourteenth century. Dean *Trench in his highly influential addresses (*On Some Deficiencies in Our English Dictionaries*) to the Philological Society in 1857 used both the strengths and weaknesses of these dictionaries to provide a model for the future *OED*. A second major influence, acknowledged by Trench, were the '*historical principles' of lexicography defined in an 1812 essay by the German scholar Franz *Passow, together with the recognition of the *Indo-European family of languages and a more scientific and factual approach to etymology.

The *OED* became, and remains, the most comprehensive and complete record of the usage and meaning of the English language from the twelfth century until the present day. The task of maintaining and augmenting this storehouse has been vastly aided by the computer, which not only creates a lexicographical database for revision and updating, but also enables lexicographers to search other full text databases that record the use of language (see DATABASE, NEW OED PROJECT).

library research. The process of checking, verifying, and, where necessary, augmenting quotations in order to illustrate fully the sequence of development of a word or sense, or of obtaining further information for definitions, etymologies, and other entry components, by the use of both in-house and external library resources.

When the editorial offices were re-established for the **Supplement* (1972–86), one important objective was to build up a library, consisting of reference books such as dictionaries and other texts relating to language, as well as copies of many of the general books and other material read for the quotation files. This collection is the first resource checked by the lexicographer, but frequently, given that the potential research material is the entire body of works published in English, it is necessary to call on the services of the library network established for that purpose. The *OED* employs staff and freelance library researchers in the Bodleian Library at Oxford, and also in major library and bibliographical centres such as London, Washington, New York, and Boston. In addition, it maintains links with language centres in other English-speaking countries such as Australia, Canada, and New Zealand.

The library researchers' work includes a range of complex tasks such as verifying the accuracy of quotations, converting references from a later edition to a first edition, confirming publication details, *antedating (or postdating) quotations, and checking the linguistic origins, pronunciation, or exact meaning of a word form. The work is seldom routine and requires an expert knowledge of resources and subjects, combined with resourcefulness and imagination. (See also READING PROGRAMME.)

Liddell & Scott. The name usually given to the *Greek-English Lexicon* (1843), compiled by Henry Liddell (1811–98) and Robert Scott (1811–87).

The *Lexicon* was notable not only for its importance to classical studies, but also because it was based on the Greek-German Lexicon compiled by the German scholar Franz *Passow. Passow's name, in fact, appeared on the title page of the first three editions of the *Lexicon*, but was omitted in the later editions since they represented a considerable expansion of his original work. The *Lexicon* was the first dictionary published in England that embodied Passow's *historical principles of lexicography which later influenced the format adopted by the *OED*. The *Lexicon* underwent eight revisions during Liddell's lifetime, and was extensively revised from 1925 to 1940 when the ninth edition was published.

ligature. A typographical symbol representing a single sound and consisting of two letters joined together. Examples include the ligatures æ and œ, employed in some words, for the Latin *diphthongs 'ae' and 'oe'. In general, the *OED* adopts a conservative policy and uses ligatures for words of Latin or Greek origin which are not fully *naturalized, for some *scientific and technical terms, and for a few classical Greek and Latin proper names where usage favours retaining the symbol.

loanword. See NATURALIZED WORD.

logical order. An alternative method (as compared to the usual *chronological order) for ordering senses within an entry. See SENSE DEVELOPMENT.

M

machine-readable. A term used to describe data or text which is encoded in electronic form in order for it to be processed by a computer. In the case of the *OED*, the text was initially converted by a key-to-tape system in which each character manually typed (in computer terms, 'keyboarded' or 'keyed in') by operators was magnetically recorded on tape. This encoding can then be 'read' and processed as electrical impulses, and used to re-create the original input for editing, searching, or printing. (See also DATABASE and NEW OED PROJECT.)

main entry. An entry which contains the complete information about its headword's history and meaning, as opposed to a *cross-reference entry. The subject of a main entry is sometimes referred to as a 'main headword' or 'main word', in particular to distinguish it from its *derivatives, *combinations, or from *phrases incorporating its use, which may also be included and defined within the same entry.

MAX-MÜLLER, Friedrich. See MÜLLER, FRIEDRICH MAX.

metathesis. A term that refers to the transposition of successive sounds in the course of the development of a word. Examples include 'dirt', 'bird', 'third', from *Middle English *drit, bridde*, and *thridde*, and Modern and Middle English 'tusk' from the *Old English *tux*.

metonym, -y. Occasionally used to refer to the use of a word in a particular type of *transferred sense, when the name of an attribute or adjunct is substituted for the thing meant. For example, the word 'palace' can be used to denote the monarch. Similarly, the Quai d'Orsay, the name of a Paris embankment, is used to refer to the French Ministry of Foreign Affairs whose offices are located there.

Middle English (ME.). The language of England from approximately 1150 to 1500. The reign of Henry III (1216–71) was often taken, particularly in the nineteenth century, to have marked the 'revival' of the native language (see OLD ENGLISH). In fact, the latter had continued to be widely spoken; the major change in the thirteenth century was one of status and acceptance rather than revival. The French legacy of the Norman Conquest is increasingly apparent in written Middle English with the gradual adaptation of many French words and spelling conventions to replace outmoded Old English words and forms. Thus, by the end of the Middle English period, the vocabulary and spelling of the language had undergone a marked change. However, Middle English, both in its written and spoken form, also varied widely from one region of the country to another. The numerous dialects account for the number of *variant forms recorded for that period since, until the end of the fifteenth century, all such forms are considered by the Dictionary as having a literary standing (see also DIALECT). It was not until after the invention of printing and the beginning of the *Modern English period that the language became more standardized, at least in its written and printed form, although spoken English continued to diversify.

The *OED* sometimes further defines the Middle English forms as 'Early' or 'Late'. As noted in the 'General Explanations' in Volume I, the thirteenth century is considered Early Middle English, the fourteenth century as Late Middle English, with the fifteenth century identified as 'Middle English Transition'.

MINOR, William Chester (1835–1920). American physician and a principal contributor of quotations to the first edition of the Dictionary. Minor had served as a surgeon-captain in the Northern army during the American Civil War, but had a history of mental instability. His persistent delusion was that unknown persons were attempting to injure him, and, during a trip to England in 1872, he shot and killed a man, apparently in the belief that he was being threatened. He was committed to Broadmoor Criminal Lunatic Asylum where he remained for the next thirty-eight years. He was allowed to have his own room and to buy books, and was obviously a man of considerable intellectual ability. His particular scholarly interest was sixteenth- and seventeenth-century literature, which he systematically read and from which he extracted numerous words and quotations for the *OED*. Although ill-health forced Minor to give up his Dictionary reading in 1902, James *Murray, who knew his story, continued to be concerned for him. When in 1910, Minor, at the request of his family, was permitted to return to America, Murray and his wife went to Broadmoor to bid him farewell. Minor spent the remainder of his life in custody in Washington.

The story of the unfortunate doctor and his initial meeting with Murray has been somewhat romanticized, in particular as a result of an inaccurate article by an American journalist, Hayden Church, which appeared in the *Strand Magazine* in 1915. Church maintained that Murray had invited Dr Minor to a Dictionary Dinner in 1902. Minor refused the invitation, pleading illness, but he invited the editor to visit him in Berkshire. Upon his arrival by train, the story continued, Murray found a handsome liveried carriage awaiting him and he was subsequently delivered to a large country house. It was only when he entered and was met by a gentleman who identified himself as the Governor of Broadmoor that the astonished editor, according to Church, learned that Minor was an inmate of an asylum. The article was strongly condemned by Henry *Bradley in a letter to the *Daily Telegraph* (8 Sept. 1915) in which he stated:

> 'The article contains several misstatements of fact, the correction of which will considerably reduce the sensational effectiveness of the narrative. Dr. Minor . . . was simply a man of education and literary tastes, whom his enforced leisure and the possession of a library, including many out-of-the-way books, enabled to contribute an extraordinary number of quotations to the Dictionary. . . . The story of Dr. Murray's first interview with Dr. Minor is, so far as its most romantic features are concerned, a fiction.'

However, despite Bradley's matter-of-fact account and his tactful reference to the doctor's 'enforced leisure', Minor himself remains as an interesting, and tragic, figure in the *OED*'s history.

modern (mod.). An abbreviation widely used in the Dictionary either as a descriptor or qualifier (mod. science, mod. Gr., mod. dialect, etc.) in the obvious sense of identifying the relative currency of a word's use or meaning. However, it is also used in a special context in quotations within entries compiled for the first edition. The abbreviation 'mod.' in these instances implies that the word was known to be in current use, but since no recent quotation could be located, the editor devised an appropriate sentence. Normally no date is given, although when the 'quotation' is no longer the most recent, the date of the *fascicle in which it appeared has been inserted. *Mod.* is also used in the same way in the phrase *Mod. Prov.* (Modern Proverb) in the second edition when a well-known saying is quoted that was not located in a printed source.

In addition, 'mod.' is occasionally encountered in the context of 'in mod. Dicts.' (in modern Dictionaries) in quotation paragraphs. This reference informs the reader that the word or sense under discussion was located in these sources. However, since the phrase was used only within entries for the first edition, the word 'modern' should be interpreted as referring to the immediate nineteenth-century predecessors of the *OED* (see also DICTIONARIES, EARLIER).

Modern English. A term generally applied to the language from approximately the end of the fifteenth century onwards.

In the Dictionary's introductory 'General Explanations', Modern English is categorized by centuries with the sixteenth century designated as Early Modern (or Tudor), the seventeenth as Middle Modern English, and the eighteenth century onwards as Recent English.

modern formation (*mod. f.*). A *label originally assigned to words of modern origin that have common forms in English and one or more Continental languages and where it is uncertain in which language the word was first used. A number of *scientific and technical terms fall into this category. If the first appearance seems to have been in a foreign language, this information is normally given in the etymology. For example, the counterpart of the English word 'terminology' was used in German in 1786 according to its etymology, although the first recorded appearance located in English, as shown in the illustrative quotations which follow, was in 1801. The implication is that the word may have been in use in scientific circles prior to its recorded English usage. However, there are times when a new word has immediate international currency and it would be difficult to ascribe a definite language of origin. (See also COINAGE.)

modern Latin (mod.L.). See LATIN.

MÜLLER, Friedrich Max (1823–1900). Philologist, orientalist, prolific writer, and an influential *Delegate of *Oxford University Press at the time of the *OED*'s inception. Müller was born in Dessau, Germany and attended the University of Leipzig, where he studied a range of subjects, including the classics, modern languages, and, in particular, the languages of ancient India. By the age of twenty, he had earned a Ph.D. and translated a major collection of Sanskrit fables. He later studied under Franz Bopp and became an ardent supporter of the new comparative *philology which Bopp had helped to develop.

In 1845 Müller spent time in Paris, and in 1848 he settled in Oxford as professor of modern European languages and later as a curator of the Bodleian Library. His primary interest, however, was Sanskrit and he produced his *History of Ancient Sanskrit Literature* in 1859. He turned his attention to comparative philology when he failed to secure a vacant chair in Sanskrit (largely, it is said, for political reasons) in 1860. Subsequently, Müller gained considerable recognition for his writings and lectures in comparative philology, and in 1868 he was awarded a new chair in the subject, created in his honour. He retired from the position in 1875 to initiate one of his major projects, the editorship of the fifty-two volumes of *The Sacred Books of the East*, published by Oxford University Press.

As a Delegate of the Press who was involved in decisions regarding the *OED*, and as a respected member of the *Philological Society, Müller's opinions carried considerable weight. Initially, his scepticism about the inclusion of etymologies in the Society's projected Dictionary caused James *Murray considerable concern. In the final negotiations, however, it was Müller who suggested a compromise which resolved the conflict between the Delegates and the Dictionary's prospective editor.

MURRAY, James Augustus Henry (1837–1915). Lexicographer and principal editor of the *OED* from 1879 until his death. Murray was responsible for providing the original model and setting the standards for the Dictionary, as well as for personally editing half of the first edition.

Born in the Scottish border village of Denholm, Murray was the eldest of five children of a tailor. He attended parish schools until he was fourteen, after which he embarked on a remarkable programme of self-education. For ten years from the age of seventeen, he was employed as a schoolmaster in nearby Hawick. His early pursuits included natural history and archaeology. His interest in languages (he could read 'in a sort of way' twenty-five or more), and his own native dialect, attracted him to *philology.

In 1864, aged twenty-seven, he took a post in London as a bank clerk, in order to find a milder climate for his consumptive wife, Maggie Scott, whom he had married in 1862. A child, born in 1864, died when only eight months old and Maggie herself passed away the next year. Murray's second marriage, to Ada Ruthven, proved a happier union. It ultimately produced eleven healthy children, and incidentally, provided a steady stream of 'child labour' to alphabetize *Dictionary slips.

Although the bank position was unrewarding, Murray, through his membership of the *Philological Society and its publication of his book *The Dialect of the Southern Counties of Scotland* (1868), made many important scholarly contacts in his six years in London, including *Sweet, *Furnivall, *Skeat, and *Gibbs. He also edited texts for the *Early English Text Society.

In 1870, Murray returned to his first career as schoolmaster at Mill Hill School near London, while continuing his philological interests. In the spring of 1876, at the suggestion of the Philological Society, the publishers

Macmillan asked Murray to edit a proposed new standard English dictionary. Discussions eventually centred on using the Society's material for the project. When these negotiations broke down, the Society wrote to *Oxford University Press documenting its terms for making its collected material available for the publication of a dictionary and suggesting James Murray as editor. After much hesitation and considerable misgivings owing to disagreements about criteria for the Dictionary, Murray signed an agreement with the Clarendon Press (see OXFORD UNIVERSITY PRESS) on 1 March 1879. Based on assurances that half of the Society's material was ready for publication, the contract called for a 7,000-page, four-volume dictionary to be completed in ten years. Murray's initial act was to have a corrugated iron workroom (dubbed the '*Scriptorium') built adjacent to his Mill Hill home equipped with pigeon-holes to hold the two tons of quotations collected by the Philological Society. To these were eventually added Dictionary slips generated by a new volunteer *reading programme that Murray initiated after seeing the gaps and errors in the Society's material. The programme added greatly to his work and by 1883, it was apparent to all that the original estimate was unrealistic (the first part, *A-Ant*, of Volume I was not published until January 1884). Confrontations with the *Delegates, the governing body of the Press, almost led to his resignation as editor, but eventually, after further negotiations about finances, Murray gave up his position at Mill Hill in 1885 and moved to Oxford to devote himself full-time to the Dictionary. In 1886, *Bradley was hired to assist with *B* and in 1888 was appointed second editor.

Even with Bradley's help, the output demanded by the Press, which once threatened cessation of publication, was exhausting. Finally, by 1896 the Press resigned itself to a target of publishing 64-page quarterly sections. In 1901, *Craigie was appointed third editor, and in 1914 *Onions became fourth editor. By the turn of the century, Murray was widely recognized for his work, having received numerous honorary doctorates, and a knighthood in 1908.

Murray maintained his astonishing intellectual and physical vigour, his humour, his enthusiasm, and his capacity for work almost to the end of his life. His conviction that he was fulfilling God's purpose and that his work would stand for all time sustained him through many difficult periods. He had hoped to live to be eighty when he estimated the dictionary would be completed, but it was not to be. In 1914, after being treated for cancer, he recovered sufficiently to complete the letter *T*. Shortly after, however, he contracted pleurisy and died of heart failure on 26 July 1915. James Murray's life and the early history of the Dictionary is vividly documented in *Caught in the Web of Words* (1977), written by his granddaughter K. M. E. Murray.

N

native word. A descriptive term applied to words of direct Germanic (*Teutonic) descent which are usually traced in *OED* etymologies to their *Old English form, along with relevant equivalents in other Germanic languages. (Compare with the following entry for NATURALIZED WORD.)

naturalized word. Non-native words which are used in the English language are broadly classed as either naturalized, or partially naturalized or non-naturalized. Naturalized words are those which have been fully integrated, in terms of spelling and pronunciation, into the language and include common words such as 'inch', 'orange', 'cat', and 'street'. Some naturalized forms are *adopted without any major change from a foreign language and used as English words, while others are *adaptations, that is, they have been modified to conform to English word structure, as in the case of many Latin or Greek *stems to which English endings have been added. *Murray categorized fully naturalized words and native words as 'naturals'.

The second category, consisting of partially naturalized or non-naturalized words, retains some aspect of 'foreignness'. Murray proposed a further breakdown of this class into denizens, aliens, and casuals, although such distinctions are difficult and subject to change over time. Denizens were classed as words which are fully naturalized as to use, but not as to form, *inflection, or pronunciation. Aliens include names of foreign objects, titles, etc. for which there are no English equivalents. Finally, casuals were identified as foreign words which are not in habitual use, but are used for special purposes such as references in travel books. Except for the mention of these classes in the original explanations, the Dictionary does not attempt to differentiate them, but it does identify the broad category of non-naturalized words by prefacing them with a *status symbol in the form of parallels or 'tramlines' (‖). (p. 16)

NED. See *NEW ENGLISH DICTIONARY.*

neologism. See NEW WORDS.

New English Dictionary (NED). The *OED*'s original, separately published parts or *fascicles and the first printing of the complete Dictionary in 1928 carried the title *A New English Dictionary on Historical Principles*, followed by the statement 'Founded mainly on the materials collected by the Philological Society'. The title was changed to the *Oxford English Dictionary* when the Dictionary was reissued with a one-volume supplement in 1933, although the words 'Oxford English Dictionary' had appeared above the *NED* title on the cover of fascicles beginning with the issue of 1 January 1895.

The initials '*N.E.D.*', together with a date, are occasionally attached to etymologies or definitions in the second edition, when a phrase such as 'at present' or 'recent' is used. The date, which is that of the original fascicle in which the statement appeared, e.g., 1910, alerts the reader to the context in which the statement was originally made. This convention is followed when it is felt that the contemporary comment or opinion may give the reader useful or interesting information that would not otherwise be available. Another instance of an '*N.E.D.*' reference is when the oldest located use of a word appeared within the text of the first edition, for example, in a definition or etymology of another word. Thus the Dictionary is used as a source in the same way as any other text.

New OED Project. A project encompassing the conversion of the *OED* to *machine-readable form, the *integration of the first edition and the **Supplement*, the development of a *database, the scheduling and production of the second edition in its print and electronic forms, and the planning of necessary revisions and updates to produce interim publications and, ultimately, a revised edition.

The New OED Project at *Oxford University Press was initiated in 1982, before the completion of the four-volume *Supplement*, in recognition of the need to consider the future of the Dictionary. Several major issues had to be addressed. First, it was obvious that to continue to issue supplements was an unsatisfactory solution for both editors and readers. Secondly, the first edition and the *Supplement* volumes had been typeset in hot metal. Not only had the old plates for the first edition deteriorated, but new computer-driven printing processes called for text in machine-readable form. Although conversion of the *OED* text was an immense undertaking, the advantages were many. Once the text was converted, or 'captured', in this form, it could be used not only for printing purposes, but also to create a database that could be constantly updated and revised. It could also serve as the basis for developing computer software to search the Dictionary, both for editorial purposes and for *OED* users in general if the Dictionary was made available in one or more electronic forms.

Once the feasibility of such an undertaking was established, a project team was set up to identify institutions or individuals interested in participating in the computerization and merging of the two texts. By early 1984, three partners had been selected. International Computaprint Corporation (ICC), a subsidiary of Reed International located in Fort Washington, Pennsylvania, was selected to convert the Dictionary to machine-readable form by keyboarding the two texts. IBM United Kingdom Ltd. undertook to supply computer hardware and three systems personnel to assist the Press's Computer Group to design software for amalgamating the two texts into one, and, in Canada, the University of Waterloo in Ontario was chosen to design a database system suitable for searching and for distribution in electronic form.

Rigorous planning was necessary to complete Phase I of the project (publication of the second edition) by the target date of 1989. In just eighteen months, both texts, containing some 350 million characters, were keyed in by ICC's team of keyboarders. Not only did these operators type the entire text, they also inserted identifiers, referred to as 'tags', to indicate the various typefaces used in the Dictionary, as well as fifteen of its most frequently occurring structural elements. With data capture under way, a team of freelance proof-readers was recruited at Oxford to check the copy generated from the magnetic tapes that ICC sent at regular intervals. By June 1986, the text had been entered into the computer and proofed.

In the meantime, computer equipment had been installed and once the text was captured electronically, it was loaded on to an IBM 4341 mainframe computer at OUP. It was decided to transform the text to conform in principle with a system known as SGML (Standard Generalized Mark-up Language), in which text is identified by its function, not simply its printed appearance. This required identifying the structural elements within Dictionary entries, following which the text was analysed automatically by tools created by computer scientists at the University of Waterloo. This process resulted in the conversion of most of the typographical coding previously inserted by the keyboarders, and also added a great many new tags, resulting in a highly flexible database (see DATABASE for an example of tagged text).

Next the main and *Supplement* texts had to be integrated, which necessitated, among other things, ensuring that the thousands of cross-references in the *OED* were properly adjusted where necessary. It was found that much of this work could be done automatically, but manual editing was still required in many instances (see INTEGRATION for an outline of the process and the types of additions and changes addressed).

Even before Phase I was completed, attention was being given to Phase II. In 1983, a small editorial team had begun compiling new entries and additions to existing entries as part of the process of updating the Dictionary, and it was decided to include some 5,000 new words and new senses from this collection in the second edition (see also NEW WORDS). As well as continuing to collect new words and uses, Phase II also addresses a number of other concerns. These include some modernization of the Dictionary's style; updating of linguistic nomenclature; improvements to the cross-referencing system; revision of scientific and technical definitions, as well as definitions in some general entries which need to be reworked to take into account changes in social and cultural attitudes; the addition of more recent quotations for words in current usage; changes in anachronistic references to countries, currency, institutions, and persons; and increased coverage of English outside the United Kingdom and the United States. The members of the New OED Project team continue to give their attention to these and other concerns as part of their commitment to maintaining a comprehensive inventory of the English language.

new words. The English language is currently growing at such a rate that it is virtually impossible for any printed dictionary to keep pace with all the new words entering the language. In addition, dictionary editors must decide whether words and phrases that become quickly dated and abandoned should be included at all. With the proliferation of printed material and rapidly shifting terminology in areas such as computer technology and popular culture, modern lexicographers have to deal with a flood of material far exceeding that facing their nineteenth-century counterparts. For the *OED*, as a historical dictionary that attempts to record the language as it exists, or existed, at any point in time, decisions for inclusion are especially difficult. In general, the policy is that a new word or new sense of an old word is not included until it appears, on the evidence of quotations, to have gained a firm foothold in the written language. Obviously, such a policy leaves ample room for editorial judgement, but it should be emphasized that decisions are based on usage, not on some arbitrary criterion of 'correctness', since the Dictionary records language as it exists and does not prescribe how it should be used.

The present structure of the *OED* editorial staff provides for the continuous collection of new words and senses (see READING PROGRAMME), as well as the drafting of new entries. Because the editorial team for the *OED* was disbanded in 1933, it was necessary for the new **Supplement* staff to be trained to draft entries and for the quotation files to be reconstituted and updated. In order to avoid a similar situation in future, towards the end of 1983, a small editorial team was assembled to begin compiling new entries. It was from this collection that 5,000 new words and new senses were selected for inclusion in the second edition, and it will also provide much of the material required, both for a complete revision of the Dictionary and for any interim supplementary publications in print or electronic form.

next. see PRECEDING.

nonce-word, -use. A *label or designation assigned to a non-standard word or sense used 'for the nonce', that is, to suit a particular purpose or perceived need. Many words in this category are formed by the addition of a *prefix, *suffix, or *inflection to existing words, or by a slight alteration to an existing word, for example, *disinvent* as the reverse of 'invent', *villarette* to refer to a small villa, *televisible* from 'televisable', or Dylan Thomas's *oystered beer* to refer to beer with oysters. The substitution of an unexpected word in a familiar phrase such as *multiplying way* for 'family way' also qualifies as a nonce-use. (Compare with INVENTED WORD.)

non-naturalized. See NATURALIZED WORD.

O

obsolete (*Obs., obs.*). A status *label attached to a word, sense, *combination, or *phrase no longer in current use. The *Obs.* designation normally appears in conjunction with a dagger (†) *status symbol preceding the relevant headword or sense. Readers of the second edition will notice that many words and senses in current use are not supported by recent quotations. In the majority of cases, this does not mean that no recent examples were located and that the word may therefore be obsolete, but rather that the entry was compiled for the first edition and has not yet been updated. It should also be realized that language is dynamic, and that labels such as 'obsolete' and 'colloquial' are not absolutes, but rather judgements based on contemporary usage, and thus, susceptible to change. (See pp. 16 and 19 for examples.)

offensive words. See TABOO AND OFFENSIVE LANGUAGE.

Old Ashmolean. A building on Broad Street in Oxford, which originally housed the Ashmolean Museum, the oldest public museum of antiquities and natural history in Britain, but which later provided quarters for *OED* editors and their staffs.

Designed by Thomas Wood, the museum first opened its doors in 1683 to display objects and curiosities donated to the University by Elias Ashmole. By the mid-nineteenth century, the collection had grown to such a size that a new museum building was constructed on Beaumont Street. Throughout James *Murray's lifetime, the senior editor and his staff remained in the *Scriptorium adjacent to his home, but *Bradley, who became second editor in 1888, worked initially in the British Museum in London. When Bradley and his staff moved to Oxford in 1896, they were first housed in the Clarendon Press building. However, more space was urgently needed when *Craigie became third editor in 1901. The Old Ashmolean was then vacant and the two *OED* editors and their staffs (and later *Onions and his staff) were given space on the ground floor. After Murray's death in 1915, the Old Ashmolean became the Dictionary's sole headquarters until the completion of the 1933 **Supplement*. An article in the 15 February 1928 issue of *The Periodical* reported on some of the 'lighter side of lexicography' in the old museum building. Apparently, when the Dictionary staff first moved in they were plagued by visitors inquiring for the Ashmolean Museum. The following account is given of their attempt to resolve the problem:

> 'One assistant who was specially exposed to such inquries finally took a sheet of cardboard, printed on it in large capitals, "This is not the Ashmolean Museum",

and hung it on the inner door. As this did not prevent inquiry being made for other University buildings, he successively added, in alternate lines of black and red ink, "Nor the Sheldonian Theatre", "Nor the Bodleian Library", "Nor the Clarendon Building", and at last "Not the Martyrs' Memorial—as yet". Unsuspecting sightseers sometimes read this aloud from beginning to end and departed wondering.'

The article also noted that the staff often pinned up quotations submitted by readers which were inadvertently relevant to their profession or situation, one of which was a 1722 extract from Macky reading 'The Museum Ashmoleanum is adorned within with a noble collection of natural Curiosities'. And a quotation from the preface to the 1611 *Bible* was obviously irresistible to lexicographers inundated with Dictionary slips since it assured them that 'a man may be counted a vertuous man, though he haue made many slips in his life'.

The Old Ashmolean building now houses the Museum of the History of Science.

Old English (OE). The language of England prior to the twelfth century, that is, the speech of the Germanic tribes (identified by the historian Bede as the Angles, Saxons, and Jutes) and their descendants who came to Britain in the fifth century from Denmark and the northern coastal region of Germany; sometimes referred to as *Anglo-Saxon in general usage. A considerable body of literature in Old English has survived in manuscript form, including the epic *Beowulf*, a varied collection of shorter poems, translations of Latin scholarly works, laws, charters, sermons, saints' lives, and the *Anglo-Saxon Chronicle*. A number of Latin words were later introduced by the gradual process of Christian conversion beginning in the sixth century. Later, Old Norse borrowings were made as a result of the Viking raids and Danish settlements which began in the mid-eighth century. Following the Norman Conquest, *Anglo-French (Anglo-Norman), together with Latin, dominated the written record, although the Anglo-Saxon language continued to be widely spoken. The *OED* uses 1150 as its starting point, excluding words obsolete by that period. However, OE. words still in use at that date are included. (See also MIDDLE ENGLISH.)

ONIONS, Charles Talbut (1873–1965). Grammarian, lexicographer, fourth editor of the first edition, and co-editor (with *Craigie) of the 1933 **Supplement*. Onions was born in Edgbaston, Birmingham, the son of a designer and embosser of metals, and exhibited an early interest in grammar. He obtained a London BA in 1892 and an MA in 1895, both while attending Mason College, Birmingham. A professor of English at the college introduced Onions to James *Murray and in September of his final year, Murray invited Onions to join his staff, during which time he also compiled *An Advanced English Syntax* (1904). Later, from 1906 until 1913, he worked under *Bradley and *Craigie and prepared portions of *M*, *N*, *R*, and *S*. In 1914, he was appointed as the fourth editor and was responsible in that capacity for the sections *Su-Sz*, *Wh-Working*, and *X*, *Y*, *Z*. Onions enjoyed saying that he contributed the final entry to the Dictionary—a cross-reference, **Zyxt**, which, since it was 'the last word', was later made the name of a soap. His time as editor was interrupted by a stint in naval intelligence in 1918, and he was also a reader in English at Oxford from 1927 to 1949. In addition, he edited several dictionaries for *Oxford University Press, the most important of which were the *Shorter Oxford English Dictionary* (1933) and the *Oxford Dictionary of English Etymology* (1966), to which he devoted his last twenty years. Onions was known for his etymological skill and his analytical powers which were demonstrated in his organization of the longest entry '*set', and the complex entries for 'shall', 'will', and the interrogative pronouns. He maintained his interest in the *OED* throughout his life. From 1940 to 1945, Onions served as Librarian at Magdalen College and students often profited from his constant presence in the Dictionary bay of the library. Because of his friendship with *Burchfield, the editor of the **Supplement* (1972–86), Onions was always a welcome visitor to the *Supplement*'s editorial offices, as well as a valuable adviser.

onomatopoeic. See ECHOIC.

opprobious, -ly. See TABOO AND OFFENSIVE LANGUAGE.

Oxford University Press (OUP). The publishing and, until recently, printing house of the University of Oxford. Its history began in 1478 with the first itinerant printer in Oxford, Theodoric Rood of Cologne, although a permanent printing press was not established until 1584, when Robert Dudley, Earl of Leicester and Chancellor of the University, granted the University the licence to print. The formal establishment of a 'press' (in the sense of a printing and publishing house) took place in 1636 when Archbishop Laud, who was then Chancellor, revised the statutes of the University to provide for such a body, confirmed by Royal Charter. Subsequently, John Fell, Dean of Christ Church and then Bishop of Oxford, who is often considered the real founder of the Press, charted its course to encompass three major publishing areas—academic, educational, and the *Bible*, and instituted the famous Fell types. (Unfortunately, Fell, whose domineering manner made him an unpopular figure, is probably best remembered, not for his accomplishments, but as the subject of Samuel *Johnson's famous lines which begin—'I do not love thee, Dr Fell . . .'). In 1989, the Press discontinued its printing operations, but it retains its role as one of the world's leading publishers of reference, academic, educational, and religious texts, and since the late nineteenth century, a wide range of general books. (For an interesting account of the Press's history see P. Sutcliffe, *The Oxford University Press*, Oxford (1978).)

OUP is organized in Publishing Divisions. The division presently handling arts and reference works was known for centuries as the Clarendon Press and was responsible for initiating many of the Press's great reference works, including the *OED*. Thus, the *Philological Society's original negotiations and the contract for the production of a New English Dictionary were with the Clarendon Press, although, in practice, this designation is used interchangeably with 'Oxford University Press', 'OUP', or simply 'the Press'. The Clarendon imprint still appears on the *OED* and many other publications, signifying that a book has been produced under the direct authority of the *Delegates, a committee of senior members of the University who direct the Press's affairs. It was the members of this body who, after considerable negotiating, agreed to undertake the Philological Society's project to compile a historical dictionary which became the *OED*. Initially anticipating a venture that would be completed in ten years, the Press soon found itself involved in a costly and frustrating undertaking that took over fifty years to complete. Despite the heavy cost, the Dictionary's inestimable value as the most comprehensive existing record of the English language has been recognized by OUP in its decision, first, to compile the **Supplement* (1972–1986), and more recently, to convert the text to *machine-readable form in order to produce the consolidated and revised second edition, and to implement future updating, both in print and electronic form (see DATABASE, NEW OED PROJECT).

P

parasynthetic. A term used to describe a *combination or *derivative in which a suffix is added to the final element to create a noun or adjective. For example, *black-eyed* and *rabbit-hearted* are not combinations of black + eyed and rabbit + hearted, but rather result from the addition of the suffix *-ed* to the phrases 'black eye' and 'rabbit heart'. (See also SIMILATIVE.)

parent. See ROOT.

participial adjective (*ppl. a.*, ppl. adj.). A part-of-speech label used to identify an adjective that resembles a present or past participle in its origin and form (by the addition of *-ing* or *-ed* to the verb *stem), but not in function. Its use as a modifier or adjective also distinguishes a participial adjective ending in *-ing* from a *verbal substantive (noun) which is similarly formed from a verb by the addition of *-ing*. These distinctions may be more readily understood by considering the following uses of the word 'reading' derived from the verb stem 'read'—'the *reading* public rejected his book' (participial adjective); '*reading* the Dictionary, he discovered a new word' (present participle); and '*reading*, writing, and arithmetic are the three basics' (verbal substantive). A simple test to determine whether a word is a participial adjective is to try to substitute an unambiguous adjective for the word in question.

participial stem (ppl. stem). See STEM.

part of speech. The grammatical category of a word or phrase, for example, noun, verb, adjective, pronoun, etc. Usually given in abbreviated form in italics following a headword or *subordinate headword appearing within an entry, such as a *combination or *derivative. When the latter forms are printed in italics, the part of speech may appear in roman type. In the numerous instances where no part of speech is given, the word form may be assumed to be a noun (*substantive). Generally, the designation *sb.* for 'substantive' is used only to differentiate a noun entry from an entry for a word with the same spelling but a different part of speech. The part-of-speech label may also be followed by a *homonym number to indicate that it is one of several forms with the same spelling and same part of speech, but different meanings and histories (see p. 19 for examples). When a word form is used as more than one part of speech, such as noun and adjective, but both share a common history, the two grammatical forms may be included within the same entry, rather than being allocated separate entries (see pp. 35–36).

PASSOW, Franz Ludwig Karl Friedrich (1786–1833). German classical scholar, educated at Gotha and Leipzig. In 1807, he was appointed to a Greek professorship at Weimar, and in 1815 to the chair at Breslau. Passow's *Handwörterbuch der griechischen Sprache* (Greek-German Lexicon) (1819–24) provided the basis for the *Greek-English Lexicon* (1843) compiled by *Liddell and Scott. His work is especially notable because his original lexicon, and that of his English successors, followed the historical principles which Passow first stated in his 1812 essay, *Über Zweck, Anlage, und Ergänzung griechischer Wörterbücher*. (See HISTORICAL PRINCIPLES for a summary of Passow's canons.)

pejorative, -ly. A descriptive term applied to a word or phrase which is used in a depreciatory way to express contempt or to belittle. It is often employed with reference to a particular class or group of people. The terms *townees* for townspeople, *Boy Scout* as a negative reference to someone who is considered excessively helpful or good, or the phrase *knowledge factory* for a university that places undue emphasis on vocational training, are examples of pejorative usage.

Philological Society. A scholarly society formed in 1842 'for the investigation of the Structure, the Affinities, and the History of Language'. Although the Society initially favoured traditional, classical *philology, its members, including scholars such as *Trench, *Sweet, *Skeat, and *Furnivall, were instrumental in promoting the new 'scientific' comparative philology imported from the Continent. Most significantly, the Society was responsible for initiating activities that resulted in the compilation of the *OED*.

In 1857 the Society, concerned by the number of early words omitted in existing dictionaries, recruited volunteer readers with the objective of compiling a supplement, in particular to *Johnson's and *Richardson's dictionaries. However, two papers delivered by Dean Trench in November, later published as *On Some Deficiencies in Our English Dictionaries*, so impressed the membership that early in 1858 a resolution was passed to compile a complete New English Dictionary. The following year, the Society made public 'A Proposal for the Publication of A New English Dictionary by the Philological Society', drawing heavily on Trench's suggestions. The document called for a comprehensive dictionary of English from the end of the thirteenth century. The authorities were to be 'all English books', except for treatises that were purely scientific and technical, and pre-Reformation works illustrating 'provincial dialects'. Most importantly, it stated 'the *historical principle will be uniformly adopted'. The Dictionary would attempt to fix the epoch in which each word first emerged, or, in the case of obsolete words, when it disappeared. Finally, it noted the urgent need for the improvement of etymologies.

Herbert *Coleridge was appointed editor and a final plan (the 'Canones Lexicographici') was drawn up calling for a dictionary in three parts. The following year, when the unfortunate Coleridge died, Furnivall assumed the editorship. The immensity of the task was becoming apparent and Furnivall almost immediately suggested that a concise version precede the major work. The reasons were practical since an earlier agreement with Trübner for publication had lapsed and no other publisher for the full work was on the horizon. The new editor, at his own expense, contracted with the publisher John Murray, for the completion of the concise dictionary by the end of 1865, but the scheme was abandoned. However, in anticipation of publication, Furnivall employed a number of sub-editors to organize the material for individual letters and to compile etymologies. The programme was initially very active, but as Furnivall's interests diversified, sub-editing lagged and was often marred by the inexperience of those employed for the task. In 1871, Furnivall persuaded Henry Nicol to take over the editorship, but illness and other work interfered, and by 1875, Furnivall was proposing James *Murray, who had gained some prominence in the philological community, as a possible candidate.

The Society's interest in the project revived in 1876 when Murray was approached by the publisher Macmillan to edit a new standard English dictionary. Use of the Society's material was proposed and negotiations began between Macmillan and the Society, but again no agreement could be reached. The Society now began to cast about for another publisher to undertake the original project which, it was apparent, required considerable financial support. Using the earlier Macmillan negotiations as a model, Sweet, as president of the Society, wrote to *Oxford University Press (OUP), outlining the Society's proposal. After considerable debate, a contract was signed by both parties on 1 March 1879, as well as between the Press and Murray as editor. The projected dictionary was to take ten years to compile and was not to exceed 7,000 pages. These terms soon proved to be highly unrealistic, in part because the Society's material, half of which was supposed to be ready for publication, proved to be inadequate. Editors had died, material had been dispersed, stored, lost, or even eaten or inhabited by mice. Shocked by the condition of the two and a half million *dictionary slips, Murray instituted a new call for voluntary readers to supplement, replace, and update the existing material.

As the work progressed, the Society's role lessened, but individual members, in particular Furnivall and *Gibbs, continued to figure actively in the affairs of the Dictionary, especially in the stressful early years when both editor and publisher threatened from time to time to withdraw from the project. The first edition of the Dictionary carries the significant words 'founded mainly on the materials collected by the Philological Society'. While the Society's material indeed provided a foundation, it formed a very small percentage of the Dictionary's total collected words and quotations, most of which were the result of Murray's new *reading programme. Nevertheless, the *OED* owes its existence in large part to the ideas, enthusiasm, energy, and persistence of those members of the Society who inspired and committed themselves to the initial project.

The Philological Society is still active and publishes twice-yearly *Transactions*.

philology. Before the nineteenth century, philology, as a discipline, usually meant the study of a nation's cultural and spiritual life through an analysis of thought and meaning as expressed in its language, and particularly its literature. Traditionally, it dealt with Greek and Roman literature, and was comparable to classical studies. In the late eighteenth and early nineteenth centuries, the relationship of modern European languages to Sanskrit and their common *Indo-European roots was recognized. On the Continent, philology increasingly meant the scientific study of the structure and development of language. By the time the *Philological Society conceived its idea of compiling a *New English Dictionary*, English scholars were beginning to discard the philosophical philology of Horne *Tooke and to adopt the new Continental comparative philology, based on the systematic comparison of languages, and specifically grammatical forms and sound systems, by Danish and German scholars (see also ETYMOLOGY).

By 1879, when the Society reached an agreement with the *Oxford University Press for the publication of its *New English Dictionary* (later to become the *OED*), English philology was fortunately committed to the study of 'what is', rather than the earlier speculative approach which had impeded its progress. (For a comprehensive account of this transitional period, see H. Aarsleff, *The Study of Language in England, 1780–1860*, Princeton (1967).)

The present use of the term Philology depends on how it is defined within a particular academic setting. In some circles, it is still applied to the textual analysis of literature in its original historical sense. In addition, while the analysis of the formation and structure of modern languages is commonly referred to as Linguistics, with the term Historical Linguistics often applied to the study of the development of one language and Comparative Linguistics to the development of a group of related languages, some institutions, such as Oxford, still frequently use the name Philology to refer to the latter disciplines.

phonetic descent (:—). As a word form is passed from one generation of speakers of a language to another it tends to undergo slight variations in pronunciation. If the language has a written form at the time, the changes are often also reflected in the spelling of the word. These variations accumulate over time until the phonetic structure becomes markedly different from what it was at an earlier period. The symbol :— is used in etymologies to indicate that the form on the left of it is derived by such a process of direct descent from the form on the right, rather than by means of borrowing from outside the language or by formation from other words and forms. As an example, in the entry for the adjective 'old', it is noted 'Early ME. *old*:— OE. *ald* (W.Saxon *eald*)', meaning that the Early Middle English *old* was phonetically descended directly from the Old English *ald* (which in West Saxon was *eald*). (See also p. 25 for a further example.)

phonetic transcription. A system that uses a set of symbols to indicate the way in which a word form is pronounced; also referred to as phonetic notation. In effect, the written form of the word is transcribed, or translated, into a phonetic, or sound-based, alphabet, in which each symbol consistently represents the same spoken sound in the dialect or language being transcribed. The system for transcribing *pronunciation in the second edition of the *OED* is the *IPA (International Phonetic Alphabet).

phrase (*phr.*). A group of words held together by a preposition, conjunction, adverb, or verb (and hence not a *combination or a *collocation) that has a more specific meaning than the individual components might suggest. The *OED* includes innumerable phrases, proverbs, idioms, and other similar expressions which use a word in an established context. A few such word forms are given main entries in their own right: for example, 'by and large', 'how-do-you-do', and 'no-can-do', as well as commonly used foreign phrases such as 'à la carte'. The vast majority, however, are included within the entries for their main or 'key' word and are normally printed in bold italics. It is difficult to generalize on their treatment because there are numerous variations in the way in which they appear. For instance, a phrase may be included as the last item within a definition in much the same way as a simple *derivative, as in the case of *the groves of Academe* which is noted in sense **2** of the noun 'academe'. Several phrases may also be listed within a *sub-sense, or they may even appear within a list of *combinations, e.g., the phrase *in the fast lane* from the combination *fast lane* which appears in the entry for 'fast'. Alternatively, in very long entries for words that occur in many different expressions, a separate section of the entry may be devoted to defining and illustrating phrases. For instance, the many phrases using the noun 'head' are listed in section **IV** of its entry. The expressions are first subdivided by their grammatical construction, such as 'phrases with a preposition' which include, among others, *off one's head, on one's own head, out of one's head*; followed by 'phrases used with another substantive', such as *from head to foot* and *head over heels*; 'phrases with adverbs' (*head first, head foremost*); 'with a verb' (*to get ahead, to lose one's head*); and, finally, 'various figurative and proverbial phrases' such as *two heads are better than one*.

preceding (prec.). Used as a *cross-reference to instruct the reader to refer to the entry (or sometimes the sense) immediately before the one presently being read. Similarly, the term 'next' indicates that the user should refer to the entry or sense immediately following the one under consideration. The terms are also occasionally found within a list of *combinations to refer to the previous or following item in the list. (See pp. 26, 38 for specific examples.)

pre-dating. See ANTEDATING.

predicative (*pred.*). Relating to the part of a sentence that forms the predicate (that is, the part, normally consisting of a verb with or without an object, an adverb, or complement, that tells something about the subject or topic of the sentence); also sometimes referred to as the 'subject complement'. In the *OED*, the abbreviation *pred.* as a label is most often applied to an adjective, a *participial adjective (*ppl. a.*), or an adjectival phrase that follows a verb. Many adjectives in English can be used both predicatively and *attributively (good, bad, right, wrong, hungry, thirsty, etc.) as, for example, 'the man is good' (predicative) and 'the good man' (attributive). Sometimes the part-of-speech label *adv.* and *pred. a.* may be encountered with words, such as 'ablow', 'afire', 'aflame', and 'afloat', which function either as adverbs or predicative adjectives. In addition, other parts of speech, such as participles and nouns, are frequently used 'predicatively'.

For example, in the sentence 'that man is a professor', the noun 'professor' is employed predicatively.

prefix (*pref.*). An element added to the beginning of a word to change its meaning or function and to form a new word (see AFFIX).

privative (priv.). Literally, denoting the quality of depriving or taking away. In grammar, especially applied to a negative participle or *affix. The term is usually employed in the *OED* with particular reference to words formed with the Greek negative prefix *a-* (*ἀ*), which functions in the same way as the prefix 'non-'. For example, the etymology for the word *amental*, meaning denying or dispensing with the existence of mind or intelligence, reads '[f. Gr. *ἀ* priv. + MENTAL]', indicating that the word was formed by the addition of the negative prefix to the existing word 'mental'.

pronunciation. The *OED* gives the pronunciation of most current words which appear as *headwords of *main entries, with the exception of *derivatives and *combinations, and some single-syllable words, for which pronunciation is considered to be self-evident. Where pronunciation is not included, *stress-marks indicating emphasis are sometimes included. Main entries for *obsolete words do not normally give pronunciation, although stress is frequently indicated. *Cross-reference entries do not generally include pronunciation or stress. When indicated, pronunciation normally appears in round brackets immediately following the headword. The pronunciation shown for native words is in accordance with educated standard southern British speech, although alternative British or non-British usages are sometimes included. A parallels symbol (‖) precedes foreign headwords that have not been fully *naturalized in their pronunciation or form, or may precede a foreign pronunciation which is given as an alternative. (For specific examples of pronunciation and stress, see pp. 17–18.)

The system used in the second edition for *phonetic transcription, or notation, is the *IPA (International Phonetic Alphabet), in contrast to James *Murray's notation (see following article), which was employed in the first edition and the **Supplement* (1972–86). Because IPA has been increasingly employed in modern dictionaries and is standard for most of the other dictionaries published by Oxford University Press (and thus familiar to many users) the conversion of the older system was considered a priority for the second edition. Given the time limitations, such an undertaking would have been impossible without the aid of sophisticated computer programs which translated Murray's phonetic symbols and stress-marks into their IPA equivalents. Although it was recognized that it was desirable to augment the existing coverage of alternative pronunciations, the extensive research and documenting of variants had to be reserved for the future. Therefore, the translation from the Murray system to IPA was reasonably straightforward, although it was necessary to make adjustments for some peculiar characteristics of Murray's system. The alterations that were made were largely related to unassimilated foreign words, dialect and regional forms, and reconstructions of earlier English, where given. It was also necessary to devise computer algorithms to assist in the process of substituting stress-marks preceding the stressed syllable for the stress dots which *followed* the vowel(s) of the stressed syllable in the older system. In total, over 137,000 phonetic transcriptions and a similar number of stress-marked words were automatically converted to IPA.

The particularly noteworthy features or exceptions in the transcription are summarized in the 'General Explanations' in Volume I (p. xxxiii), and, together with an account of specific problems encountered in the conversion, in the 'Introduction' (pp. xviii–xxi). A *Key to Pronunciation* which illustrates with English, or, where necessary, foreign words, the sounds symbolized by each element of the phonetic alphabet is found at the front of each volume of the Dictionary.

pronunciation: first edition. A *phonetic transcription system devised by James *Murray was used to indicate pronunciation in the first edition and the **Supplement* (1972–86). Murray had a long-standing interest in transcription, or notation systems which could be used to record the way words sounded. As a young man, in 1857, he had formed a friendship with Alexander Melville Bell from whom he had taken a course in elocution. In fact, it is said that Murray gave Bell's young son, Alexander Graham, his first instruction in electricity. Melville Bell had developed a system called 'Visible Speech' to record the sound of human speech. Murray saw its potential for recording his local Scottish dialect, as well as for the phonetic key to Jamieson's *Etymological Dictionary of the Scottish Language* which he was attempting to develop. Later, as a member of the *Philological Society, Murray came in contact with men such as Henry *Sweet, the leading British phonetician, and Alexander Ellis who, together with Isaac Pitman, had developed a notational scheme using letters rather than special symbols.

As editor of the *OED*, Murray almost immediately found himself in conflict with the *Delegates of the Press on a number of questions, including whether or not pronunciation should be given in the Dictionary. The Delegates felt that since no one system was sufficiently established and phonetic theory was in a state of flux, it would be unwise for the Dictionary to commit itself to a scheme. Sweet agreed with the Delegates, and both he and *Skeat attempted to convince Murray that he was creating unnecessary work for himself. The editor, however, was so convinced that it was both worthwhile and possible to transcribe pronunciation, that he worked for three years to perfect a system which made its appearance in the first section published in 1884. The system was both complex and precise and, given the considerable controversy under which it was developed, it stood the test of time remarkably well. (For a detailed critique of Murray's notation, see MacMahon, *Transactions of the Philological Society* (1985), pp. 72–112, as well as the 'Introduction' in Volume I of the Dictionary (pp. xvii–xii).)

Privately, Murray's attitude towards both the use of language and the pronunciation of words was far from rigid. He once made his position clear to a correspondent when he remarked 'it is a free country, and a man may call a *vase*, a vawse, a vahse, a vaze, or a vase, as he pleases', adding that we do not all think, walk, dress, etc. alike, so 'why should not we use our liberty in speech also' (quoted in K. M. E. Murray, *Caught in the Web of Words* (1979), p. 189).

proprietary name. A name given to a product or process which is legally protected by registration with a Patent Office; a trade mark. *OED* editors attempt, to the best of their ability, to determine the status of all words which are known to be, or are suspected of being, proprietary names or trade marks, and to include this information in the word's definition. However, the Dictionary does not claim to make any judgement concerning the legal status of such words. The present practice is to capitalize the initial letter of all current trade marks. In addition, some word forms which are still proprietary have been adapted as generic terms in general usage, and sometimes appear in quotations without initial capitalization. In the case of words that were once proprietary, but are no longer registered, their former status and origin, where known, are given. Note also that occasionally proprietary names derived from a previously existing word, such as 'caterpillar' or 'penguin', may be trade marks in one sense, but not in others, and that some names may only be proprietary in one country. (See pp. 64–68 for examples.)

proto-. In Linguistics, a prefix used to indicate the reconstructed or hypothetical, and hence unrecorded, earlier form of a language, e.g., Proto-Germanic, the common ancestor of all Germanic languages, or Proto-*Indo-European.

proverb. See PHRASE.

pseudonymous works. An author who chooses to write under an assumed or 'pen' name is normally cited by his or her pseudonym, which appears within single quotation marks. Some exceptions are made for well-known pseudonyms such as George Eliot, which usually appears without the quotation marks.

Many authors, of course, have written both under their actual name and under one or more pseudonyms. The Victorian writer Sir Arthur Quiller-Couch wrote books both under his full name and under the sobriquet 'Q.'.

In these cases, he is usually cited by the name under which a particular title was published.

In some instances, the real name of the author is not known, but when it is, the **Bibliography* at the end of Volume XX normally lists works by the pseudonym (in single quotation marks) under which they were published followed by the real name in parentheses as, for example, 'Carroll, Lewis' (C. L. Dodgson).

The numerous authors who write, or wrote, under initials can cause confusion, especially when the same initials have been used by several authors. Referring to the *Bibliography*, for instance, one finds that the initials 'J. H.' have been used by John Hall, Joseph Hall, J. Hammond, James Harvey, J. Healey, J. Heath, J. Humfrey, and J. Hutton. For the reader who wishes to determine the author, the search is complicated by the fact that there are several John Halls, and a John, James, and Joseph Hammond. The only recourse in such cases is to match the title or date to the appropriate author. (See also ANONYMOUS WORKS.)

Q

quotation. An example selected from a printed source illustrating the use, form, meaning, or development of a word, phrase, etc. in a given sense. Quotations are normally listed in *chronological order starting with the earliest example located, and represent one of the most important features of a historical dictionary. The source of each quotation is cited, and the standard order in which the information appears is the date of publication or writing, author, title of the work, edition cited (if appropriate), location within the work (chapter, page, act, scene, line, verse, etc. as applicable), and, finally, the exact text, including the original spelling and punctuation, of the quotation. The second edition contains almost two and a half million quotations representing the contributions of hundreds of readers (see READING PROGRAMME).

For the first edition, which covered most of the 'core' words of the English language, the policy was to include at least one quotation per century for each sense. However, this ratio was considerably increased for the **Supplement* (1972–86) since the original figure was considered inadequate to keep pace with the rapid proliferation of contemporary language; a figure of one quotation per decade was suggested by the editor as probably being more appropriate.

Quotations are carefully selected from existing files and, when necessary, they are augmented by further searches by *library researchers or through the use of computerized text databases. It is considered particularly important that the quotations should not be simply examples of the word or sense used in its fully developed form, but that they should also illustrate how a particular sense or word evolved and became separated from preceding senses or related words. In effect, the quotations must justify the lexicographer's decision to divide and subdivide a word's senses.

Although quotations had been used to illustrate the use of words in earlier English dictionaries, such as *Richardson and *Johnson, the magnitude of the *OED*'s undertaking and its employment of numerous readers to methodically extract and record the use of all manner of words over such an extended period of time was unique. (For conventions relating to quotations, see articles under the individual entry elements, as well as pp. 39–46.)

R

rare. A status *label applied to a word or *sense indicating that very few examples of its use have been found. The term is sometimes further defined by the addition of a superior number or superscript preceded by a dash (*rare*$^{-0}$ or *rare*$^{-1}$) to indicate, in the first instance, that the word or sense was found only in an earlier dictionary or dictionaries, or, in the case of '*rare*$^{-1}$', that only one quotation (from a text other than a dictionary) was located. In the first case, the quotation paragraph may include the text of the definition found in the earlier dictionary, or it may simply note that it was included in that source ('**1847** in WEBSTER' or '**1858** in MAYNE *Expo. Lex.*'). It may be observed that the label 'rare' is sometimes used without the '-1' superior number when only one quotation is given; this normally indicates that more quotations existed, but were not printed.

Rare also frequently appears as a secondary label to the status designation *Obs.* (obsolete), or alternatively the phrase 'now *rare*' may be used. The distinction here is that in the first instance, the word or sense is obsolete, but it was rare when it did exist, while, in the second case, the word form is rare *now* regardless of what it was in the past.

readers. See CONTRIBUTORS.

Reading Programme. The nucleus of the 1.8 million quotations contained in the first edition was the result of a programme to recruit volunteer readers, established by the *Philological Society in 1857, to select words and quotations from literary works for its projected **New English Dictionary*. The first editor, Herbert *Coleridge, divided the collection programme into three chronological periods between 1250 and 1858. The response was enthusiastic and it was soon reported that seventy-six individuals had volunteered to cover 121 works of English authors.

The programme continued for twenty years, largely under the direction of the second editor, Frederick *Furnivall, until agreement was reached with *Oxford University Press in 1878 to undertake the printing and publication of a historical dictionary. It was anticipated that the Society's *dictionary slips, on which quotations were recorded, would provide sufficient material for the compilation of the projected dictionary. However, the newly appointed editor, James *Murray, soon discovered that the coverage was inadequate and, in 1879, established a new programme, appealing initially for 1,000 readers for a period of three years. Once again, the response from both sides of the Atlantic was remarkable, with an estimated eight hundred British readers and four to five hundred American readers contributing approximately a million quotations in the three years prior to the publication of the first volume. Murray's programme, in the end, provided the majority of quotations included in the first edition.

After the publication of the supplementary volume included with the 1933 reissue of the *OED*, the Dictionary staff was disbanded and the quotation files were stored and even dispersed to other locations. A number of slips were sent to Ann Arbor, Michigan, for example, to support a projected dictionary of Early Modern English. When it was decided in 1957 to compile the **Supplement*, a new Reading Programme, covering nineteenth- and twentieth-century printed sources of all kinds, was established by the editor Robert *Burchfield. In keeping with cultural changes, the programme was designed to cover a broader range of general, popular, and scientific sources than the first edition (see also VOCABULARY, SCIENTIFIC AND TECHNICAL TERMS). The new *Supplement* also made use of some 140,000 quotation slips left over from the 1933 volume and several valuable private collections. A great deal of other material was excerpted from periodicals such as *Notes and Queries, American Speech*, and a variety of regional, slang, and technical and scientific dictionaries. Combined with the excellent response of contributors, these resources produced a quotation file approaching three million slips by the time the fourth and final volume of the *Supplement* was completed.

The Reading Programme was continued and enlarged after the *Supplement*'s publication, and provided material for the new entries added to the second edition. The importance of the quotation file as a resource, not only for a future third edition of the *OED* and for interim publications in print and electronic form, but also for all other Oxford dictionary projects, is fully recognized by the Press. A North American base was established in 1989, to take over the extensive coverage of American and Canadian sources, with the expectation that the programmes on each side of the Atlantic would each add roughly 300,000 citations per year to the central file.

While readers still voluntarily collect quotations from their own personal reading, the majority are now part of a 'directed' programme whereby readers are employed to cover certain subject areas or specific publications. Quotations continue to be submitted on the traditional 6″ × 4″ slips, or in the form of marked-up books and other materials assigned for reading. However, since its inception in 1989, the North American operation has stored its collected quotations in *machine-readable form, and, at the same time, the British programme also began computerization of new submissions. The gradual conversion of the previously existing files to create a valuable machine-searchable corpus of the English language is a long-term desideratum. In addition to the Reading Programmes, a variety of full text databases are routinely searched for occurrences of particular words and phrases.

Received Pronunciation (RP). Broadly speaking, educated standard southern British pronunciation, and the model followed by the *OED*. In a few cases, alternative British or non-British pronunciations are given. Although it was recognized that a greater inclusion of such variants might be desirable, the translation of Murray's pronunciation system used in the first edition into the more widely accepted *IPA (International Phonetic Alphabet) was all that could reasonably be undertaken for the second edition. (See also PRONUNCIATION.)

reduplicating (redupl.). A descriptive term used in *OED* etymologies or definitions in several ways. Commonly, it identifies a word that is repeated to describe a repetitive action, such as 'thrump' and 'glug' ('the heavy thrump, thrump of marching feet', and 'Lord Mergwain listened to the glug-glug in the long neck of the decanter'), or, alternatively, a form in which the first element is repeated in a rhyming fashion, such as 'boogie-woogie', 'dingle-dangle', and 'ziggety-zaggety'. Very rarely, reduplicating is used in etymologies to describe a class of *Old English *strong verbs descended from *Indo-European ancestors whose past tense was formed with reduplication of the initial consonant. For example, 'held' and 'fell' from OE. *heold* and *feoll* are believed to descend from Germanic *hehald-* and *fefall-*.

refashioned, -ing (refash.). A term used in etymologies to describe the remodelling of an *adopted word so that it resembles more closely an ancestral form rather than its immediate source. This is especially common with words of *Latin origin that were first borrowed in their mediaeval French form and later changed to resemble the original Latin form, often with a pronunciation change as well. For example 'Arctic' in its older English forms, such as *artik*, *artick*, or *artique*, was adopted from the Old French *artique*. In the seventeenth century, however, the English form was 'refashioned' after the Latin form *articus*, *arcticus*. Refashionings are sometimes based on a misapprehension. For example, 'abnormal' is a refashioning of *anormal* in the belief that the latter was formed on the Latin *a-*, *ab-* prefix plus 'normal', whereas it is actually a corruption of the Latin and Greek adjective from which 'anomalous' is derived.

reflexive (*refl.*). Applied to a verb or pronoun in instances where the object of the action indicated by the verb is also the subject of the sentence. A reflexive pronoun (the object) is typically formed with the addition of *-self* or *-selves* to the objective form of the pronoun (herself, himself, themselves, etc.). The designation 'refl.' is most often applied to an individual sense or sub-sense, rather than to an entire entry or main division of an entry, since a verb's history may involve several shifts in its grammatical categories, or a verb may be used both reflexively and intransitively. For example, the verb 'surrender' in 'he surrendered himself to the enemy' is reflexive (and employs the reflexive pronoun 'himself'), but in 'he surrendered to the enemy', it is intransitive. (See also TRANSITIVE for further examples of intransitive verbs used in a reflexive sense.)

regional label. See LABEL.

regular, -ly (reg.). The term 'regular' or 'reg.' is used in the Dictionary to describe the linguistically most common forms or uses; examples are 'the reg. south. form after 1200'; 'still in reg. use in the north', or 'the regular form of'. The opposite form, irregular (irreg.) usually identifies a grammatically atypical word form or formation process: for instance, an irregular *combining form, an irregular *back formation, or an irregular *adaptation of (irreg. ad.). In general grammatical use, the two terms are often employed specifically to differentiate verbs with normal *inflectional forms (that is, which incorporate the changes that are most commonly employed in a language to indicate tense, person, etc.) from those with an atypical pattern. (See also STRONG.)

RICHARDSON, Charles (1775–1865). Lexicographer, scholar, and ardent supporter of the philosophical *philology of Horne *Tooke. In 1818, the first part of his English lexicon, which was issued serially, appeared in the *Encyclopædia Metropolitana*. The lexicon, with some additions and corrections, was later published between 1835 and 1837 under the title *A New Dictionary of the English Language*.

Richardson's work is significant for its quasi-historical approach and for its inclusion of a greater number of illustrative quotations than any previous English dictionary. This feature was noted with approval by Dean *Trench in his thoughtful criticism of existing English dictionaries presented to the *Philological Society in 1857, and the use of quotations later became one of the distinguishing features of the *OED*. However, while Richardson deserves credit for his use of quotations to support his concept of word development, his underlying lexicographical principles left much to be desired because of his attachment to Tooke's conviction that each word could be demonstrated to have only one immutable meaning. This idea was so prevalent that Noah *Webster's 1837 criticism of Richardson substantially accepted the principle, but found Richardson lacking because he often failed to find the original meaning or to advance his work beyond that of Tooke. Webster also noted that Richardson's etymologies were incorrect, although, with the development of the new scientific philology, the same criticism was later aimed at Webster himself. Despite its many shortcomings, Richardson's dictionary was well received and reviewed, and published in abridged form in 1839.

root. A term frequently defined, in a general sense, as a basic, meaningful unit of a language which cannot be further analysed and which may be used in word formation. In the *OED*, the term is applied in the specific sense of the primary word or word form in a parent language, that is, the language of origin or the earliest source traced by the Dictionary. For example, the word 'angle' is from the hypothetical Aryan root *ank-* meaning 'to bend', and the word 'engine' was *adapted from the Old French form *engin*. The latter and similar words in other languages can be traced to the Latin word *ingenium* which, in turn, was developed by combining the Latin *in* (in)+*gen-*, the root of the verb *gignere*, meaning 'to beget'. Note that root forms are sometimes preceded by an asterisk (*) indicating that their existence has been reconstructed from later evidence.

S

scientific and technical terms. The coverage of the language of science and technology in the second edition of the *OED* is extensive, reflecting the rapid proliferation of terminology and the extent to which it has penetrated popular media such as newspapers, magazines, and fiction. This is not to say that the first edition ignored specialized vocabulary, but its emphasis was undoubtedly more 'literary' with a tendency to regard many scientific terms as somewhat outside its perimeters. The most famous and most publicized instance of its cautious approach was *Murray's decision, based on the advice of medical experts, to omit the new term 'appendicitis' from the first volume of the Dictionary. Much was made of the fact when the term came into considerable prominence in 1902 because Edward VII's coronation was delayed while the future monarch underwent an appendectomy. Even today, however, the editors cannot necessarily predict which of the hundreds of new scientific and technical terms will survive and which will be quickly forgotten.

The second edition continues the more generous policy of the **Supplement* (1972–86) in expanding the circumference of what Murray referred to as 'the circle' of the English language (see also VOCABULARY). However, modern science and technology has produced such highly esoteric sub-specialities that their terminology is principally of interest only to the few specialists for whom the definition of a term would have meaning. Obviously, the Dictionary cannot hope, or indeed wish, to include this level of specialization. Nevertheless, educated readers in fields such as medicine, biology, engineering, etc. are likely to find most terms that they would encounter in their general reading.

While the overall policy is flexible, certain specific boundaries are observed. For example, Latin names of plants or animals at the generic level are only included if there is sufficient evidence of their use in an English context with reference to an individual and not as the name of a genus, while above the generic level, names of groups are only included in their anglicized forms, if there is evidence of the use of such forms.

Finally, while some entries for basic scientific and technical terms that were written for the first edition have not yet undergone general revision, some obvious anachronisms have been omitted or changed. (See also COINAGE, MODERN FORMATION for policy regarding the origin of scientific terms first used in a foreign language.)

SCOTT, Robert (1811–87). See LIDDELL & SCOTT.

Scriptorium. The name given by James *Murray to each of the two structures in which he and his staff worked on the compilation of the first edition, with reference to the word's original meaning of a writing room where early scribes copied manuscripts. When Murray was appointed editor in 1879, he was living in Mill Hill, where he was a schoolmaster. His immediate concern was to house the mass of material he anticipated receiving from the *Philological Society. There was no additional space in his home, and, at his wife's suggestion, he decided to have a portable fireproof building constructed adjacent to his house at a cost of £150. The structure, which was approximately thirty by fifteen feet, was made of corrugated iron and equipped with skylights. The walls of the utilitarian room were lined with over a thousand pigeon-holes to hold *Dictionary slips, but these were later converted to shelves because the bundles of slips had to be shifted so frequently. Murray had a foot-high platform constructed on which to place his own work table, with the sorters at a lower level. The editor often received visiting academics in the Scriptorium, wearing, as he always did, the black velvet academic cap of the University of Edinburgh.

In 1885 when the Murrays moved to Oxford, the original Scriptorium was presented to the Mill Hill School as a study room. Unfortunately, despite its construction, it was destroyed by fire in 1902, but was replaced by a Murray Reading Room attached to the school library. In the garden of the Murrays' new home at 78 Banbury Road in Oxford, a larger Scriptorium was erected. In order not to interfere with a neighbour's view, the building was sunk about three feet in the ground, which added to the dampness and cold in the winter, while in summer it was poorly ventilated and often stuffy. Although there was a stove, it was extinguished at night for fear of fire and Murray often worked in an overcoat with his feet in a box to protect them from the cold draughts. Murray and his staff continued to work in these unhealthy and spartan circumstances until his death in 1915. One suspects that the 1907 quotation from the *Times Literary Supplement*, supporting the entry for 'Scriptorium' in the Dictionary, was selected for its appropriateness; it reads, 'Drowsy intelligence and numbed fingers in a draughty scriptorium will easily account for deviations'. The Banbury Road Scriptorium was eventually torn down, although a small plaque marks the place where it stood. (See also OLD ASHMOLEAN.)

semantic label. See LABEL.

sense. An element of a Dictionary entry, identified (where there is more than one) by a *sense number that defines, and illustrates with quotations, a meaning, form, or function attached to a headword, or a *subordinate headword such as a *combination or *derivative. Senses may contain, if appropriate, a symbol, preceding the sense number, indicating its status in the language (*status symbol); a *label identifying special status or usage, or grammatical or semantic form or function; a definition; a *definition note; and *chronologically arranged quotations in a single paragraph, illustrating usage and development of the sense. Occasionally, a comment may be included regarding the etymology or the pronunciation of an individual sense. (See also pp. 28–52 for an explanation and examples of each of the elements.)

sense development. The way in which a word form's meaning changes over time. Identifying, defining, and documenting a word's *senses in the order in which they developed in a language is one of the major objectives of historical *lexicography. The *OED* builds this structure on the foundation of an immense collection of quotations drawn from the written word in almost all of its printed forms.

In writing an entry, the lexicographer works from the quotation files (and from other sources such as period dictionaries and glossaries for older words), sorting, selecting, dividing, and subdividing the quotations into groups by their contextual meaning. Using the most descriptive of the quotations as evidence, the lexicographer begins the further task of writing a definition for each identified group, and of arranging them in the order of their development, which is most often chronological (that is, by the date of the earliest quotation for each defined group). Each sense must then be assigned a *sense number consistent with the Dictionary's hierarchical numbering and lettering scheme. This, in itself, often challenges the lexicographer's skill because, especially if a word form has many senses, decisions must be made as to whether a usage qualifies as a main sense, or whether it represents an aspect or special application of a main sense, and should thus be considered a *sub-sense. Senses may also diverge into two or more parallel branches and the numbering system must be adapted to identify these separate sense groupings. No hard and fast rules other than the hierarchical framework exist for this process. The statement that James *Murray originally made in his 'General Explanations' that 'every (such) word must be treated in the way which seems best suited to exhibit the facts of its own history and use' still applies.

While sense development is usually chronological, the reader will encounter some entries in which senses are arranged in what is termed 'logical order', because the lexicographer or editor, on the basis of his or her knowledge of word development, has decided that the historical record of the quotations at hand must be incomplete. This kind of practical decision-making may be a simple assumption that a derivative, such as an adverb formed with *-ly*, must have been developed after its adjectival form, even though the available quotations give chronological precedence to the adverb. There are instances in the Dictionary, however, when logical order may be more open to debate. Some scholars have questioned whether Murray was at times unduly influenced, particularly in his entries for native words, by the assumption that word development must necessarily follow a pattern from simple to complex, and from concrete to abstract.

There are also instances where chronological order is deliberately maintained even though it deviates from a pattern of logical development. This sometimes happens, as Murray was careful to point out, with foreign words that are *adopted or *adapted into the English language in a way that differs from the actual historical development in their language of origin. The entry for 'agony' clearly illustrates this problem in a preliminary statement which observes that the word's meanings in Greek evolved as follows: 1. a struggle for victory in games, 2. any struggle, 3. mental struggle, as exemplified by Christ's anguish in Gethsemane. The word is first recorded in English usage, however, in the third, abstract sense of mental struggle, followed by Christ's 'agonye' as described in Wyclif's version of the *Bible*; a death struggle; extreme bodily suffering; and finally, a kind of contest. Since the Dictionary is first and foremost a history of the *English* language, it retains the order of the word's sense development in that language.

sense number. The unique number and/or letter assigned to a particular sense or *sub-sense of a headword in order to provide it with an 'address' for reference or cross-referencing purposes. Thus, references are often made to a specific sense *within* an entry for a headword, as well as simply to the headword itself. The assignment of numbers is based on a hierarchical scheme of letters and numbers devised by James *Murray to provide a framework for listing senses and subdivisions of senses in the order of their development. The scheme is also sometimes used as a means of grouping sets of senses when a word's development is not straightforwardly linear. For example, two branches of senses which developed simultaneously from the same origin, or use of the word as two *parts of speech (for example, noun and adjective), may be contained in a single entry. (For an explanation of the scheme and its variants, see pp. 30–36.)

sense section. The term currently applied to that section of an entry documenting the history of a headword's meaning in the language by listing its various senses and *sub-senses, usually in *chronological order. The sense section is typically made up of a series of sense units identified by *sense numbers. *Combinations derived from the headword, which do not have a main entry of their own, normally appear as the last numbered sense or senses of an entry, or section of an entry. *Derivatives are usually listed as a final unnumbered element. This pattern may vary somewhat in either very short or very long entries. (Also compare with SIGNIFICATION and see pp. 74–78 for an example of the organization of a lengthy entry.)

set. The longest entry in the Dictionary is for the verb 'set'. The initial sorting and sub-editing of the entry was done by P. W. Jacob. In a report presented in 1881, *Murray gave the following account of Jacob's struggle with the unwieldy verb:

> 'In returning to me his last batch, Mr. Jacob mentioned to me that the division of the meanings of the verb *Set*, and the attempt to put them in satisfactory order, had occupied him over 40 hours. In examining his results, with 51 senses of the simple verb, and 83 phrases, like *set out*, *set off*, *set down*—134 divisions in all—I do not wonder at the time: I suspect that the Editor will have to give 40 more hours to it, for the language seems not to contain a more perplexing word than *Set*, which occupies more than two columns of Webster, and will probably fill three of our large quarto pages.'

The entry was subsequently prepared by *Onions and finally appeared in 1912 in a section edited by *Bradley, where its 154 divisions and numerous subdivisions occupied more than eighteen pages.

SHAKESPEARE, William (1564–1616). The most frequently quoted author in the *OED*. The number of *quotations taken from the collected works of Shakespeare totals appoximately 33,300, which probably exceeds by roughly ten thousand the number of quotations extracted from various versions of the **Bible*. Approximately 1,970 of these are listed as the earliest quotations located for a particular entry (note that this figure is for the entire *entry* and does not take into account instances where Shakespeare is credited with the first use of a word form in a particular sense). The single work of Shakespeare with the greatest number of citations is *Hamlet*. Some scholars, however, have questioned the emphasis given to Shakespeare, arguing that, in some instances, these first recorded uses may be susceptible to *antedating. The reader should also be aware that the citations, as well as the dates attributed to them, were taken from all works recognized as Shakespeare's at the time the original inventory was made for the first edition. The **Bibliography* at the end of Volume XX lists the titles, although the question of the editions originally used in particular cases is not clear. The numerous quotations also represent the *OED*'s original policy of literary inclusiveness for selected early authors. Therefore, the quotations cover an estimated 200 *hapax legomena*, that is word forms of which only one record exists.

Shakespeare's name as the author is usually given as 'Shaks.' and the titles of plays, sonnets, etc. appear in a shortened or abbreviated form, such as *A.Y.L.*, *L.L.L.*, *Ham.*, and *Mids.* for *As You Like It, Love's Labour's Lost, Hamlet,* and *A Midsummer Night's Dream*, respectively. The way in which the same title is cited varies considerably, which is of concern principally to users who may be searching the Dictionary text in electronic form. The brief title is followed by the act, scene, and line number, as in '**1597** SHAKS. *2 Hen. IV* III. ii. 52' for *Henry IV, Part 2*, Act III, scene ii, line 52.

Shorter Oxford English Dictionary (SOED). The two-volume abridgement of the *OED*, first published in 1933. From the time of the *OED*'s inception by the *Philological Society, the idea of an abridgement had been contemplated, and it was, in fact, included as one of the provisions of the 1879 contract with *Oxford University Press. In 1903 its compilation was begun by William Little who continued the work until his death in 1922, after which it was completed by H. W. Fowler and Jessie Coulson. C. T. *Onions, one of the editors of the *OED* and the 1933 **Supplement*, revised and edited the work.

The *SOED*, also familiarly known as 'the *Shorter*', has been frequently reprinted with additions and corrections, and has appeared in three major editions (1933, 1936, and 1944). It contains about two-thirds of the *OED*'s headwords, and its historical coverage and format are similar, on a reduced scale, to the parent Dictionary, including features such as pronunciation, etymologies, dates of origin of senses, and illustrative quotations (usually limited to one per major sense). The *SOED*, both in its own right and also as a 'key' to the *OED*, is one of the most popular of OUP's English language dictionaries.

signification. A term used to refer collectively to the *senses, excluding their illustrative quotations. The word 'signification' is also sometimes used as a heading in very long entries to differentiate the section containing the senses and quotations from an initial section documenting the head-word's form history (see p. 77 for a further explanation of this usage in 'Lengthy Entries').

similative. A term that describes the use of a word, in combination with another word, to paraphrase a simile (that is, to express likeness or similarity). For example, 'rock' and 'feather' are used similatively in the *combinations *rock-hard*, *rock-fast*, *rock-firm* and *feather-light*, *feather-soft*, *feather-white*, as alternatives to the similes 'hard as a rock', 'light as a feather', etc. Some *parasynthetic combinations (created by the addition of an ending or *suffix) are also similative, e.g., 'rabbit-hearted'.

SKEAT, Walter William (1835–1912). Scholar, editor, philologist, founder of the *English Dialect Society (1873), and long-time friend and supporter of James *Murray and the *OED*. Although he studied theology and mathematics at Cambridge and became a lecturer in mathematics, his interest in and knowledge of early English led to his appointment in 1878 as the first holder of a chair in *Anglo-Saxon. He also edited works for the *Early English Text Society and is especially well known for his editions of *Piers Plowman* (1886) and the 7-volume *Chaucer* (1894–7).

An active member of the *Philological Society, Skeat undertook the compilation of etymologies, originally as part of the Society's project to produce a New Dictionary. When the likelihood of publication seemed remote, Skeat negotiated independently with *Oxford University Press to publish his *Etymological Dictionary* (1879–82). Inadvertently, since this had not been Skeat's intention, its acceptance almost led the *Delegates of the Press to dispense with etymologies in the *OED*, a possibility that Murray vigorously opposed. However, Skeat remained Murray's firm friend and adviser, even though the two men sometimes differed in their attitudes towards their work. Skeat was a dedicated scholar, but he was also a highly practical man who believed in setting limits which sometimes disturbed the meticulous Murray. Three hours, Skeat argued in the introduction to his *Etymological Dictionary*, were enough to spend on a word and during that time, he said, 'I made the best I could of it and then let it go'. In spite, or perhaps because, of his attitude, his scholarly accomplishments were many. Always kindly and optimistic, Skeat often wrote humorous letters and verses to Murray to lift his spirits, including a poem celebrating the completion of the letter **C** which began:

> Wherever the English speech has spread
> And the Union Jack flies free,
> The news will be gratefully, proudly read
> That you've conquered your ABC!

slang. Normally used as a *label to indicate a word or usage that is an informal alternative for standard vocabulary. Slang terms are often created and popularized, at least initially, by a particular age group, profession, trade, etc., although they may eventually become more universal. Slang is also often short-lived and quickly replaced by new words or expressions.

The *OED*'s coverage of slang was considerably augmented by the **Supplement* (1972–86); in particular, a number of words labelled *coarse slang* were added (see TABOO AND OFFENSIVE LANGUAGE). This more open policy (in comparison to the first edition) was continued in the second edition. Note also that the label *vulgar* (or the term 'vulgarly' used in some definitions) is applied primarily to some words or senses compiled for the first edition, and is used in the sense of 'common' or unrefined, rather than 'impolite'. (Compare with COLLOQUIAL.)

special English characters. The Germanic tribes which invaded Britain in the fifth century brought with them the runic alphabet which was used to scratch and carve inscriptions (known as runes) on stones and artefacts. When the Latin alphabet was adapted for the writing of Old English, it was augmented by the inclusion of two runic characters *thorn* (þ), with the sounds of *th* as *thin* and *bathe*, and *wynn* (ƿ), which stood for *w*. The sounds of *th* were also often symbolized by an adaptation of the ordinary letter *d* known as *edh* or *eth* (ð). *Thorn* and *edh* were more or less interchangeable. Old English had two *a*-sounds, roughly as in *father* and *cat*. The ordinary *a* was used for the former sound, while the latter, for which there had been a symbol in the runic alphabet, was represented by the Latin æ which took over the runic name *ash*. In the modern printing of Old English, þ, ð and æ are retained, but ƿ is usually replaced by *w*.

In Old English, the letter g represented a number of different sounds. In phonetic terminology, these are defined as: (1) the velar plosive *g* in *gate*, (2) the velar fricative (ɣ), the voiced equivalent of *ch* /x/ in *loch*, (3) the palatal semivowel *y* /j/ in *young*, and (4) the palatal affricate as *dg* /ʤ/ in *bridge*. The letter in the Old English 'insular' script had a distinctive shape ᵹ. When English began to be written according to Norman scribal practices, the Continental shape of g was introduced for the two sounds of *g* which were familiar in French: (1) as in *gate* and (4) as in *bridge*. The insular ᵹ was retained for the other two sounds but in *Middle English was modified in shape to ȝ, and this character was called *yogh*. ȝ was also extended to symbolize the voiceless /*x*/ sound (as in *loch*) which in Old English had been written *h*. In Later Middle English ȝ was gradually replaced by *y* in initial positions and by *gh* in other places: so OE *geong*, ME *ȝong*, Modern English *young*; OE *niht*, ME *niȝt*, Modern English *night*. Modern printing of Middle English normally retains ȝ.

In Old English forms and text cited in the *OED*, in contrast to the usual modern practice, a distinction is drawn between g and ᵹ.

The former is used in places where the Middle English spelling would be with g, the latter where it would be with ᵹ. Example: On ðisum ᵹere wæs swyðe mycel hunger (in this year was very great hunger) in the 1044 quotation under the entry for 'dear' *a.*[1],**6.a.**

specifically (*spec.*). See GENERAL.

spelling. In general, the spelling of headwords in the *OED* represents the most current or common form for the word, *combination, *abbreviation, etc. under discussion, and the most typical of later spellings in the case of *obsolete words. When two or more forms are widely used, the alternative spellings are given as a double headword. One of the outstanding features of the Dictionary is that it also lists the principal variant spellings throughout a word's history (including less widely accepted contemporary forms) identifying them chronologically by the centuries in which they prevailed and illustrating their usage with quotations (see VARIANT FORM).

Broadly speaking, the Dictionary gives preference to what is recognized as 'British' spelling. Typically, 'colour' and 'honour' are the first listed alternatives, rather than the 'American' forms 'color' and 'honor'. However, a few instances will be found when the *OED*'s 'preferred spelling' (in the sense of the first form listed) appears to run counter to what is commonly thought of as predominantly British usage. Such examples, while rare, may interest readers because they reflect James Murray's 'rational' approach to spelling, based on a word's etymology or pronunciation, rather than the national standard. For example, the spelling 'program', the usual form in England before the nineteenth century and in standard use in America, is listed before the contemporary English spelling 'programme', adopted from French in the nineteenth century. It is argued that the earlier spelling is analogous with other representations of the Greek *gramma* in words such as 'anagram', 'telegram', 'cryptogram'. Similarly, with words that are alternatively spelled with an *-ize*, *-ization*, or *-ise*, *-isation*, such as 'organize/organization' or 'organise/organisation', the *OED* recognizes the 'z' form, rather than the 's' form which is used by many present-day English printers, since 'z' is consistent with the suffix's Greek origin, and with its pronunciation. Note, however, that some words, such as 'advertise' or 'surprise', which are not Greek in origin, have no valid alternative to 's'. Another example is the entry for 'jail, gaol', which lists the two alternative spellings of the headwords with preference given to what is sometimes assumed to be American spelling. The Dictionary notes that while both forms have survived ('jail' from Old Parisian French and *Middle English, and 'gaol' from Norman French and Middle English as well), only the 'jail' pronunciation survives in the spoken language

An interesting deviation from most contemporary British spelling, since it is widely used in Dictionary etymologies in the grammatical sense, is *inflexion*, in place of the more common *inflection*. The entry for this word and several similar forms gives preference to the use of *x* rather than *ct*. A rationale for this spelling can be found in the entry for 'connexion, connection'.

spurious word. In the *OED*, 'spurious' is applied to words which are erroneous, false, or cannot be authenticated. There are fewer than 400 entries for spurious words in the Dictionary, all of which were compiled for the first edition. Spurious entries are readily identifiable because they are entirely enclosed in square brackets. Their purpose was mainly to correct errors made by earlier dictionaries in recording and defining words that were actually copyist's or translator's errors, misprints, or misreadings of text. (See pp. 72–74 for examples.)

status label. See LABEL.

status symbols. Three types of symbols are used in the Dictionary to distinguish *word forms which have special status. The dagger (†) precedes headwords or senses which are considered to be *obsolete. These forms are usually further identified by the *label *Obs.* (obsolete). Parallels or 'tram-lines' (‖) signify non-*naturalized words or pronunciations. In the case of non-naturalized words, the symbol precedes the headword or *sense, whereas for pronunciations, the symbol immediately precedes the original foreign pronunciation. A third indicator, the so-called '*catachrestic' symbol (¶), which is the reverse of the symbol occasionally used to indicate a paragraph within quotations, is employed only with senses, usually to indicate a use that is considered to be confused or erroneous (see pp. 16, 29, 30, and also compare with SPURIOUS WORD).

stem. A term used to refer to that part of an inflected word that remains unchanged; in other words, the part to which *inflections (grammatical modifications used to form plurals of nouns, tenses of verbs, etc.) are added. In the *OED*, the term most frequently appears in the context of the 'participial stem' (ppl. stem) of a Latin verb (specifically, the base to which endings are added to form present and past participles) within etymologies. For example, the word 'fugitive' comes from *fugit-*, the participial stem of the Latin verb *fugere*, meaning to flee.

stress-mark. A symbol used to indicate a syllable that is emphasized or accented when a word form is spoken (the term 'syllable' is employed here in the sense of a sound or set of sounds that are articulated as one element). The second edition of the Dictionary follows the International Phonetic Association's stress-marking system, whereby the syllable that receives the main stress is preceded by a superior stress mark (ˈ). When necessary to indicate secondary stress, an inferior stress mark (ˌ) is used. In both cases, the stress-mark *precedes* the stressed element, in contrast to the first edition and the **Supplement* (1972–86) which employed stress-dots *after* the stressed vowel. Stress-marks are either incorporated in the *IPA pronunciation which appears in round brackets following the headword, or, where pronunciation is not given, within the headword itself. They are also used to indicate stress on some subordinate headwords. It should be emphasized that syllabification in the above explanation refers to stressed sounds and should not be confused with word-break syllabification which is typically used to hyphenate words or combinations at line endings. The *OED* does not indicate syllabification in the latter sense. (See PRONUNCIATION for further comments on the use of stress-marks and p. 17 for examples.)

strong (str.). A term (German *stark*) originally used by *Grimm together with its opposite 'weak' (wk.) (German *schwach*), to describe certain *Old English or Germanic grammatical forms. By extension, the terms are sometimes applied in the Dictionary to English verbs. Strong verbs form their past tense and past participle by changing the vowel within their *root, as in the English 'drink', 'drank', 'drunk', and frequently form their past participle with the addition of *-en* ('break', 'broke', 'broken'). Weak verbs form the same part of speech by the addition of a dental suffix, typically *-ed*, *-d*, or *-t*, and as in 'call', 'called'.

The term 'weak' is also applied to the old Germanic declension of nouns or adjectives in which the *stem was formed with *-n*, surviving, for example, in the modern English plural 'oxen' in which the suffix *-en* represents the Old English termination of the weak declension, *oxa*, *oxan*. (See also REGULAR.)

sub-editors. See CONTRIBUTORS, DICTIONARY SLIP.

subject label. See LABEL.

subordinate headword. In present *OED* terminology, a word form which appears within an entry, either in bold type or in bold italic type. Word forms printed in bold type, such as *derivatives and major *combinations are normally defined and illustrated by quotations. Most bold italic forms, such as minor combinations are listed without definitions, but are followed by illustrative quotations. Items such as *phrases and idioms, which also appear in bold italics, are defined when their meaning would otherwise be unclear, and have supporting quotations. The two kinds of bold typeface are designed to assist the reader to find the word form which, because it shares the history of the headword under which it is listed, does not warrant an entry of its own. Subordinate headwords are included under entries for their main word, that is, normally the first word, or the *stem in the case of combinations and derivatives, or the most important word in the case of phrases and idioms.

Note that in the first edition, a typographical distinction was made between two types of headwords in what were referred to as 'main' and 'subordinate' entries. Headwords of subordinate entries, a category largely consisting of *cross-reference entries, were printed in lighter bold type than main headwords. This distinction was abandoned in the *Supplement* and the second edition, and all headwords are now shown in bold type. The earlier meaning assigned to subordinate headword, therefore, no longer applies. (See also TYPOGRAPHY.)

sub-sense. A subdivision in the hierarchical scheme used by the Dictionary to present the historical development of a word's changes in meaning. In documenting the *sense development of a word, the lexicographer identifies the separate meanings given to it. In some cases, the recorded usage may not clearly represent a separate sense, but rather an offshoot of an existing sense, such as an application in which the word is used **figuratively*, **allusively*, or **specifically* in reference to some object, action, etc. Like main senses, sub-senses are normally listed in chronological order and each is illustrated by quotations.

A typical example of the use of sub-senses is found in the entry for 'scarf' which has seven main senses. The first two define military and clerical uses. Sense 3, however, has six sub-senses which, in keeping with the Dictionary's conventions, are lettered **a** to **e.** The initial definition is 'a strip of silk . . . hung loosely over the shoulders'. Senses **3. b, c, d, e,** and **f** cover, respectively, the obsolete meaning of 'a bandage for the eyes, or a veil'; a *figurative (*fig.*) use as in Shelley's phrase 'Iris her many-coloured scarf has drawn'; a *specific use (*spec.*) as something black worn over the shoulders by mourners at a funeral; the familiar meaning of a band of material worn around the neck in cold weather; and a tie or cravat. The order in which these sub-senses are listed is governed by the date of their earliest quotations (1562, 1587, 1610, 1739, 1823, and 1865). Three final, separate senses define the word as a support for an ailing limb, a heraldic device, and an inscribed scroll. This entry is a good example of the decisions that must be made in identifying sub-senses, particularly as they relate to figurative and specific uses which, depending on their importance or history, may sometimes warrant treatment as senses in their own right.

substantive (*sb.*). A grammatical term used consistently throughout the *OED* in place of 'noun', and in its abbreviated form as a *part-of-speech label. The term comes from *noun substantive*, the Latin *nomen substantivum*, meaning a name denoting a substance or thing. It was also common in early grammars to distinguish between two types of nouns—the 'noun substantive' and the 'noun adjective' (now referred to simply as an 'adjective'). The latter was so called because it was an attribute of the thing named and could not stand on its own.

suffix (*suff.*). An element added to the end of a word to change its meaning or function (see AFFIX.)

Supplement (1933). Edited by C. T. *Onions, the *Supplement*, containing additions to the *OED*, was issued as a thirteenth volume when the first edition was reprinted in 1933 in twelve volumes (see EDITIONS). The idea of producing a supplement to the first edition had long been envisaged as a possibility and, in fact, by the time the Dictionary was completed in 1928, a great mass of unused quotations and information had been collected.

Initially, a supplement on the grand scale which would not only add new words, but also correct and revise existing entries, was contemplated. When the magnitude of such an undertaking was fully recognized, it was decided to issue a one-volume work to cover primarily new words and senses that had emerged in the preceding fifty years. In its final form, however, the 1933 *Supplement* also enlarged the categories of *vocabulary covered by the first edition. For example, more *colloquial idiom and *slang, especially American, was added, as well as earlier evidence of American usage of words, largely as a result of William *Craigie's work in Chicago on the *Dictionary of American English*. Many more technical and scientific words were also included, and the coverage of proper names used *allusively was increased.

The *Supplement*, as originally printed in its 800-page format in 1933, also contained a revision of the 'List of Additions and Emendations', which had prefixed the ten-volume 1928 printing; a 'List of *Spurious Words'; and a 'List of Books Quoted in Volumes I–XII' (reproduced in the second edition as the **Bibliography*). Subsequent printings of the first edition, however, reduced the size of the *Supplement* to just over 300 pages by including the three lists at the end of Volume XII.

When the *Supplement* was completed, the *OED* staff was disbanded and Onions, the last remaining editor of the first edition, went on to other work. Left behind were numerous unused quotation slips to be dispersed or stored, some 140,000 of which were retrieved in 1957 when work on the four-volume **Supplement* (1972–86) was initiated. The new work effectively replaced the 1933 *Supplement* by incorporating almost all of its additions.

Supplement (1972–1986). A four-volume work whose 69,000 entries added new words and senses to the coverage of the first edition and its one-volume 1933 **Supplement*, and considerably expanded their coverage. After the conclusion of the Second World War, the *Delegates of *Oxford University Press recognized the need to update the *OED*. In 1955, the first steps were taken to establish editorial offices at No. 40 Walton Crescent, and in 1957 an editor, Robert *Burchfield, a New Zealander who was then a Lecturer in English Language and Literature at Christ Church, Oxford, was appointed. The new work was originally planned as a single-volume revision of the 1933 *Supplement*, comprising some 1,300 pages. It was estimated that it would take approximately seven years to compile.

In addition to appointing staff, Burchfield's most urgent task was to recruit readers to contribute words and quotations. Some twenty-five years had elapsed since the Dictionary's editorial offices had closed their doors, and the 140,000 quotations left behind, although useful, were inadequate both in quantity and range. A new *Reading Programme was inaugurated which included a wide selection of literary, popular, and specialized sources. Editorial policy was extended to encompass more coverage of North American vocabulary in particular, as well as other English-speaking areas such as Australia and the West Indies. After careful consideration, it was decided that taboo words, omitted in the first edition, should be included, as well as other potentially offensive vocabulary. By the late 1960s, science graduates in various specialized areas were appointed to assist in the revision and preparation of entries in those disciplines. An *OED* reference library was established, and researchers were also appointed in major libraries in London and Washington. Many of the *Supplement*'s policies relating to coverage, as well as improvements in page layout and *typography, were later carried over to the second edition.

However, despite some policy and typographical changes, the *Supplement* retained the *historical principles and structure of the main work. From the beginning, it was designed to be read in conjunction with the main volumes, rather than being conceived as a separate twentieth-century dictionary. Each addition, change, or deletion to an existing entry was identified by a *sense number consistent with the scheme in the original entry, a policy that greatly simplified the *integration of the *Supplement* with the first edition.

By the early 1960s, it was evident, because of the rapid proliferation of language, that the size and extent of the work had been underestimated. Plans were revised to encompass a three- or four-volume work. By 1964, the first copy, *A-alpha*, was delivered to the printer. In 1972, the first complete volume (A–G) was published. It was followed by the second volume (H–N) in 1976, the third (O–Scz) in 1982, and the final volume in 1986. It should be noted that these volumes included almost all the entries contained in the 1933 *Supplement*. Even before the *Supplement* was completed, consideration was being given to the future of the *OED*, and the *New OED Project was established in 1984 to consider ways and means of integrating the first edition with the four volumes of the *Supplement*, together with the conversion of the entire text of the Dictionary to *machine-readable form. (See also LIBRARY RESEARCH, SCIENTIFIC AND TECHNICAL TERMS, TABOO AND OFFENSIVE LANGUAGE, and VOCABULARY.)

SWEET, Henry (1845–1912). Phonetician and philologist, he studied at Balliol College, Oxford and Heidelberg. He has been called 'the chief founder of modern phonetics' and was a strong advocate of the new comparative *philology developed on the Continent. As president of the *Philological Society in 1878, he signed the initial, optimistic proposal for a new English dictionary. However, as discussions progressed, Sweet became increasingly disillusioned with the attitude of the *Delegates and supported *Furnivall's wish to break off negotiations over the matter of royalties. Sweet favoured *Murray's appointment as editor since he had been impressed by the latter's work on Scottish dialects. The two men later disagreed over the inclusion of pronunciation in the Dictionary, Sweet arguing against it, while Murray was convinced that he should use the system he himself had devised (see PRONUNCIATION: FIRST EDITION).

Although Sweet was the author of learned texts on phonetics, grammar, and *Anglo-Saxon, and generally acknowledged as a brilliant scholar, his only academic post was as a reader at Oxford. His failure to gain other positions for which he was well qualified has been attributed to his often stubborn and rude manner (it is said he was the model for Bernard Shaw's arrogant Professor Henry Higgins).

synchronic. See DIACHRONIC.

syncopate, -ation. A term sometimes encountered in an etymology (or, more specifically, in a *form-history) referring to the contraction of a word by the omission of one or more syllables or letters in the middle. For example, the word 'chapter' is a syncopated form of *chapiter*, and 'proctor' is a syncopated form of *procurator*.

syntactic label. See LABEL.

T

taboo and offensive language. The first edition's policy for the inclusion of words or expressions was, to some extent, governed by contemporary mores, although, even until recently, several of the so-called 'four-letter' words were considered taboo and were not included in any general English dictionary. When the **Supplement* was begun in 1957, the question of their inclusion was still being debated and it was not until 1968 that the *Delegates of *Oxford University Press agreed that two of the more notorious words should be added since 'standards of tolerance have changed and their omission has for many years, and more frequently of late, excited critical comment'. The second edition includes approximately seventy-five words with the *label *coarse slang*, a category of words, often with a long history, that largely refer to sexual organs or activities. The *Supplement* also made the decision to include words that might be offensive to certain racial and religious groups, although a number of such 'opprobrious' terms already appeared in the first edition, many of which were, or are, applied to women. The use of words or senses in this category is commonly introduced by a phrase such as 'applied opprobriously to'. The second edition also revised some instances of racial, religious, or sexual bias which were contained in definitions compiled for the first edition and which had not been so categorized. However, no attempt is made to eliminate relevant supporting quotations demonstrating such biases since they record the historical context, however offensive, in which certain words and senses were used. Thus, the *OED* often provides a useful source for social scientists, as well as general users.

Teutonic (Teut.) A term used in *OED* etymologies to identify one of the great branches of the *Indo-European (Indo-Germanic, or Aryan) family of languages. This branch includes *Old English, Old Frisian, Old Saxon, Old High German, Old Norse, and Gothic, together with their later forms. These early forms are the foundation of modern European languages such as English, Dutch, German, Danish, Swedish, and Norwegian. In modern linguistics, the term 'Germanic' is normally employed instead of 'Teutonic'. The prevalence in the *OED* of the use of Teutonic as a generic term reflects the fact that most entries for the core *native English words were written for the first edition. Note that the term 'Gothic' (Goth.) in etymologies normally means the language of the Goths (surviving only in a fourth-century translation of the *Bible* by Ulfilas), not the Teutonic or Germanic languages in general.

thorn. See SPECIAL ENGLISH CHARACTERS.

titles. The titles of works are normally printed in italics and are often cited in abbreviated or shortened form in quotations, etymologies, and other entry components in order to save space. There is routine omission of the definite articles 'the' and 'a', as well as the preposition 'of' (except when needed for the sense), and the substitution of the ampersand (&) for 'and'. However, there are further abbreviations of titles which may cause more difficulty. The original intent of the shortened references was to abbreviate them so as 'to be recognizable by those who know them', or to give sufficient information that the reader could locate them in a library or bibliographical catalogue. The statement is perhaps not as applicable to the modern general reader of the Dictionary as it was to the nineteenth-century scholars and amateur philologists who largely made up its original readership, in an age that was somewhat more familiar than our own with classical and early English literature. Full titles for most, but not all, cited works are given in the **Bibliography* at the conclusion of Volume XX. Frequently used abbreviations are also included in the *List of Abbreviations, Signs, etc.* at the front of each volume, for example, *Adv.* for Advance, -d, -s, *Dis.* for Disease, *R.* for Royal, *Q.* for Quarterly. Readers may also notice that a title is not necessarily referred to in the same form each time it is quoted (Shakespeare's *Comedy of Errors* is abbreviated as *Comm. Err.*, *C. Err.*, and *Err.*). Such irregularities are more likely to cause difficulties for the user of the electronic text than the printed text. (For further examples of the way in which titles are cited within quotations, see p. 45.)

TOOKE, John Horne (1736–1812). Philologist and political agitator. Born John Horn(e), he adopted the surname of his friend William Tooke. He became a vicar after graduating from Cambridge, but gained notoriety as a supporter of parliamentary reform and freedom of dissent. He was once imprisoned for seditious libel and later acquitted of a charge of high treason. In *philology, Tooke is chiefly remembered for *The Diversions of Purley* (1786, 1805), a projected three-volume work of which only two volumes were published. His philosophical philology attempted to demonstrate that all words, and all parts of speech, could be traced to primary nouns (or possibly verbs) that named concrete or sensible objects (or actions) with single, immutable meanings, resulting from the impression or sensation received by the mind. For example, Tooke argued that the word 'bar' invariably connotes 'defence', and it could be demonstrated that such diverse words as 'barn', 'baron', 'bargain', and 'bark' (in all its senses) contained this one radical meaning. As can be imagined, the reduction process became absurdly convoluted, especially when attempts were made to explain the 'true' meaning of parts of speech such as prepositions and conjunctions. Despite its obvious shortcomings, Tooke's theory popularized conjectural etymologies and, it has been argued, delayed the adoption by English philologists of the new comparative philology pursued on the Continent. His work influenced *Richardson whose *A New Dictionary of the English Language* (1836–37) was admirable for its use of illustrative quotations, but less noteworthy for its highly speculative etymologies. One of the objectives of the initiators of the *OED* was to implement the comparative method and to counteract the conjectural approach to word origins. (See also ETYMOLOGY, PHILOLOGY.)

transferred (*transf.*). A label applied to the use of a word or sense in other than its normal context. For example, a tower is normally thought of as a name given to a lofty structure or building in a particular style, but in Dickens's reference to 'sundry towers of buttered Yorkshire cakes', the use of the noun is extended or transferred to describe a lofty pile of cakes.

There is some indication in a quotation in the Dictionary under the verb 'transfer' that James *Murray may have originally thought of *transferred* in more general terms as a superordinate category of which non-literal applications such as *figurative, allusive*, etc. were subordinate categories. However, it seems apparent that this concept was not uniformly applied and that, for example, *figurative* and *transferred* are seen in most instances as two distinct categories. (See FIGURATIVE for an example of this distinction.)

transitive (*trans.*). A grammatical *label used to differentiate verbs (or the use of a verb) which require a direct object to complete their meaning (transitive) from those which do not (intransitive). For instance, in the sentence 'the nurse took a blood sample', the verb 'take' is transitive, whereas in the sentence, 'the skin graft did not take', the same verb is used intransitively. Frequently, for verbs used in more than one sense, the labels *trans.* or *intr.* are attached to particular senses or sub-senses (rather than to the entire entry), some of which may represent temporary, special, or rare uses in the history of a verb. Labels are not necessarily applied to every sense, but rather to the first in what may be a series of senses in the same grammatical category. Therefore, the lack of an identifying label normally means that the use in that sense is the same as the previous sense.

Grammatical shifts are often the result of the omission of an object. For example, the verb 'televise' was first used with an object (picture, programme, etc.), and later also intransitively ('they were not allowed to televise'). In addition, many verbs which were originally intransitive (answer, obey, etc.) and were followed by a noun in the dative case (that is, the equivalent of an adverbial phrase consisting of 'to' plus a noun) have over time become transitive. Sometimes a *reflexive pronoun ('myself', 'himself', etc.) may gradually be omitted, as in the Biblical quotation 'Jesus withdrew himself to the sea' which, in a later version, became 'Jesus withdrew to the sea'. Note in the first case that the use of the verb is usually identified as 'reflexive', although it is also transitive.

The abbreviation *intr.* will also be encountered in phrases such as '*intr.* and *refl.*', which does not imply that it is both at the same time, but rather that a single sense or sub-sense and the accompanying quotation paragraph cover both forms. This is often done when one of the categories is *obsolete or *rare, or when a word has only one sense. For example, the word 'overdrink' has a single sense identified as both '*intr.* and *refl.*', as illustrated by the quotations 'many of us over-eat, over-drink and over-smoke' (intr.), and 'if he is hot . . . he will over-drink himself' (refl.). A sense may also use an intransitive form reflexively ('*intr.* for *refl.*'). Thus, in the sentence 'this is not the first time women have organized for peace', the verb is used intransitively, but the reflexive pronoun 'themselves' is understood. The phrase '*intr.* for *pass.*', meaning 'intransitive for passive', may also be encountered. For instance, the verb 'televise' is used intransitively in the sentence 'some faces televise better than others', in the same sense as a passive construction such as 'some faces can be televised better than others'.

translations (tr.). The Dictionary contains numerous quotations extracted from foreign works translated into English. Since translators are responsible for the choice of English words which render the original writer's sense, the translator, when known, is cited as the author of a quotation (that is, the name appears after the date in large and small capitals), followed by the abbreviation 'tr.'. The date given is usually that of the translation. The original author's surname, when known, is included in the possessive case as part of the italicized title (for example, '**1928** E. & C. PAUL tr. *Marx's Capital*). The title is normally given in its English translation, although sometimes translated works are published under their original name, such as the early Latin work *De imitatione Christi*. In this instance, the earliest of several translations of the manuscript was made in approximately 1450 by an unknown translator and the citations from this version read '*c* **1450** tr. *De Imitatione*'. (See also p. 44.)

TRENCH, Richard Chenevix (1807–86). Philologist, churchman, author, and generally recognized as providing the inspiration for the undertaking that led to the *OED*. Educated at Trinity College, Cambridge, Trench became Dean of Westminster, and later Archbishop of Dublin. He wrote numerous books on divinity, history, literature, and *philology, including *On the Study of Words* (1851) and *English Past and Present* (1855) which popularized the scientific study of language. However, it was his presentation of two brief papers (later published under the title *On Some Deficiencies in Our English Dictionaries*) to the *Philological Society in November of 1857 which was crucial to the *OED*'s history. Largely as a result of Trench's remarks, the Society's members expanded their original project of producing a supplement to existing dictionaries to encompass the compilation of a complete, new dictionary of the English language.

Trench's papers were notable not only for his careful analysis and criticism of existing dictionaries, but also for the suggestions they contained about what should be done. He identified seven major deficiencies in existing dictionaries: 1) the incomplete registering of obsolete words; 2) the failure to include all words in the 'same family' (that is, *derivatives, *combinations, *inflected forms); 3) the failure to identify the earliest use of words or, in the case of obsolete words, when they became extinct; 4) the omission of changes in meaning and usages of words, resulting in incomplete word histories; 5) the lack of attention to distinguishing synonymous words; 6) the failure to use quotations that might assist in illustrating a word's first introduction, etymology, and meaning; and 7) the reluctance of dictionaries to recognize their own limitations by attempting to be encyclopaedic and by including too many scientific and technical terms. One of Trench's most important observations was that a dictionary should be an objective 'inventory of language'; it was not, he maintained, the role of the lexicographer to be an arbiter, or 'a self-made dictator', of 'good words', as many had attempted to be in the past.

Trench did not fail to give credit where it was due, citing the immensity of the almost single-handed undertakings of lexicographers such as *Johnson and *Richardson, but also emphasizing that any project to obtain a complete inventory of the English language must be 'by combined action'. As a model, he noted that the brothers *Grimm had already employed over eighty volunteer readers, and hoped to enlist more, to aid in the compilation of their great historical dictionary, the *Deutsches Wörterbuch*, the first part of which had just been published in 1852. It is also significant that Trench mentioned the comprehensiveness of *Liddell and Scott's *Greek-English Lexicon* (1843) based on the work of the German scholar Franz *Passow, whose *historical principles had also been adopted by the Grimms.

Although Trench left London in 1863 to become Archbishop of Dublin and terminated his association with the Philological Society, many of his concepts came to fruition in the *OED*.

typography. One of the features of the *OED* is its use of a variety of typefaces to differentiate elements within an entry and to alert the reader to their significance. The three major typographical variants from roman, which is used for the body of the text, are bold, italic, and small capitals. The following brief entry for 'framboise' illustrates many of these conventions:

> **framboise**, *sb.* and *a.* Also 6 **framboye**, 6–7 **frambois, -boys.** [a. F. *framboise* (from 12th c.), usually regarded as a corruption of Du. *braambezie* = Ger. *brombeere* blackberry, lit. bramble-berry: see BRAMBLE, BROOM, BERRY. But some French scholars doubt this.]
>
> †**A.** *sb.* The raspberry (*Rubus Idæus*). *Obs.*
>
> [**1551-62** Turner cites the word as French only.] **1578** LYTE *Dodoens* VI. v. 662 Of Framboys, Raspis, or Hyndberie. The Framboye is a kinde of bremble. **1620** VENNER *Via Recta* vii. 125 Strawberries are..to be preferred before the Framboise. **1651** tr. *Bacon's Life & Death* 31 Of this sort the chief are Borage..Frambois or Raspis, &c.
>
> **B.** *adj.* Of raspberry colour. Also *absol.*
>
> **1904** *Daily Chron.* 24 Sept. 8/3 The soft..framboise tones. **1959** *Times* 28 Sept. 13/2 It [*sc.* a suit] can also be obtained in size 18..in framboise.
>
> **frambousier** [F. *framboisier*], a raspberry bush.
>
> *a* **1648** LD. HERBERT *Life Hen. VIII* (1683) 89 A Frambousier or Raspis-Bush.

The most obvious typeface in the above entry is the heavy bold which is used for all headwords (in this case, 'framboise') in the second edition. A smaller bold type is used for *derivatives ('frambousier'), as well as major *combinations (see examples below), which are included as *subordinate headwords. Bold type is also used for the dates (1551–62, 1578, etc.) which typically introduce citations within quotation paragraphs, and for numerals and letters indicating sense divisions and major *sub-senses. In the entry for 'framboise', the letters **A.** and **B.**, signifying that two parts of speech (noun and adjective) are included within the single entry, are printed in bold. Finally, a lighter bold type identifies *variant forms, such as the sixteenth-century spelling 'framboye', and the sixteenth- to seventeenth-century variants 'frambois, -boys'. Italic type is liberally employed to indicate the significance or function of certain elements. Parts of speech (e.g. *sb.* and *adj.*), and labels (e.g. *obs.* and *absol.*), are generally italicized. Foreign words and phrases (including Latin scientific and botanical names) and foreign or related linguistic forms cited in etymologies also appear in italics. Examples are the French, Dutch, and German words *framboise*, *braambezie*, and *brombeere*, and the botanical name *Rubus Idæus*. Titles of books, essays, periodicals, and other written or printed works are normally italicized. The most frequent use of this convention is in quotation paragraphs, such as the references to *Dodoens*, *Via Recta*, *Daily Chron.*, and *Times*, but it is also used for works cited in other entry sections such as etymologies, and etymological or definition notes.

Two additional italicized elements are illustrated below in an extract from sense **3.** of the noun 'gauze'.

> **3.** *Comb.* **a.** simple attrib., as ***gauze blind***, ***curtain***, ***dress***, ***handkerchief***, ***merino***, ***ribbon***, ***silk***, ***suit***, ***veil***, ***wing***, ***wire-cloth***. **b.** objective, as ***gauze-dresser***, ***-dyer***, ***-manufacturer***, ***-weaving***; ***gauze-like*** adj. **c.** Special comb.: **gauze-lamp**, a safety-lamp in which the flame is surrounded by wire-gauze; **gauze-loom** (see quot.); **gauze ring** = *crape ring* (CRAPE *sb.* 3 b); **gauze-tree** (*West Indian*), the lace-bark tree, *Lagetta lintearia*.

First, *cross-references to combinations or phrases, either within the same entry or in another entry, are italicized. For example, following the major combination 'gauze ring' (printed in bold as noted above) there is an equals sign (=) informing the reader that this usage is equivalent to 'crape ring' (in italics) which, as indicated in parentheses, is defined in sense **3. b.** of the entry for the noun 'crape'. Secondly, darker, or bold, italics are used for phrases or minor combinations in which the main word is used *attributively and the meaning is obvious, as in the case of *gauze blind*, *curtain*, *dress*, etc., in order to differentiate them from the major combinations **gauze-loom, gauze-ring**, and **gauze-tree** which require further definition.

The third typographical convention is the use of small capitals for cross-references to *main entries as in the 'framboise' example, where the reader is referred in the etymology to the entries for 'bramble', 'broom', and 'berry', and in the extract from 'gauze', where the reference, as mentioned previously, is to the entry for 'crape'. The other use of small capitals, is to identify the author of a quotation. For example, the authors 'Lyte' and 'Venner' in the 1578 and 1620 quotations under 'framboise' are printed chiefly in small capitals with large capital initial letters.

It will also be noted that the Dictionary uses a number of special symbols and characters (see STATUS SYMBOL and SPECIAL ENGLISH CHARACTERS for examples).

V

variant form. A variant or different, and often earlier, spelling of a headword. One of the features of the Dictionary is that it attempts to give all documented variants of each headword and to identify the century range in which they occurred. Variant forms normally appear immediately before the etymology (the section enclosed in square brackets) and are often preceded by the word 'Forms' or 'Also'. The century or the range of centuries in which each form prevailed appears in abbreviated form as a single arabic number, for example '6–7' for sixteenth to seventeenth centuries. When more than one form is given, the list is chronological, with the oldest variant appearing first. Sometimes forms are grouped according to some principal feature of spelling and each group is identified by a Greek letter, and illustrated by quotations grouped in the same fashion. As a valuable aid to scholars, the majority of variant forms also appear in the Dictionary as *cross-reference entries, so that a reader who encounters an older spelling in an early text and who may be uncertain of the later form it represents is directed to the appropriate main entry. (For examples of variant form lists and conventions used to identify centuries and to group by spelling characteristics, see pp. 20–22.)

verbal substantive (*vbl. sb.*). A grammatical *label used to identify a noun (*substantive) derived from a verb by the addition of *-ing* to the verb *stem. The resultant word resembles the present participle in form, but not in function. Its form may also be identical to a *participial adjective derived from a verb. Many verbal substantives imply a continuous action or existence and take no plural ('pushing', 'sleeping', 'speaking', 'living'), or, alternatively, they may identify a single event, such as a 'wedding', 'christening', 'launching', in which case, they can be used in the plural. (See PARTICIPIAL ADJECTIVE for a further explanation of how the two forms differ and pp. 68–72 for examples.)

vocabulary. The policy of vocabulary inclusion in the *OED* underwent notable changes between the first edition and the **Supplement* (1972–86), reflecting both the cultural environment in which they were compiled and changes in the language.

James *Murray, in his 'General Explanations' written for the first edition, likened the English language to a circle with a well-defined core of literary and colloquial words, but 'no discernible circumference'. The circumference, as he viewed it, was an ever-expanding nimbus of scientific, technical, slang, dialectical, and foreign terms for which the lexicographer must 'draw the line somewhere'. In the end, Victorian conventions dictated the exclusion of certain offensive words from the first edition, although the restriction was much less stringent than has sometimes been implied. Literary works were emphasized as sources (although Murray once complained, when pressured by the Delegates to keep the Dictionary's size within reasonable limits, that he did not know what to class as 'literature'), and the coverage of scientific and technical terminology was somewhat restricted since it was argued that the more abstruse terms were the province of specialized dictionaries.

Although the principal task of the *Supplement* was to update the Dictionary's coverage of the standard vocabulary of British English, it also attempted to compensate for the gaps in the first edition. It made a special effort to include regional varieties of English, especially that of the United

States and other English speaking countries. More *slang and *dialectal words that had passed into common use, as well as more foreign terms and proper names, were added. The coverage also reflected the way in which new technologies such as computer science and space exploration, and popular culture in such areas as music, had influenced the language. In recognition of their importance in late twentieth-century vocabulary, a number of *acronyms, *abbreviations, and *proprietary terms were added, many of which were given separate entries instead of being included within entries for their initial letters. Finally, in addition to the inclusion of the sexually explicit words which had previously been considered taboo, the *Supplement* also made the decision to continue to include terms which were recognized as offensive to certain racial or religious groups (see also TABOO AND OFFENSIVE LANGUAGE.)

The second edition continued the expanded policy of the *Supplement*, adding some 5,000 new words or new uses of old words. While the importance of emergent vocabulary is recognized, it cannot, in a historical dictionary, be emphasized at the expense of other lexical categories, and *new words must demonstrate that they have an established foothold in the language before they are considered for inclusion. The coverage of English vocabulary did not cease with the publication of the second edition. The *OED* continues to maintain files, both in manual and electronic form, of new words, new uses, and revisions, and employs an editorial staff who are responsible for the preparation of new entries. The *OED* *Reading Programme, which since 1989 has included a collection centre in the US to take over coverage of North American vocabulary, is a primary contributor. Large computer databases containing texts of sources such as journals, newspapers, and legal documents are routinely searched. With the flexibility offered by computer technology, new entries and revisions can be constantly added to the OED *database, not only for the production of future editions of the Dictionary in both print and electronic form, but also to serve as a central lexical resource for other general and specialized dictionaries published by Oxford University Press. (See also SCIENTIFIC AND TECHNICAL TERMS.)

vulgar, -ly. See SLANG.

W

weak (wek.). See STRONG.

WEBSTER, Noah (1758–1843). American lexicographer and philologist. In 1806, he published his *A Compendious Dictionary of the English Language*, which claimed to add five thousand words 'to the number found in the Best English Compends'. Webster's work challenged the authority and dominance of existing English dictionaries, and sought to establish a standard for American usage and spelling, as well as adding scientific, technical, commercial, and everyday terms ignored by literary-based dictionaries such as *Johnson's. In 1828, his greatest undertaking, *An American Dictionary of the English Language*, was published in two volumes. It included 'the origin, affinities and primary signification of English words', together with their spelling and pronunciation, and 'accurate and discriminating definitions, with numerous authorities and illustrations'. Webster claimed that its 70,000 entries (all of which he had laboriously written by hand) exceeded any previous dictionary. A revised edition of the work was published in 1840 just before his death.

While many of Webster's proposed spelling and pronunciation reforms, as well as his etymologies, were questionable, the excellence of his definitions, his use of illustrative quotations, and above all the comprehensiveness of his coverage were notable. James *Murray criticized Webster's etymologies, but he also paid tribute to the American lexicographer's skills and referred to him as 'a born definer of words'.

When Webster died in 1843, the publishing rights were acquired by George and Charles Merriam who published a revised edition of Webster's final work in 1847. This became the first in the series of Merriam-Webster *Unabridged Dictionaries*, including another revision in 1864, the 1890 *Webster's International Dictionary*, and a further name change in 1909 to the current title, *Webster's New International Dictionary*. When the size of the *OED* was first discussed, it was proposed to limit it to 7,000 pages, which was defined as 'four times the size of Webster's'. The *Webster* scale often became a bone of contention between the editor and the *Delegates of the Press, especially when Murray discovered he was sometimes exceeding the length of *Webster's* entries by as much as ten times. There are over 5,000 references within *OED* quotation paragraphs, particularly in entries for scientific and technical terms, to various *Webster* editions, either noting that a word appeared, for example, '**1890** in WEBSTER', or quoting a definition from the dictionary.

women contributors. See CONTRIBUTORS.

word form. A term used throughout this guide to mean a distinct item of vocabulary, and by extension, an item that merits entry in the Dictionary either as a headword or a *subordinate headword (*combination, *derivative, *phrase, etc.). This designation was selected because many items other than what are usually considered 'words' are defined in the Dictionary. It was also thought to be less confusing to readers than equivalent technical terms, such as 'lexeme', 'lexical item', or 'lemma', which are employed by linguists and lexicographers, and are often subject to conflicting interpretations.

wynn. See SPECIAL ENGLISH CHARACTERS.

Y

yogh. See SPECIAL ENGLISH CHARACTERS.

OED FACTS AND FIGURES

The following Dictionary statistics are taken both from introductory statements contained in the printed editions and from the databases of the first and second editions. Readers may notice a slight discrepancy between figures given in the *Introduction* to the second edition and those listed below. These variations are a result of database refinements subsequent to the date by which it was necessary to prepare the introductory section for typesetting. Because of the ongoing nature of this process, most computer-generated figures have been rounded *down* to the nearest hundred and should be read as, for example, 'at least 291,500 entries in the second edition'. In addition, it should be remembered that the *OED*, although remarkably consistent in its format, was not designed to conform to the absolute consistency demanded by computerization. For example, variations in the citing of names of individual authors or in the abbreviations used for titles of works occasionally make it difficult to assure that every form has been taken into account. In a few instances, such as calculating the numbers of quotations taken from the various versions, partial versions, and translations of the *Bible*, only a rough estimate can be given until such time as a detailed analysis is undertaken.

Statistics are given for the first edition, the four-volume *Supplement*, and for the second edition. In each case, 'number of entries' is equivalent to the number of headwords allocated independent articles. However, many word forms, such as derivatives, combinations, and phrases, appear as subordinate headwords within entries for their root or main words, and are either defined and illustrated, or where their meaning is obvious, illustrated, by quotations. The figure for the total number of word forms, therefore, includes both subordinate headwords appearing in bold type (defined and illustrated) and those printed in bold italic type (illustrated).

FIRST EDITION

- proposed size: 4 volumes, 6,400 pages (with provision for 'a larger dictionary containing not fewer than 10 volumes, each containing not less than 1,600 pages')
  proposed time to complete: 10 years
  actual size: 10 volumes, 15,490 pages
  actual time to complete: 70 years (from approval date)
- publication date: 1884–1928 in 128 fascicles. Published in 10 volumes in 1928 and reissued in 12 volumes in 1933, with addition of one-volume *Supplement*
- price of fascicles: 12 shillings and sixpence for large sections
  price of bound volumes (1928): from 50 to 55 guineas for the set, depending on the binding
- number of pages edited by James Murray: est. 7,200
- number of entries: 252,200
- number of word forms defined and/or illustrated: 414,800
- number of contributors (readers): est. 2,000
- number of quotations submitted by contributors: est. 5 million
- number of quotations used in Dictionary: 1,861,200
  number of authors represented in quotations: 2,700
  number of works represented in quotations: 4,500

SUPPLEMENT (1972–86)

- proposed size: one volume, 1,300 pages
  proposed time to complete: 7 years
  actual size: 4 volumes, 5,730 pages
  actual time to complete: 30 years
- publication date: vol. 1, 1972; vol. 2, 1976; vol. 3, 1982; vol. 4, 1986.
- number of entries: 69,300
- number of quotations: est. 527,000

SECOND EDITION (1989)

- proposed size: 20 volumes
  actual size: 20 volumes, 21,730 pages
- publication date: 1989
- price per set: £1,650
  weight of text: 62.6 kilos or 137.72 lbs.
  amount of ink used to print complete run: 2,830 kilos or 6,243 lbs.
- number of words in entire text: 59 million
  number of printed characters: 350 million
  number of different typographical characters used in text: approx. 750 (660 special plus approx. 90 on regular keyboard)
  equivalent person years to 'key in' text to convert to machine-readable form: 120
  equivalent person years to proof-read text: 60
  number of megabytes of electronic storage required for text: 540
- number of entries: 291,500
- number of main entries: 231,100
  number of main entries for obsolete words (†): 47,100
  number of main entries for spurious words: 240
  number of main entries for non-naturalized words (‖): 12,200
  longest entry in Dictionary: the verb 'set' with over 430 senses consisting of approximately 60,000 words or 326,000 characters
- number of cross-reference entries: 60,400
  number of cross-references *within* entries: 580,600
- number of word forms defined and/or illustrated: 615,100
- number of pronunciations: 139,900
- number of etymologies: 219,800
- number of quotations: 2,436,600
- most frequently quoted work (in various full and partial versions, and translations): *Bible* (est. 25,000 quotations)
  most frequently quoted single work: *Cursor Mundi* (approx. 12,790 quotations)
  most frequently quoted single author: Shakespeare (approx. 33,300 quotations)

most frequently quoted single work of Shakespeare: *Hamlet* (almost 1,600 quotations)

- percentage of quotations by centuries

20th century	20 per cent
19th century	31
18th century	11
17th century	16
16th century	10
15th century	4.5
14th century	3.5
13th century	1
1st to 12th centuries	1
undated (see note)	0.5

Note: 'Undated' includes approximately 1,250 quotations from *Beowulf*, with the balance consisting of proverbs, nursery rhymes, 'made-up' illustrations, and references to the appearance of word forms 'in mod. Dicts.'.

A CHRONOLOGY

OF EVENTS RELEVANT TO THE HISTORY OF THE *OED*

1755 Publication of Dr Samuel Johnson's *Dictionary of the English Language* in two folio volumes.

1786 Publication of Volume 1 of John Horne Tooke's *Diversions of Purley*.
Sir William Jones delivers his discourse 'On the Hindus' to the Asiatic Society, Calcutta, noting similarity of Sanskrit to European languages.

1805 Publication of Volume 2 of Tooke's *Diversions of Purley*.

1806 Publication of Noah Webster's *Compendious Dictionary of the English Language*, a supplement to existing dictionaries containing 5,000 headwords, as well as tables of currency, weights and measures, lists of post offices, chronology of events, etc., and distinguishing between American and British usage.

1812 Franz Passow's essay *Über Zweck, Anlage, und Ergänzung griechischer Wörterbücher* published, outlining his historical principles of lexicography.

1818 First instalment of Charles Richardson's dictionary published as part of the *Encyclopædia Metropolitana*.

1819 Publication of Volume 1 of Jakob Grimm's *Deutsche Grammatik* incorporating observations on systematic phonetic shifts from Indo-European to the Germanic languages.
Publication of first part of Passow's *Handwörterbuch der griechischen Sprache* (Greek-German Lexicon).

1828 Thomas Dale becomes first person in England to hold a Chair in English language and literature (University of London).
Webster's comprehensive *American Dictionary of the English Language*, containing 70,000 entries, published in two volumes.

1830 Rasmus Rask reviews Grimm's *Deutsche Grammatik* in the English periodical *Foreign Review*.
Benjamin Thorpe's translation of Rask's *Grammar of the Anglo-Saxon Tongue* published.

1830–3 Publication of Sir Charles Lyell's *Principles of Geology*.

1835/7 Publication of Charles Richardson's *A New Dictionary of the English Language* in two volumes.

1840 Webster's revision of his 1828 dictionary is published.

1842 Founding of the Philological Society in London.

1843 Publication of Liddell and Scott's *Greek-English Lexicon* based on Franz Passow's *Wörterbücher*.
John Ogilvie's *Imperial Dictionary*, based on Webster's dictionary, published.

1851 Publication of Richard Chenevix Trench's *On the Study of Words*.

1853 Frederick Furnivall is appointed honorary secretary of the Philological Society.

1854 Publication of first part of Jakob and Wilhelm Grimm's *Deutsches Wörterbuch*, a historical dictionary of the German language.

1857 Dean Trench joins the Philological Society. Trench, Furnivall, and Herbert Coleridge form the Society's 'Unregistered Words Committee' to collect words for a supplement to existing dictionaries. In November, Trench presents two papers to the Society, later published as *On Some Deficiencies in Our English Dictionaries*.

1858 The Philological Society passes resolution, as a result of Trench's papers, to compile a complete New English Dictionary, and volunteer readers are recruited to contribute words and illustrative quotations.

1859 The Society publishes full details of the dictionary project in a 'Proposal for the Publication of A New English Dictionary by the Philological Society'.
Charles Darwin's *Origin of the Species* published.
Herbert Coleridge's *Glossarial Index to the Printed English Literature of the Thirteenth Century* is published and later that year he is appointed editor of the Society's proposed dictionary. He prepares the 'Canones Lexicographici; or Rules to be observed in editing the New English Dictionary'.
The Hon. G. P. Marsh of Burlington, Vermont offers to organize American contributions to the dictionary.

1860 After considerable debate and revision, Coleridge's 'Rules' are issued as a final plan for the dictionary.

1861 Herbert Coleridge dies at the age of 31, and Frederick Furnivall is appointed editor.

1862 Furnivall proposes a concise dictionary, tentatively to be completed by 1865, as a preliminary to the larger work.

1864 Publication of a new edition of Webster's *American Dictionary of the English Language* (popularly known as the Unabridged), edited by Noah Porter and published by Merriam-Webster.
Furnivall founds the Early English Text Society to transcribe and publish rare and inaccessible manuscripts, particularly of the Middle English period.

1868 James A. H Murray joins the Philological Society. His *Dialect of the Southern Counties of Scotland* is published.

1869 Murray begins editing texts for Furnivall's Early English Text Society.

1871 Furnivall appeals for a new editor for the dictionary and persuades Henry Nicol to take the job, but illness and other work prevent him from pursuing the task.

1873 English Dialect Society founded at Cambridge by Walter Skeat.

1874 Murray awarded an honorary LL.D by Edinburgh University.

1875 Furnivall again seeks a new editor and suggests Murray's name.

1876 Murray is approached by the publishing firm of Macmillan regarding possibility of editing a new standard English Dictionary for Macmillan and US publisher Harper, using the Philological Society's material. Negotiations are later terminated.
Furnivall makes overtures to Oxford University Press (OUP) for publication of the Society's dictionary.

1877 Henry Sweet, as President of the Philological Society, formally writes to the Secretary to the Delegates of the Oxford University Press, proposing that the Society make its material available to compile a historical dictionary.

1879 Philological Society signs contract with the Clarendon Press (OUP) for publication of a historical dictionary not to exceed 7,000 pages.
Murray also reaches agreement with the Press to become editor. Murray has a Scriptorium built to house the editorial staff. He decides that a new Reading Programme is necessary, and the Clarendon Press issues an appeal for 1,000 readers for three years. Professor F. A. March of Lafayette College, Pennsylvania, undertakes the organization and supervision of volunteer readers in the United States.
Publication of Walter Skeat's *Etymological Dictionary of the English Language* (1879–82).

1881 Murray urges Delegates to extend size of Dictionary to 10,000 pages. Delegates agree to a total of 8,400 pages in six volumes of

1881 1,400 pages each, instead of original four volumes of 1,600 pages each.

1882 Scheduled date for publication of Part I. Murray sends first batch of copy, consisting of some forty pages, to the printer on 19 April.

1884 Part I (A to ANT) published. Murray's suggestion that the title be revised to *A New English Dictionary on Historical Principles* (*NED*) is adopted.

1885 Murray gives up his position at Mill Hill School and moves to Banbury Road, Oxford to work on the Dictionary full time. A new Scriptorium is erected. Part II (ANT to BATTEN) published.

1886 Henry Bradley is appointed to assist on letter 'B' with the intention that he later become an independent editor.

1887 Part III of the Dictionary published.

1888 Bradley becomes the second editor with his own staff working at the British Museum in London.

1889 The first of six volumes of the *Century Dictionary*, edited by William Dwight Whitney, is published in the US.

1890 Publication of *Webster's International Dictionary*, edited by Noah Porter.

1891 Two parts of Dictionary published—Murray's part of letter 'C' and Bradley's first part of 'E'.

1895 Charles Talbut Onions joins Dictionary staff at Murray's request. The designation 'Oxford English Dictionary' appears for the first time above the title on the cover of the section DECEIT to DEJECT published on 1 January.

1896 Delegates seek to enforce policy that entries average six times length of *Webster*, instead of editors' eight times or more, but finally agree to editors' ratio. The Press adopts policy of publishing 64-page quarterly sections (352 pages to a volume) to be sold at half a crown each.
Bradley moves to Oxford and is housed, with his own staff, in the Clarendon Press building.
Publication of first volume of the *English Dialect Dictionary* (1896–1905).

1897 William Alexander Craigie joins staff and starts work on letter 'G' under Bradley's supervision.

1898 By permission, the Dictionary is dedicated to Queen Victoria.

1900 Murray gives Romanes Lecture at Oxford, entitled *The Evolution of English Lexicography*.

1901 Craigie appointed as the third independent editor. Bradley and Craigie, together with their staffs, move to the Old Ashmolean.

1902 Five out of the final ten volumes completed.

1905 Contribution of £5,000 made by Worshipful Company of Goldsmiths towards the production of the sixth volume. Dinner is held in the Company's Hall in London to celebrate completion of the volume.

1908 James Murray receives knighthood.

1909 Publication of the first edition of *Webster's New International Dictionary*.

1910 Frederick Furnivall dies.

1914 Outbreak of World War I, which deprives Dictionary of many younger staff members and delays its completion.
Charles Talbut Onions appointed third editor.
Oxford University awards Murray and Bradley honorary D.Litt. and Onions honorary MA.

1915 Murray dies on 26 July. His Dictionary staff is transferred to the Old Ashmolean.

1918 End of War and return of some of staff.

1923 Bradley dies on 23 May.

1925 Craigie accepts appointment at the University of Chicago, but continues to work on Dictionary.

1928 Work on first edition completed. Dictionary is published in ten volumes still carrying the title *A New English Dictionary on Historical Principles* followed by 'founded mainly on the materials collected by the Philological Society'. First copies are presented to King George V and to Calvin Coolidge, President of the United States.
Craigie receives knighthood for his work on the Dictionary.

1933 Dictionary reissued in twelve volumes, together with a *Supplement* volume containing new words and meanings, a list of spurious words, and a bibliography. The title is now officially changed to the *Oxford English Dictionary*, followed by the phrase 'being a corrected re-issue with an Introduction, Supplement, and Bibliography of *A New English Dictionary on Historical Principles*'.
Publication of the first edition of the *Shorter Oxford English Dictionary*, 'an official abridgement' of the *OED*.

1934 Publication of *Webster's New International Dictionary*, Second Edition.

1936 Publication of the second edition of the *Shorter Oxford English Dictionary*.

The first volume of the four-volume, historical *Dictionary of American English*, edited by Craigie (with James R. Hulbert), published.

1957 William Craigie dies.

Robert W. Burchfield accepts invitation of the Delegates of the Press to edit the *Supplement*, which it is projected will be a single volume taking seven years to complete. Editorial offices are established at No. 40 Walton Crescent, Oxford and a new Reading Programme is launched.

1961 Publication of *Webster's Third New International Dictionary*.

1964 The first instalment (A to ALPHA) of the *Supplement* is delivered to the University printer 27 May.

1965 C. T. Onions, the fourth editor of the *OED*, dies.

Estimate of the *Supplement*'s size is revised to three, or possibly four, volumes. Library researchers are employed in major libraries in Washington and London and links are established with language centres in other English-speaking countries.

1968 First graduates in science are appointed to *Supplement* staff to help prepare entries for scientific and technical terms.

1972 First volume (A to G) of the *Supplement* published.

1973 Publication of the third edition of the *Shorter Oxford English Dictionary*.

1976 Second volume (H to N) published, which includes a dedication of the whole work to Queen Elizabeth II.

1982 Publication of third volume of *Supplement* (O to SCZ).

Preliminary study undertaken by Dictionary Department to consider feasibility of conversion of text to electronic form, and of combining main *OED* and *Supplement* volumes.

1984 Edmund Weiner is appointed editor of the Dictionary.

On 15 May, OUP formally announces launching of the New OED Project and a partnership with three institutions—International Computaprint Corporation (ICC) in Fort Washington, Pennsylvania, IBM United Kingdom, Ltd., and the University of Waterloo in Canada.

The British Department of Trade and Industry announces subvention towards cost of project.

Decision is made to include approximately 5,000 new words or new senses in the proposed second edition; a complete revision of the Dictionary is planned for Phase II of the project.

1985 First batch of magnetic tapes and proofs arrive from ICC in January.
The Centre for the New OED established at the University of Waterloo with the aid of Canadian Government funding.

1986 John Simpson becomes co-editor of the Dictionary.
Publication of the final volume of the *Supplement*.
Data capture of the text of the first edition and the *Supplement* in machine-readable form completed.

1987 Automatic integration of the two texts begins in March and is completed by end of May.

1989 The 20-volume second edition of the *OED* published on schedule on 30 March.
Phase II begins, including planning for publication of second edition on CD-ROM, as well as its release on magnetic tape.

1991 Compact version of the second edition published.

1992 CD-ROM of the second edition released.

BIBLIOGRAPHY

Much of the information contained in this volume was supplied by the present editorial staff of the *OED* or by the electronic searching of the Dictionary database, using computer facilities and software developed at the Centre for the New OED at the University of Waterloo. In addition, the introductions to the first and second editions of the Dictionary and to the *Supplement* (1972–86) were extremely helpful. Biographical and historical material was also obtained from standard reference texts such as the *Dictionary of National Biography* and various encyclopaedias. Over and above these resources, a number of books and articles were used in the research for Part II. The following list includes a few titles which were either found to be especially relevant, or which may be of interest to readers who wish to explore a particular topic further:

Aarsleff, Hans. 'The Early History of the *Oxford English Dictionary*', *Bulletin of the New York Public Library* 66 (1962): 417–39.

—— *The Study of Languages in England, 1780–1860*. Princeton, NJ: Princeton University Press, 1967.

Albright, Robert W. *The International Phonetic Alphabet; its backgrounds and development*. Bloomington, Ind.: Indiana University Press, Research Centre in Anthropology, Folklore and Linguistics, 1958.

Bailey, Richard W. 'Materials for the History of the *Oxford English Dictionary*', *Dictionaries* 8 (1986): 176–250.

Barker, Nicholas. *The Oxford University Press and the Spread of Learning, 1478–1978: An Illustrated History*. Oxford: Oxford University Press, 1978.

Berg, Donna Lee, Gaston H. Gonnet, and Frank Wm. Tompa. *The New Oxford English Dictionary Project at the University of Waterloo*. Waterloo, Ontario: UW Centre for the New Oxford English Dictionary, 1988 (OED-88-01).

Burchfield, Robert. 'Data Collecting and Research', *Annals of the New York Academy of Sciences*, 211 (8 June 1973): 99–103.

—— *The English Language*. Oxford: Oxford University Press, 1985.

Burchfield, Robert. *Spoken Language as an Art Form: An Autobiographical Approach*. New York: English Speaking Union of the United States, 1981 (Occasional Papers 1).

Dutton, Marsha L. 'Lexicography and Popular History: Readers and Their Slips for the *New English Dictionary*', *Dictionaries* 9 (1987): 196–210.

Landau, Sidney I. *Dictionaries: The Art and Craft of Lexicography*. New York: Scribner, 1984.

Leavitt, Robert Keith. *Noah's Ark: New England Yankees and the Endless Quest*. Springfield, Mass.: G. & C. Merriam Company, 1947.

'The Making of the Dictionary'. *The Periodical*, XIII 143 (15 Feb. 1928): 3–32.

MacMahon, M. K. C. 'James Murray and the Phonetic Notation in the *New English Dictionary*', *Transactions of the Philological Society* (London: 1985): 72–112.

Mathews, M. M. *A Survey of English Dictionaries*. New York: Russell & Russell, 1966.

Murray, James A. H. *The Evolution of English Lexicography*. Oxford: Clarendon Press, 1900.

Murray, K. M. Elisabeth. *Caught in the Web of Words: James Murray and the Oxford English Dictionary*. Oxford: Oxford University Press, 1979.

Quirk, Randolph, *et al. A Comprehensive Grammar of the English Language*. London: Longman, 1985.

Raymond, Darrell R. *Dispatches from the Front: The Prefaces to the Oxford English Dictionary*. Waterloo, Ontario: University of Waterloo Centre for the New Oxford English Dictionary, 1987 (OED-87-04).

Schäfer, Jürgen. *Documentation in the OED: Shakespeare and Nashe as Test Cases*. Oxford: Clarendon Press, 1980.

Sutcliffe, Peter. *The Oxford University Press: An Informal History*. Oxford: Oxford University Press, 1978.

Trench, Richard Chenevix. *On Some Deficiencies in Our English Dictionaries; being the substance of two papers read before the Philological Society, 5 and 19 Nov. 1857*. London: John W. Parker and Son, 1857.